STEVEN RAICHLEN'S GUIDE TO BOSTON RESTAURANTS

DINING IN BOSTON COOKBOOK

STEVEN RAICHLEN

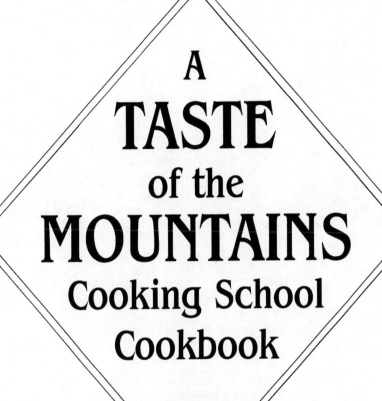

A
TASTE
of the
MOUNTAINS
Cooking School
Cookbook

POSEIDON PRESS · NEW YORK

A Poseidon Press Book
Published by Pocket Books, A Division of Simon & Schuster, Inc.
Simon & Schuster Building
Rockefeller Center
1230 Avenue of the Americas
New York, New York 10020
POSEIDON PRESS is a registered trademark of Simon & Schuster, Inc.
Designed by Helene Berinsky
Manufactured in the United States of America

1 3 5 7 9 10 8 6 4 2

Library of Congress Cataloging in Publication Data
Raichlen, Steven.
A Taste of the Mountains Cooking School cookbook.

Bibliography: p.
Includes index.
1. Cookery, International.   2. Taste of the
Mountains Cooking School (Glen, N.H.)   I. Title.
TX725.A1R28   1985   641.59   85-17033
ISBN: 0-671-54428-4

This book is dedicated to my grandparents
Sarah Goldman
Ethel Raichlen
Samuel "Dear" Raichlen

CONTENTS

◇

DESSERTS

REFERENCE

"Dinner last night was superb, but you will make me die of indigestion."
—the Prince Regent

"My duty, Sir, is to tempt your appetite, not control it."
—Antonin Carême (royal chef, 1783–1833)

ACKNOWLEDGMENTS

◇

The most enjoyable part of writing any book is thanking the people who helped make it possible. This one involved a small army of helpful friends, family members, former students, and associates.

My first thanks go to my agent, Meg Ruley, who planted the seed; to my editor, Pat Capon, who nurtured the plant; to Susan Mattmann, who made it blossom with her lovely drawings (and to Matthiew Morse, who lived with Susan's deadline); to Barbara Sause and Jim Daly, who pruned it with skillful editing; and to Margaret Crane, who helped bring it to fruition by living up to her nickname, "Girl Wonder."

The book grew out of my cooking classes in Cambridge and New Hampshire. I would not have survived without the tireless assistance of Linda Wong, Carol Powers, Paula Senese, and Chris Kauth. Recipe testers included some of my star alumnae: Ann Boynton, Debbie Donahey, Linda Folts, Kathy Hawley, Margot LaStrange, Lisa Lipton, Diane Mann, Linda McGurk, Uta Renz, Carole Stephenson, Susan Wittpenn, and Christa Wilm. Any mistakes are, of course, my own.

The Taste of the Mountains Cooking School owes much of its success to my partners, Ted Wroblewski and Cronan Minton. Sharon Wroblewski and Penny Minton deserve thanks for their patience. I have certainly learned much from Bernerhof chefs Howard Friedland, Rick Spencer, and Chuck Doolittle. Innkeepers Kim Babineau and Katheryn Friedland provided all the comforts of home, including expertly made gin gimlets.

The Taste of the Mountains has had many loyal friends, including Ginger Blymer, Birdy Brooks, Holly Collins, Jeanne (Patty) Delia, Joe Kropp, and Kay Reed. Thank you, Bill Bergman, whom we sorely miss for your humility and zest for life. It is a pleasure to acknowledge Zacke Hanle and Susan Hubley, whose fine articles in *Bon Appetit* magazine and the *Portland Press Herald* helped put the cooking school on the map.

No one learns to cook in a vacuum. My career got its start with a grant from the Thomas J. Watson Foundation. (Yes, they actually paid someone to eat and drink his way through Europe!) I was equally fortunate to train with such excellent chefs as Anne Willan, Fernand Chambrette, Albert Jorant, Claude Vauguet, and Louis LeRoy.

Last but not least are the people who helped the writing machine become human again when the book was finished. Thanks to Linda, Marty, Martha, and Andy Millson, who ate strange meals in Wellfleet. A grand thanks to Barbara Klein, who fed me home fries when I was sick of *gratin dauphinoise*. Thanks to Sonny and Cecille Raichlen, for their moral and material support. And thanks to Fran Raichlen, too, who contributed as she could.

This book was written on a Kaypro computer in Massachusetts, New Hampshire, and Florida.

INTRODUCTION

◇

It's 5 P.M. of a Friday in late October. The setting is a rambling clapboard structure in the heart of New Hampshire's White Mountains—the Bernerhof Inn. Bernerhof owner Ted Wroblewski is in the kitchen, preparing our traditional "welcome" fondue. Cronan Minton, the school's "social director," shows incoming students to the Zumstein lounge for cocktails by a blazing fireplace. I have just arrived from Boston, my chef's whites starched, my car loaded with goat cheese, wild mushrooms, fresh herbs, and whole salmon. Welcome to the Taste of the Mountains Cooking School: you are just in time for dinner.

ABOUT THE SCHOOL: The Taste of the Mountains is a unique cooking school located in the Mount Washington Valley in New Hampshire. The school was founded by Ted, Cronan, and myself on a wintry evening in 1981. Ted had recently purchased the Bernerhof and he was interested in hosting a cooking school. I had been holding classes in Cambridge and welcomed the opportunity to teach cooking in the spacious kitchen of a 100-year-old country inn. The lounge with its oak paneling, the dining rooms with their rustic elegance, would be ideal for socializing and feasting.

Ted's job would be to run the inn, while I would teach the actual classes. As the third partner, Cronan would be responsible for our brochures, public relations, and student admissions. He quickly became the school's "social director," introducing our guests to Mount Washington Valley's excellent recreational facilities. Our goal was simple: to provide serious culinary instruction in the congenial atmosphere of a New England country inn.

In the fall of 1981 we held our first session—with a grand total of four students! Each morning after breakfast, we would file into the Bernerhof kitchen. At the start of each class, I demonstrated the day's cooking techniques: how to chop an onion, truss a duck, or wield a piping bag. The students themselves did the actual cooking under my tutelage. Knives flashed, sauté pans sizzled, and even the novice joined in the creation of whipped-cream swans and of a rack of lamb with goat cheese pesto. At 1 P.M., exhausted but exhilarated, we took our seats at a smartly set table to sample the fruits of our labors.

The students told their friends about the school; the press wrote glowing reports; every season, the Taste of the Mountains prospered. We expanded our original program to include wine-tasting, a gourmet picnic, a guest-inn dinner, and "student" night, on which the pupils prepared specialties of their own for the staff. Ted renovated the Bernerhof kitchen. Swing dancing became a regular part of our program, as did hot-tubbing, horseback riding, and a trip to the top of Mount Washington.

The Taste of the Mountains Cooking School is now in its fourth year. We have graduated students from all over North America, ranging in age quite literally from eighteen to eighty. Some of our students are professional chefs; others have scarcely set foot in a kitchen; most are, like the school's directors, devotees of cooking and fine dining. More gratifying than the steady growth of the school is the fact that a full 40 percent of our alumnae return for a second session.

ABOUT THE TEACHER: As long as I can remember, I have been impassioned by fine food and cooking. As a youngster, I looked forward to the times when my parents would leave the house, for I could then turn myself loose in the kitchen. I suppose it was self defense: as a child in the fifties, I was raised on TV dinners.

Curiously, it was my interest at college in medieval French literature that led to my becoming a full-time food writer. In 1975, I received a Thomas J. Watson Foundation Fellowship for a year's study of medieval cooking in Europe. For the next eighteen months, I pored over antique cookbooks in the great libraries, studied traditional methods of beer-, wine-, and cheese-making, and visited kitchens in castles and monasteries.

I was fascinated by the role that food has played in human history. Through the centuries, food preparation has influenced our art, literature, language, technology, social organization, and commerce. You'll find that I have included lots of food history in *A Taste of the Mountains Cooking School Cookbook*. The headnotes to the recipes won't necessarily make you a better cook, but you'll be better informed about food.

My practical training came from the Cordon Bleu and La Varenne cooking schools in Paris. I was fortunate enough to work with chefs of the old school, chefs who had apprenticed at the age of thirteen and had learned to do everything—from slapping brioche dough to pureeing fish mousses—by hand. They instilled in me the conviction that any cook should master the rudiments of classical cuisine before attempting contemporary innovations.

Thus, when I set out to write *A Taste of the Mountains Cooking School*

Cookbook, I knew that it must be firmly rooted in the classical French tradition.

At the same time, I was lucky to be in France in 1976, a year that was as revolutionary in the world of cooking as 1789 had been in the history of politics. After a hundred years of domination, classical French cuisine was being shaken at its roots by pioneers of *la nouvelle cuisine,* the "new" cooking. An unquestioning faith in tradition gave way to a spirit of innovation; striking plate presentations replaced stuffy French service; and for the first time in five centuries, chauvinistic French chefs turned to the Orient and even the New World for inspiration. The advent of a machine called the food processor brought the efforts of the imperious chef within easy grasp of the home cook.

Like any revolution, *nouvelle cuisine* had its "Reign of Terror," and few chefs today would starve their clients with minuscule portions, or serve such outlandish creations as liver with chocolate or monkfish with raspberries. Much of *nouvelle cuisine* has become old hat, like the use of green peppercorns, exotic lettuces, and barely cooked string beans. Nonetheless, contemporary chefs share a spirit of innovation that would have been unthinkable thirty years ago. I have tried to infuse this cookbook with this spirit of innovation.

When I returned to the U.S. in 1977, I remained a French clone, turning heavy cream into *crème fraîche,* doing even the most menial kitchen tasks by hand, inveighing against my fishmonger for not carrying European species. At the end of six months, I realized the futility of trying to cook like a Frenchman in America. I discovered that my New England home had marvelous seafood, produce, and other native provender, not to mention a rich and long culinary tradition. Boston, with its extensive Chinatown and Italian quarter, made me take a fresh look at ethnic cooking.

Like many chefs of my generation, I began to adapt my French recipes to American ingredients, and traditional American recipes to classical techniques. As a journalist, I helped create, and as a cook, I became a part of, what has come to be called the " 'new' American cooking."

I have tried, then, to write a cookbook based on classical European cooking techniques, infused with a spirit of innovation and tied to American ingredients and culinary traditions. To the extent that I have succeeded, I owe my thanks to such excellent teachers as Anne Willan, Albert Jorant, Fernand Chambrette, Claude Vauguet, and Louis LeRoy. I have been equally influenced by my students over the past eight years, who challenged the traditional methods and brought me a wealth of new ideas.

I hope you will enjoy the individual recipes in *A Taste of the Mountains Cooking School Cookbook.* They have been chosen to illustrate key cooking techniques that can be applied to a wide range of dishes. Because I believe that the presentation of food is as important as its preparation, you will find instructions and illustrations for serving as well as preparing many of the dishes in this cookbook. You'll also find lots of food and cooking lore of the sort our students discuss over dinner. More importantly, I hope that you will use my recipes as a starting point, to help you create culinary masterpieces of your own. So pour yourself a glass of wine and pull your chair near the fire. Here at the Taste of the Mountains, the show is about to begin.

HOW TO USE THIS BOOK

As director of the Taste of the Mountains and food columnist for *Boston Magazine,* I have devoted much of my time to teaching people how to cook. My method might be called the "themes and variations" approach to cooking: learn a relatively small number of fundamental techniques and basic culinary preparations, and you will be able to create a myriad of delectable dishes. I have always stressed cooking techniques, not recipes; the process, not the end product. The goal of my cooking classes is to wean people from cookbooks by awakening within them an intuitive understanding of how to combine whichever ingredients are best at a given time.

Learning to cook is like acquiring a new language. The individual ingredients are the words. The basic culinary preparations, such as clarified butter or *bouquet garni,* are the idiomatic expressions. The actual cooking techniques—chopping, sautéing, cake decorating—comprise the "grammar." Put them together, and you have a language as rich and varied as that of Shakespeare. The cook who relies exclusively on recipes is no better than the linguist who never transcends the dialogue in his textbook.

A Taste of the Mountains Cooking School Cookbook comprises fifty-three lessons. Each lesson focuses on a particular technique or set of techniques, or on a specific family of dishes. We start with a discussion of the individual techniques, touching on social history, special ingredients, and potential stumbling blocks for neophytes. We move next to a "master" or "theme" recipe, designed to illustrate the basic principles. The lesson concludes with a series of "variations" based on the techniques developed in the master recipe.

Thus, *A Taste of the Mountains Cooking School Cookbook* is designed for three levels of cooks. The beginner can work through the lessons sequentially, building from simple techniques to sophisticated specialties. The intermediate cook may wish to refresh his or her memory about a particular process—for example, making soufflés. The master recipe in this lesson explains in exhaustive detail how to make a cheese soufflé. The expert can skip the explanatory sections entirely, moving directly to specific recipes. I have tried to select recipes that show the cross-cultural connections between foods and ways to prepare them. Bouillabaise, after all, is nothing more than an elaborate fish chowder. "Pizza" can be made with smoked cheese and leeks, as well as with anchovies and tomatoes.

Each of the cooking techniques, special equipment, and exotic ingredients used in the book is defined where it first appears in the text. For the convenience of people who use the recipes out of order, I have included a glossary of cooking terms at the end. For people who wish to do further reading, I have also included a bibliography of references I have found useful.

Some final observations:

◇ Read any recipe from beginning to end before you attempt it. This will help you be more organized and perhaps will spare you the discovery at the last step that the dish can't be served for twenty-four hours.

◇ Assemble all your ingredients and equipment before you start cooking. Except for pinches and splashes, measure your ingredients beforehand. This will save you time once you start.

◇ Measure accurately, especially for sauces and pastries. To measure flour and other dry ingredients, dip the spoon or cup into the container, and level the top with your finger. Do not pack the ingredient down.

◇ When a recipe calls for butter, use unsalted butter. Salt is added as a preservative, so unsalted butter is usually fresher. Besides, salted butter robs you of your right to season a dish to taste.

◇ When a recipe calls for flour, unless otherwise directed, use unbleached, all-purpose white flour.

◇ Eggs should be large, not extra-large, or jumbo.

◇ Heavy cream is preferred to whipping cream.

◇ You'll notice that most of the recipes call for a high cooking temperature: why take 1 hour to cook a dish when it can be ready in 20 minutes? It is policy in my house that no meal take longer to cook than it takes to eat. (At the very least, this guarantees leisurely dining!)

◇ Use the proper-sized utensil for the recipe. If you expect to wind up with 4 cups of stew, don't sauté your beef in a 2-cup skillet. It is as hard to chop a head of cabbage with a tiny paring knife as it is to whisk a sauce with a wooden spoon.

◇ Remember that a cook's most important tools are his hands and tastebuds. All too many novices forget the latter. You can't tell whether a dish is correctly seasoned unless you taste it. As tastes differ, I do not, except with pastries, give precise measurements for salt and pepper. To me "correctly seasoned" means that a dish does not need additional salt and pepper at the table.

◇ Finally, cooking is *not* brain surgery. The following recipes are intended as a guide, not gospel. If you don't like curry powder, substitute saffron. If you don't like fish, try the recipe with chicken or some other seafood. With the possible exception of a few pastries, I never slavishly follow a recipe. Nor do I expect you to. We strongly believe at the Taste of the Mountains that cooking should be fun.

And now, dear reader, put on your apron and tie a dish towel around your waist. The first class begins on page 23!

Steven Raichlen
The Taste of the Mountains
Cooking School
Glen, New Hampshire

SOUPS

AND

SALADS

L E S S O N 1

Stocks

◇

Technique:
MAKING STOCK

Master Recipe:
CHICKEN STOCK

Variations:
CHICKEN NOODLE SOUP
BROWN-BONE CHICKEN STOCK
VEAL STOCK
FISH STOCK

◇   ◇   ◇

The French word for "stock" is *fonds*, from the same Latin root as our word "fundamental." Stock is the cornerstone of fine cooking, providing backbone and richness to soups, stews, and sauces. It is easy to make; it perfumes your whole house; and a large batch can be frozen in 1- or 2-cup containers for convenient future use.

Stock is not unlike tea except that its flavor comes from bones, herbs, and vegetables instead of tea leaves. To make a light stock use raw bones; to make a brown stock roast the bones and vegetables in a hot oven. To make broth (enriched stock), use a whole chicken and/or beef shin.

Five root vegetables provide additional flavor: onions, carrots, celery, garlic, and leeks. These vegetables appear together in a multitude of soups, stews, and braises: together they comprise what the French call a *mirepoix.*

We also add an herb bundle (*bouquet garni* in French), an assortment of aromatic herbs and spices, including bay leaf, thyme, parsley, black peppercorns, cloves, and allspice berries. Traditionally, the herb bundle is tied in cheesecloth. I never seem to have cheesecloth on hand, however, so I wrap the herbs in a square of aluminum foil, poking holes in the foil with a fork to release the flavor. The wrapping keeps the herbs together and spares the diner the potential displeasure of choking on a whole peppercorn or bay leaf.

◇   ◇   ◇

Chicken Stock

In this recipe we use chicken bones, but we could just as easily make stock from veal or fish bones (see below). Whenever you cut up a chicken, save the neck and back in the freezer; when you have enough bones, make stock. Alternatively, you can buy chicken backs or necks from your butcher.

Makes 2 quarts stock

> 3 pounds chicken bones
> 1 large onion, peeled and quartered
> 2 carrots, washed and coarsely chopped
> 2 stalks celery, coarsely chopped
> 1 leek, washed and chopped as described on page 29
> 2 cloves garlic, peeled
> 1 *bouquet garni* (see page 23)
>   approximately 3 quarts cold water

1. Remove any lumps of fat from the chicken bones. If using necks, pull off the skin. Place the bones, vegetables, and *bouquet garni* in a large (at least 6-quart) stockpot, and add cold water to cover.

2. Bring the stock to a boil over high heat. The pot should not be covered. Reduce the heat and gently simmer the stock for 3 hours, adding cold water as necessary to keep the bones covered.

3. As the stock cooks, you must skim off the impurities that rise to the surface. Use a shallow ladle for skimming, not a slotted spoon, and hold it just under the surface. Remove all the fat and foam: don't worry about discarding the top inch of stock. The important thing is to remove the impurities. Skim stock at 20-minute intervals and just after you add any cold water. (The cold water will drive the fat to the surface.) The key to good stock lies in conscientious skimming and slow, long, steady simmering.

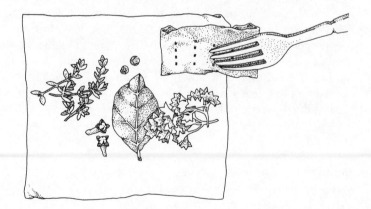

Failure to skim, or boiling rather than simmering stock, will cause the fat to homogenize with the liquid, resulting in a stock that is cloudy rather than clear and clean-tasting.

4. At the end of 3 hours, you should have a golden, full-flavored broth. Strain it into 1- or 2-cup containers and let it cool to room temperature. Do not attempt to refrigerate stock until it has come to room temperature. A hot stock or sauce in a cold refrigerator is a breeding ground for bacteria.

Stock will keep for 3–4 days in the refrigerator and 1–2 months in the freezer. To use frozen stock, simply melt it in a saucepan or add it directly to a soup or stew.

◇   ◇   ◇

CHICKEN NOODLE SOUP: Prepare the recipe above, using a whole chicken instead of bones. You need only cook the soup for 1 hour. Season the broth with plenty of salt and pepper. Cook 1 pound slender noodles separately in rapidly boiling salted water and add them at the last minute. (Cooking the noodles directly in the broth will make it cloudy with starch.) Serves 6–8.

BROWN-BONE CHICKEN STOCK: Roast the chicken bones in a hot (425°F.) oven for 1–1½ hours or until very brown, adding the vegetables halfway through so that they brown as well. Leave the skins on the onions for color. Transfer the bones to the stockpot with a slotted spoon. Discard any remaining fat. Place the roasting pan over a high heat and add 1 cup dry white wine, scraping the bottom of the pan to dissolve the congealed meat juices. (This is called "deglazing.") Add this mixture and 2 tablespoons tomato paste to the pot. Prepare the stock as described above. Brown-bone duck, goose, and veal stocks are prepared the same way.

VEAL STOCK: Substitute veal bones for chicken bones. Try to use bones with some meat on them, such as neck or back bones. For extra flavor, add a pound or two of veal shin.

FISH STOCK

Fish stock, like chicken or veal stock, is an aromatic infusion of vegetables, herbs, and bones. It is cooked for only 20 minutes, however, because fish bones become bitter when simmered too long. The best bones to use are those from a fine-flavored white fish, like halibut, sole, or snapper. Avoid dark, oily fish, like mackerel, herring, and bluefish, or your stock will be unpleasantly fishy. You can use either the "frames" (the skeleton of the fish) or the heads to make fish stock. If you are feeling simply squeamish, you can make fish stock with inexpensive "chowder fish" (bony scraps trimmed from fish carcasses). Remove the gills from behind the head, taking care not to cut yourself on the sharp ridges. (I use the hooked end of a ladle to extract the gills.)

Makes 1–1½ quarts fish stock

2 pounds "frames" or heads from fine-flavored white fish
3 tablespoons butter
1 onion, finely chopped
1 small leek, finely chopped
2 stalks celery, finely chopped
1 clove garlic, minced
   approximately 1 quart cold water
1 large *bouquet garni*

1. Remove the gills and wash the fish frames thoroughly to eliminate all traces of blood. Using a cleaver, cut the frames into 4-inch pieces.

2. Melt the butter in a large (at least 4-quart) pot and sauté the chopped vegetables and the minced garlic over medium heat for 3–4 minutes, or until soft. Add the fish bodies, increase heat to high, and cook for 1–2 minutes, or until the fish starts to turn opaque. Add cold water to cover and the *bouquet garni.*

3. Bring the stock to a boil and skim off the white foam that forms on the surface. Reduce heat and gently simmer the stock for 20 minutes, skimming often to remove any impurities. Strain the stock and discard the bones. If the flavor of the stock is not concentrated enough, continue boiling the stock *without* the bones, until it is reduced to the taste and consistency you desire.

Note: Noticing a reluctance on the part of my students to handle fish heads and bones, I experimented with bottled clam broth. The results are excellent, but you have to cut back on the salt in the recipe in which fish stock is called for. Either the fish stock or clam broth can be used for the recipes in this book.

LESSON 2

Vegetable Soups

◇

Techniques:
CHOPPING ONIONS, CARROTS, LEEKS, GARLIC
"SWEATING" VEGETABLES

Master Recipe:
POTAGE GARBURE (VEGETABLE SOUP FROM SOUTHWEST FRANCE)

Variations:
POTAGE GARBURE GRATINÉ
BEET BORSCHT

◇   ◇   ◇

The first dish in any cook's repertory is soup. This lesson focuses on a hardy French vegetable soup called *potage garbure. Potage garbure* (pronounced "po-tahj gar-buhr") was the traditional supper of peasants in southwest France. Eugène Le Roy describes a humble version in his *Jacquou le Croquant,* the moving story of a poor nineteenth-century Périgourdine peasant:

> Having lit a fire, my mother peeled an onion, cut it into small pieces, and put it in a pan with a spoonful of bacon fat over the fire. When the onion was fried, she filled the pan with water, and put some sliced bread in our soup bowls. When the water boiled, she poured it over the bread. To say that this meager broth served over hard black bread was good would be an exaggeration, but it was hot and it was better than the plain dry bread or cold potatoes we usually ate.

Today's *garbure* is a different story—a robust dish made with beans, root vegetables, and cabbage. A fancy version would include country ham or even cured duck or goose.

Making *potage garbure* offers an excellent opportunity to learn the proper technique for chopping vegetables. Good knifsmanship greatly increases your efficiency in the kitchen and makes your food look better. Every cook should own at least three knives: a short paring knife, a slender, flexible boning knife for filleting fish, and a long, heavy "chef's" or chopping knife for finely chopping vegetables. If you already know how to sharpen a knife and chop vegetables, proceed directly to the recipe on page 31.

HOW TO CHOP VEGETABLES

ONIONS AND OTHER ROUND VEGETABLES: Use a paring or filleting knife. To chop an onion, cut it in half from the pointed end to the root end. Cut off the pointed end, leaving the root end intact (it will serve as a handle). Peel back the skin. Lay the onion on the cutting board, cut side down. Make a series of parallel, vertical cuts from the pointed end to root end, but do not cut all the way through the root end: You want the slices to hold together. Now, guiding the front half of the knife against your knuckles, make a second series of parallel vertical cuts, this time perpendicular to the first cuts. The onion should fall into a pile of small, neat cubes. Use this technique for chopping all round vegetables, like shallots, turnips, and potatoes. When chopping shallots, however, you will have to make an additional cut, holding the knife blade parallel to the cutting board. (The natural layers make this unnecessary for an onion.)

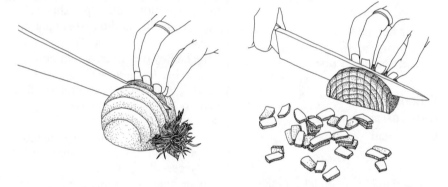

CARROTS, CELERY, AND OTHER LONG, THIN VEGETABLES: Use a chef's knife to cut a carrot in half lengthwise almost to the end. Turn the carrot 90 degrees and again cut it in half lengthwise almost to the end. (If the carrot is really large, make 1 or 2 more lengthwise cuts.) Now, holding the blade perpendicular to the vegetable, and raising and lowering the heel of the knife, make a series of ¼-inch slices, guiding the blade with your knuckles. The end you left intact will now serve as a convenient handhold (hold it with your thumb). Note that when chopping round vegetables, we use the pointed end of the knife; when chopping long, skinny vegetables, we use the heel end. Celery stalks, leeks, and parsnips are chopped in this fashion.

LEEKS: The tastiest part of a leek is the white, sun-starved root, but because it remains underground, it is usually riddled with dirt. To clean and chop a leek, cut off the dark-green leaves. Slice the outer layer of the leek lengthwise and remove it as you would an onion skin. Using a chef's knife, cut the leek in half lengthwise almost to the root; rotate the leek 90 degrees and cut it in half again. Now, plunge the leek up and down in a bowl of cold water, like a plumber's plunger, until the layers are completely cleansed of grit. Shake the leek to dry it out and chop it with a chef's knife as you did the carrot. Be sure to wipe off the cutting board, because grit often remains behind.

GARLIC: To skin garlic, lay the clove on the cutting board and lightly smash it with the heel of your palm. This loosens the skin so that you can slip it off. To mince garlic, cut each clove into ¼-inch slices and stand these on edge. Lay the widest part of a chopping knife over each slice, and hit the blade sharply with the heel of your palm; the garlic will be pulverized. Work at the edge of the cutting board, because the heel of the knife must extend well beyond the edge. Angle the blade downward to avoid cutting your hand.

CABBAGE: Cut the cabbage in half lengthwise (through the stem end). Make a V-shaped cut along either side of the core and remove it. Place the cabbage on a cutting board cut side down and chop it as you would an onion.

◇

To sharpen a knife, hold the blade at a 15-degree angle to the steel. Pull the blade toward you along the steel, first on one side, then on the other. Alternatively, you can sharpen the knife away from you, slicing at the steel the way you would sharpen the point of a pencil. Knives should be professionally sharpened at least once a year.

◇   ◇   ◇

Potage Garbure

VEGETABLE SOUP FROM SOUTHWEST FRANCE

To make vegetable soups, we employ a technique called "sweating." The vegetables are cooked in a tightly sealed pan over a low heat so that they sweat, or stew, in their own juices. (This concentrates their flavor.) The soup can be prepared with water, but, naturally, it will have more flavor if made with stock.

Serves 10 generously

1 onion
1 large carrot, peeled
2 stalks celery
2 leeks
2 cloves garlic, peeled
1 small turnip, peeled (turnips are white with a purple tinge;
    rutabagas are yellow)
1 parsnip, peeled
1 large potato, peeled
1 small green cabbage
4 strips bacon, finely chopped
½ cup white beans, soaked in water overnight
8 cups chicken stock, light veal stock, or water
    generous *bouquet garni*
1 ham hock or ¼ pound finely chopped smoked ham
    salt and plenty of fresh black pepper
1 cup heavy cream (optional)

1. Finely chop all the vegetables as described on pages 28–30.

2. Render the bacon (cook it over a medium heat to melt out the fat) in a large (6-quart) pot; do not let it brown. (If you prefer, use 4 tablespoons butter or chicken fat instead of the bacon.) Add the chopped onion, carrot, celery, leeks and garlic and sauté, stirring from time to time, for 3–4 minutes, or until the onions soften. Stir in the remaining chopped vegetables, press a piece of buttered foil on top of them, and tightly cover the pan. Sweat the vegetables over low heat for 15–20 minutes, or until limp and shiny.

3. Drain the beans and add them, the stock, *bouquet garni,* ham hock, and seasonings to the soup pot. Bring the soup to a boil. Reduce heat and simmer for 1 hour or until the vegetables are soft and the soup is well flavored. Remove the *bouquet* and ham hock, discarding the former. Remove and chop the meat from the latter and put it back into the soup. Stir in the cream, bring the soup to a boil, and adjust the seasonings.

Note: Potage Garbure can be served right away, but like most soups it improves with age. The peasants of the southwest of France have a curious way of serving *potage garbure:* a glass of wine is poured into the last quarter bowlful of soup. The soup is eaten with a spoon. One good wine for this would be a Cahors, a dry, earthy red from the southwest of France.

POTAGE GARBURE GRATINÉ: To turn this soup into a main course, serve it *gratiné,* topped with grilled bread and cheese. Lightly brush ten ½-inch slices of French bread with melted butter. Bake them in a preheated 400° oven, turning once, for 15 minutes, or until golden brown. Cool on a cake rack. Arrange the toasts on a baking sheet and sprinkle with 1 cup grated Gruyère cheese. Just before serving, melt the cheese under the broiler. To serve, float a cheese-topped piece of toast on each bowl of soup.

BEET BORSCHT

Borscht is a Central European version of *potage garbure,* made with beets and flavored with caraway seed. Borscht can be served hot or cold, coarse or pureed. The traditional accompaniments include sour cream, finely chopped scallions, and finely chopped, peeled, seeded cucumber served in bowls on the side.

Serves 4

>   5 tablespoons butter, bacon fat, or chicken fat
>   1 onion
>   1 leek
>   1 carrot
>   1 stalk celery
>   2 cloves garlic
>   1 bunch (1 pound) beets, peeled and chopped
>   4 cups chicken stock
>   generous *bouquet garni*
>   ½ teaspoon caraway seeds
>   2 teaspoons red wine vinegar, or to taste
>   salt and fresh black pepper

Prepare as described in the preceding recipe.

LESSON 3

Cream Soups

◇

Techniques:
THICKENING CREAM SOUPS
PUREEING CREAM SOUPS

Master Recipe:
CREAM OF JERUSALEM ARTICHOKE SOUP

Variations:
CURRIED CREAM OF BROCCOLI SOUP
CREAM OF WATERCRESS SOUP WITH
    PARSNIPS AND PEARS

◇   ◇   ◇

I must admit, cream soups make me nervous. Perhaps as a child I ate too much Campbell's. A cream soup can be as smooth as silk, rich as cream, and sophisticated as a Noel Coward heroine. But as often as not, it's a starchy paste unworthy of a spoon.

Cream soups are always thickened. There are three main thickeners: potatoes; starch thickeners, such as roux and slurry; and a cream and egg-yolk *liaison*. Each of these recipes uses at least one.

Potato is my favorite thickener. The starch naturally found in potatoes (and other starchy tubers, like parsnips and Jerusalem artichokes) thickens a soup without leaving a floury taste or a skin on the surface. The potatoes need only be cooked till soft, then pureed with the other vegetables.

Roux (flour and butter) and slurries (cornstarch or arrowroot dissolved in water) are often used to thicken cream soups made with stringy or watery vegetables, like lettuce or tomatoes. Of the two, I prefer roux, because it is added at the beginning. (The flour thus has longer to cook, reducing the chance of a floury taste at the end.) Slurries are whisked into a boiling soup at the last minute. (This is how the Chinese thicken hot and sour soup). The result always seems rather gelatinous to me.

The traditional thickener of French soups is an egg yolk and cream mixture called a *liaison*. The egg yolks are cooked to the point where they thicken but not so much that they scramble. (The principle is the same as in *crème anglaise*—see page 287). This method is tricky, because if the soup boils, the yolks will curdle. The safest way is to place the yolks in a large heatproof bowl. Add the cream and bring the soup just to a boil, then, whisking constantly, pour it in a thin stream into the egg yolks. (This way the temperature of the soup never exceeds the boiling point.) A yolk *liaison* produces a soup of unequaled creaminess.

◇ ◇ ◇

Cream of Jerusalem Artichoke Soup

The Jerusalem artichoke is neither from Jerusalem nor an artichoke. This small, lumpy tuber, also known as a "sunchoke," is actually a member of the sunflower family. Native to North America, the Jerusalem artichoke was introduced to Europe in the seventeenth century, an age when an exotic foodstuff had better sales appeal if its name suggested Near East or Oriental origins. (This is how turkey and Guinea fowl got their names, although both are in fact from America.) So someone, hearing the Italian word for "sunflower," *girasóle,* transformed it into the exotic-sounding "Jerusalem."

As for artichokes, the taste of this vitamin-rich tuber does indeed resemble its namesake. Its earthy flavor makes it delicious in soups, gratins, and purees. But feel free to substitute sweet potatoes, parsnips, or yams.

Serves 4–6

1½ pounds Jerusalem artichokes
4 tablespoons butter
1 onion, finely chopped
1 carrot, finely chopped
2 ribs celery, finely chopped
1 clove garlic, minced
2 cups chicken stock
2 cups milk
½ cup cream (optional)
  bouquet garni
  salt and plenty of fresh white pepper
6 sprigs fresh dill or parsley for garnish

1. Peel the Jerusalem artichokes with a paring knife or vegetable peeler. (This is no easy task, and it helps to buy smooth, round tubers.) Place the chokes in cold water to cover to keep them from discoloring.

2. Melt the butter in a large saucepan and cook the other vegetables over medium heat for 3 minutes or until soft. Dice the Jerusalem artichokes and add them. Press buttered foil over the vegetables, cover the pan, and sweat the vegetables over a low heat, stirring occasionally, for 10 minutes or until the chokes are soft.

3. Add the stock, milk, cream, *bouquet garni,* and seasonings, and simmer the soup for 15–20 minutes. Remove the *bouquet garni* and puree

the soup in a blender or food processor. NOTE: If using the processor, puree the solids first, adding the liquid gradually. If you want a perfectly smooth soup, force it through a China cap—a fine-meshed conical strainer that takes its name (*chinoise* in French) from its resemblance to a coolie's hat. The soup can be prepared ahead to this stage. Just before serving, reheat the soup, correct the seasoning, and garnish each bowl of soup with a sprig of dill or parsley.

Note: When substituting yams, parsnips, or sweet potatoes for the Jerusalem artichokes, alter the flavorings accordingly. Freshly grated ginger and a touch of maple syrup would, for example, be delicious with yams or sweet potatoes.

CURRIED CREAM OF BROCCOLI SOUP

Because broccoli is a relatively fibrous vegetable, we thicken this soup lightly with flour. Curry is not a single spice, of course, but a skillful blend of dozens of herbs and spices, including turmeric, cumin, coriander, cardamom, fenugreek, ginger, and cinnamon. Light frying intensifies the flavor of curry.

Serves 6

2 pounds broccoli
4 tablespoons butter
1 onion, finely chopped (about ¾ cup)
2 leeks, washed, trimmed, and finely chopped (about ¾ cup)
2 stalks celery, finely chopped
1 tablespoon fresh high-quality curry powder
2 tablespoons flour
4 cups chicken stock
1 clove garlic, minced
  bouquet garni
  salt, fresh black pepper, cayenne pepper
1 cup heavy cream

1. Cut the woody stems off the broccoli and discard. Cut the prettiest florets (green buds) off the other end until you have about ¾ cup. Cook the florets in rapidly boiling salted water for 3 minutes, or until crispy-tender. Refresh under cold water. Reserve these for garnish. Chop the remaining broccoli as finely as possible.

2. Melt the butter in a large saucepan. Sauté the onion, leeks, and celery over medium heat for 2 minutes. Add the curry powder and flour and sauté for 2–3 minutes more or until the onion is soft. Add the chopped broccoli, press a piece of buttered foil on top, cover the pan, and sweat the vegetables over low heat for 10 minutes.

3. Stir in the stock, garlic, *bouquet garni*, seasonings, and cream. Bring the soup to a boil, stirring constantly. Reduce heat and simmer for 15 minutes, or until the broccoli is very soft. Remove the *bouquet garni* and puree the soup in a blender or food processor. Again, if you want a *really* fine-textured soup, force it through a fine-meshed strainer. The soup can be prepared ahead to this stage.

4. Just before serving, reheat the soup and adjust the seasoning. Garnish each bowl with a few broccoli florets. Curried cream of broccoli soup calls for a big wine, like a California Chardonnay or a Riesling from the Pacific Northwest.

"Crispy-tender" describes a vegetable that is fully cooked but left a little bit crisp. The cooking time varies with the vegetable. The proper way to determine if a vegetable is crispy-tender is to taste it.

CREAM OF WATERCRESS SOUP WITH PARSNIPS AND PEARS

This soup is a variation on the traditional French cream of watercress soup. The parsnip adds a pleasant sweetness, not to mention the starch necessary to thicken the soup. The pear provides an unusual contrast to the cress. The size of a bunch of watercress varies widely from city to city: you want about 4 cups. The egg yolks will produce a soup of dizzying richness; omit them if your conscience so dictates.

Serves 4–6

      2 large or 4 small bunches watercress
      4 tablespoons butter
    3–4 shallots, finely chopped (about ¼ cup)
      2 leeks, trimmed, cleaned, and finely chopped (about ½ cup)
      2 parsnips, peeled and finely chopped (about 1 cup)
      4 cups chicken stock
        bouquet garni
      1 cup heavy cream
        salt and fresh black pepper
      2 very ripe pears
        juice of ½ lemon
      3 egg yolks (optional)

1. Wash the watercress, cut off the thick stems and reserve them. Finely chop the remainder. (The stems take the longest to cook, so they will go into the soup first.) Remove 25 of the prettiest leaves and reserve for garnish. Finely chop the remaining cress.

2. Melt the butter in a large non-aluminum saucepan. Sauté the shallots, leeks, and watercress stems over medium heat for 2–3 minutes, or until soft. Do not let the shallots brown. Add the parsnips and remaining watercress (minus the reserved leaves). Press a piece of buttered foil on top, cover the pan, and sweat the vegetables over low heat for 10 minutes, stirring occasionally.

3. Add the stock, *bouquet garni*, cream, and seasonings, and simmer the soup for 10–15 minutes, or until all the vegetables are very soft. Remove the *bouquet garni* and puree the soup in a blender or food processor. Strain if desired.

4. Just before serving, peel, core, and dice the pears, sprinkling the pieces with lemon juice. Add the pear to the soup, and bring it to a boil. Correct the seasoning. If using the egg yolks, place them in a large heatproof bowl and, whisking constantly, pour the hot soup in a thin stream into the yolks. Garnish each bowl with a few reserved watercress leaves and serve at once. A Minho Verde from Portugal or Gavi from Italy would make a nice accompaniment.

LESSON 4

Chowders

◇

Techniques:
SHUCKING CLAMS
TRYING SALT PORK

Master Recipe:
NEW ENGLAND CLAM CHOWDER

Variations:
BRETON SEAFOOD CHOWDER
SMOKED FISH CHOWDER

◇   ◇   ◇

Let the French have their bouilla-baisse, the Creoles, their gumbo. When it comes to fish soup, I raise my spoon for chowder. No dish is more typical of New England than chowder, introduced by the first Europeans—Breton fishermen —who plied our icy waters. Indeed, our word "chowder" comes from the French *chaudière,* the cast-iron cauldron in which these hardy fish stews were simmered.

Chowder began with the three ingredients seafarers always had on hand: salt pork, ship's biscuit, and sea-food. It wasn't until the mid-1800s that the milk, clams, and potatoes entered the picture, resulting in the soup we know today. New Yorkers added tomatoes (heresy to a New Englander), and the Portuguese fishermen who settled Provincetown contributed saffron, cumin, and vinegar. The lack of fresh seafood did not deter chowder makers in the western parts of New England: nineteenth-century cookbooks abound with recipes for corn, chicken, and veal chowders, and even a chowder of parsnips. Melville wasn't far off when he described life at the Try Pot Inn in Nantucket: "Chowder for breakfast, and chowder for dinner, and chowder for supper, 'til you began to look for fishbones coming through your clothes."

Chowder is one of the simplest of all soups to make, but woe betide the cook whose clams are tough or whose broth curdles. Some years ago, I received an anonymous note from a reader of *Boston Magazine* about a story I had written on chowder. The advice represents a concise treatise on the art of chowder making.

"Clam chowder will not curdle if made correctly, but it has to be 'built up.' We fry the pork scraps, brown the onion, add the clams or cod. The milk must be heated separately and then added to the other hot ingredients. You cannot add cold to hot or it will curdle. Cool air should not be allowed to hit the chowder while it is cooking, for that will curdle a chowder, too. True chowder can only be made with clams with bellies—the clam strips served widely today have no more flavor than rubber."

Wherever you are, anonymous reader, thank you!

SHUCKING CLAMS

For the best results, clams should be freshly shucked. Grasp the bivalve firmly in the palm of your left hand (or right hand if you are left-handed), hinge tucked into the base of your thumb. Place the blade of a shucking knife or butter knife flat against the crack where the shells meet. Insert the knife between the shells by pulling the blade with your first and second fingers toward your thumb. Once the adductor muscles are cut, the shells will open. Slide the knife along the inside of the shell to loosen the meat. I always place a pot holder between my hand and the shellfish to protect my palm. Be sure to work over a bowl to catch the clam liquor.

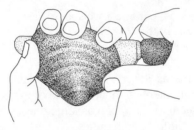

LAZY MAN'S METHOD: Place clams in a large pan with ¼ inch water. Tightly cover the pan, place over high heat, and steam the clams for 3 minutes or until the shells just begin to open. Remove clams from pan, and as soon as they are cool enough to handle, shuck them as described above. In many parts of the country, you can buy freshly shucked clams—a boon for the chowder maker. Canned clams should be used only as a last resort; they are not nearly as flavorful as the fresh.

Note: A full discussion of the various types of clams is found on page 147. For the following recipe we recommend quahaugs—a hard-shelled clam larger than a littleneck or cherrystone.

◇   ◇   ◇

New England Clam Chowder

The secret to New England clam chowder lies in the unexpected combination of land flavors and sea flavors in the form of salt pork and quahaugs (large hard-shelled clams). Salt pork was traditionally favored over butter as a frying fat because it was virtually unperishable. (For an interesting twist, try bacon.)

Serves 4–6

16 littleneck or cherrystone clams or 14 quahaugs (about 1½
      cups clam meat and liquor)
 1 2-inch cube (2 ounces) salt pork, or bacon
 1 onion, finely chopped (about ¾ cup)
 1 cup fish stock or bottled clam broth
 2 potatoes, peeled and cut into ½-inch cubes
   pinch of thyme
 1 cup light cream
 1 cup heavy cream
   fresh black pepper and a whisper of salt
 4 tablespoons butter for serving
   oyster crackers for serving

1. Open the clams as described above, working over a bowl to catch the liquor. Finely chop the clam meat by hand or in a food processor. (Small clams need not be as finely chopped as large ones.) Cut the rind off the salt pork, rinse, and cut it into ¼-inch cubes.

2. "Try" the salt pork in a large saucepan over medium heat; that is, sauté it for 3–4 minutes to render the fat and crisp the cubes. Reduce the heat slightly, add the onion, and cook for 3 minutes or until the onion is soft and translucent. Add the stock or broth, reserved clam liquor, potatoes, and thyme. Bring the mixture to a boil, reduce the heat, and gently simmer for 10 minutes or until the potatoes are almost tender. Add the light cream to the chowder five minutes after you add the potatoes.

2. To finish the chowder, add the clam meat and heavy cream to the chowder and simmer for 3 minutes. Season with salt and pepper, if necessary. You can serve the chowder right away (float a pat of butter on each portion), but it will taste even better if you let it "ripen" for a day. Let it cool, uncovered, to room temperature before refrigerating.

Serving: Serve New England quahaug chowder with oyster crackers and the best imported ale or stout money can buy.

BRETON SEAFOOD CHOWDER

Brittany is the westernmost province of France, a peninsula with brooding forests and craggy shores that juts far into the Atlantic. It was here that King Arthur supposedly dwelled, and many of the natives still speak a Celtic language that is closer to English than French. For centuries (perhaps even before the time of Columbus), Breton fishermen fished the waters of Greenland, Nova Scotia, and Maine.

Breton fish soup was probably the ancestor of our chowder. Sorrel is a lemony herb that adds color and piquancy—substitute spinach for the color but not for the flavor. This recipe was inspired by Parisian chef Fernand Chambrette, instructor at La Varenne cooking school.

Serves 6

> 2 pounds mixed white fish fillets, including cod, haddock, halibut, fluke, or monkfish, skin removed
> 2 pounds mussels, threads removed and scrubbed as described on page 148
> ¼ cup dry white wine
> 3 tablespoons butter
> 4 leeks, washed, green leaves discarded, and chopped (about 1 cup)
> 1 onion, finely chopped
> 1 clove garlic, finely chopped
> 5 cups fish stock, clam broth, or water reserved mussel broth
> 2 potatoes, peeled and cut in half lengthwise, then in ¼-inch slices
> *bouquet garni*
> 1½ cups heavy cream
> fresh black pepper and a little salt
> 1 bunch fresh sorrel or spinach (4 ounces), washed and cut widthwise into ¼-inch strips

1. Remove any bones and cut the fish into 1-inch chunks. Steam the mussels in the wine until the shells just open (see instructions on page 148). "Beard" the mussels, place a few back in the shells for garnish, and strain and reserve the mussel broth.

2. Melt the butter in a large saucepan over medium heat. Add the leeks, onion, and garlic and sauté for 4–5 minutes or until the vegetables are soft. Add the broth, potatoes, and *bouquet garni* and bring to a boil. Reduce heat and simmer until the potatoes are half-cooked, about 5 minutes. Add the fish and cream and boil rapidly for 5 minutes or until the fish flakes easily. Add the mussels, seasonings, and sorrel or spinach and simmer

for 30 seconds. Remove the *bouquet garni* and stir the soup well before serving.

Serving: Serve Breton chowder with crusty French bread, a green salad, and an acidic dry white wine like Muscadet or Gros Plant.

◇

In traditional recipes, the mussels would not be steamed separately but would be cooked directly in the soup. As many mussels sold in North America are sandy, we recommend steaming them separately to reduce the likelihood of getting sand in the soup. If you are feeling lazy or you know your mussels to be sandless, you can cook them directly in the chowder, adding them 3–4 minutes before you add the fish.

When cooking any fish soup, keep in mind the cooking time for each ingredient. Bivalves take longer to cook than fish (clams longer than mussels). Firm-fleshed fish, like monkfish or halibut, need more cooking time than flimsy fish, like cod or haddock. Add the fish in the proper sequence so that each will be done at the same time.

SMOKED FISH CHOWDER

We created this smoked fish chowder for *Bon Appetit* magazine during their visit to our school in May 1983. Feel free to use whatever smoked seafood is available in your area—a variety is nice—but avoid lox, which is not smoked at all but simply salted.

Serves 4

      3 tablespoons butter
      1 small onion, finely chopped
      1 celery stalk, finely chopped
      2 tablespoons flour
   1½ cups clam broth, fish stock, or water
      1 large potato, peeled and cut into ½-inch cubes
        bouquet garni
   1½ cups milk
      ½ pound boned smoked fish (salmon, whitefish, bluefish,
           scallops, oysters, etc.)
      ½ cup heavy cream
        fresh ground pepper and perhaps a little salt
      1 tablespoon chopped fresh chives
        prepared white horseradish (optional)

1. Melt the butter in a large saucepan over medium heat. Add the onion and celery, and cook for 3–4 minutes, or until soft. Stir in the flour to make a roux. Add the clam broth, potato, and *bouquet garni,* and bring to a boil. Reduce heat, and simmer the chowder for 6–8 minutes or until the potato is almost soft. Meanwhile, bring the milk to a boil in a separate pot and add it gradually to the chowder. The chowder can be prepared ahead to this stage.

2. Just before serving, add the smoked fish, cream, and pepper (and salt). Gently simmer the chowder for 5 minutes or until the fish flakes easily. Remove the *bouquet garni.* Garnish each bowl of smoked fish chowder with chopped chives and, if desired, a spoonful of horseradish.

Salads and Simple Dressings

◇

Techniques:

UNDERSTANDING LETTUCES, OILS, AND
  VINEGARS

WASHING LETTUCE

MAKING VINAIGRETTE SAUCE

SQUEEZING LEMONS

ASSEMBLING SALADS

Master Recipe:

GREEN SALAD WITH VINAIGRETTE SAUCE

Variations:

RASPBERRY WALNUT VINAIGRETTE

WATERCRESS AND BELGIAN ENDIVE AND
  WALNUT DRESSING

STEVEN RAICHLEN'S CAESAR SALAD

HOT GOAT CHEESE SALAD

SPINACH SALAD WITH MONKFISH AND
  GREEN PEPPERCORNS

◇   ◇   ◇

Cooking teachers are a finicky lot. Nothing raises my hackles like a poorly made salad. Alas, that's all one seems to find these days —flavorless iceberg lettuce, anemic tomatoes, and boxed croutons drowned in bottled dressing.

There are two basic kinds of salad: composed salads and green salads. What most Americans mean by salad is the former—lettuce garnished with vegetables, bacon, cheese, cold cuts, etc., served as an appetizer or even a light entrée. When the French say *salade,* they mean a simple green salad—lettuce demurely dressed with oil and vinegar, served after the entrée to refresh the palate. With the advent of *nouvelle cuisine,* the French have adopted the composed salad, lavished with foie gras, crayfish tails, fresh truffles, and other exotic ingredients. But before we can talk about salads—composed or simple—we must understand the basic ingredients: salad greens, oil, and vinegar.

SALAD GREENS

Iceberg lettuce may be fine on a sandwich, but when it comes to salad, I prefer a lettuce with flavor. This commonly means one of the *butterhead* lettuces, distinguished by their soft, curly, delicately flavored leaves. Popular varieties include *Boston* lettuce and *Bibb* lettuce, named for John Bibb, who developed it in Frankfort, Kentucky, in the 1850s.

The *loose leaf* lettuces, with their short, curly leaves that grow away from the stalk, are another good basic green. Popular species include *green leaf* lettuce and *red leaf* lettuce: the reddish edges of the latter are ideal for lining plates. *Romaine,* with its long, crisp, full-flavored leaves, is an essential component of Caesar salad. Fresh *spinach* is also delicious in salads; the young, flat leaves are the most succulent.

You may also wish to use what I call "condiment greens"—leafy vegetables that are too bitter to eat by themselves but compliment the milder lettuces. The most famous is *Belgian endive,* distinguished by its cylindrical, ivory-colored leaves tipped with green, and its nutty, mildly bitter flavor. Related to Belgian endive botanically, if not in appearance, is *chickory,* a bitter green with long, slender, jagged leaves. *Endive* is somewhat milder than chickory, with crisp, green, curly, jagged-edged leaves. *Escarole* has a similar flavor and is distinguished by a light-green hue, and broad, round, fleshy leaves.

This brings us to what I call "gourmet greens"—rare lettuces whose high prices make them fare for special occasions. A few years ago, such exotica as *mâche* and *radicchio* were eaten only in Europe, but with swift air freight and growing demand, these luxury lettuces can now be found in most major U.S. cities.

Lamb's lettuce (also called *corn lettuce* and *mâche* in French) has small, dark-green spoon-shaped leaves and a flavor most aptly described as buttery. *Trevisse* is a French lettuce the size of a single brussels sprout, with burgundy-colored leaves, bone-white stalks, and a taste vaguely reminiscent of cabbage. *Radicchio,* darling of today's chefs, has curly red leaves prettily marbled with white and is the size of a tennis ball. (It tastes faintly bitter.) *Rocket,* better known by its Italian name *arugula,* has peppery leaves the shape of those of a radish plant. Similarly peppery are *watercress* and *mustard greens,* both of which add zing to an ordinary salad.

OILS

Olive oil is the traditional anointment for salads. It comes in three grades: pure, virgin, and extra-virgin. *Extra-virgin* is the best, made from hand-culled olives that are cold-pressed (crushed between stones, not in a machine) and filtered through cloths rather than purified with chemicals. Most extra-virgin olive oils come from small farms in southern France and Italy, and their incredible fragrance makes them worth their astronomical price. (Fortunately, a little goes a long way.) The French oils are lighter and more delicate than the Italian oils, which increase in flavor the farther south they are made.

Virgin olive oil is inferior to extra-virgin in that it is crushed in mechanical presses, the heat from which alters the natural flavor of the oil. There is nothing "pure" about *pure olive oil,* which is made from pits and pulp of previously pressed olives and is often extracted with chemical solvents.

In their search for exotic flavors, contemporary chefs have rediscovered the nut oils that French peasants have used for centuries. French nut oils include *walnut, hazelnut,* and *grape seed.* Japanese *sesame oil* is delicious, too. Nut oils have a strong, sometimes overpowering flavor, and I usually combine them with a neutral vegetable oil. Once opened, they should be stored in the refrigerator as they are highly perishable.

VINEGARS

Vinegar means "sour wine," literally. Today it is made with every imaginable sort—Cabernet Sauvignon, Chardonnay, even champagne.

Wine vinegar is not the only kind of vinegar, although it is the one I prefer for salads. *Distilled vinegar* has lots of acidity, but it lacks the depth of flavor of wine vinegar. *Cider vinegar* is rather sweet for green salads, but it sure tastes good on coleslaw and bean salad. From Spain comes *sherry vinegar*—sharply acetic and nut-flavored—ideal for salads with bitter greens, like Belgian endive or chickory. I like the mildness of Japanese *rice vinegar* for seasoning delicate greens like lamb's lettuce and Bibb.

One of the most delicious vinegars is *aceto balsamico*—Italian balsamic vinegar. Made from grape must (crushed, partially fermented grapes) rather than from fully fermented wine, *balsamic vinegar* is the color and consistency of soy sauce. It is so sweet, so rich, so mellow, you can sip it full strength without puckering. Italians like to sprinkle it on strawberries for dessert.

The increased interest in rare oils has been accompanied by a proliferation of exotic vinegars, including herb vinegars, fruit vinegars (raspberry vinegar has become the sine qua non of contemporary cooking), even vinegars flavored with lavender. There's no reason to pay astronomic prices for commercial flavored vinegars when it is so easy to make your own. To make raspberry vinegar, combine 1 quart white wine vinegar or cider vinegar with 1 pint fresh or unsweetened frozen raspberries and let stand for at least 2 days before straining. Fresh herb vinegars would be made the same way, substituting a bunch of bruised fresh herbs for the raspberries. (To bruise herbs, crush them lightly with the back of a knife.)

WASHING AND STORING LETTUCE

The best way to wash salad greens is to fill a large bowl (or the bottom of a salad spinner) with water and float the individual leaves in it. Agitate the lettuce gently to shake loose the sand. Lift the leaves out of the water, leaving the dirt at the bottom. Change the water once or twice or until the greens are clean. Do not pour the leaves into a strainer, or you will wash the dirt back onto them.

Drying lettuce was a problem before the advent of the salad spinner—a marvelous invention I rank in importance with the food processor and mixer. If you do not own a spinner, place the greens inside a pillowcase (or dish towel folded in two) and twirl them rapidly over your head for two minutes. Twirl lettuce out-of-doors, as the centrifugal force will spray the water in every direction.

To store greens, wrap them loosely in a paper towel moistened with cold water. Place in a plastic bag, but do not seal the end, so the lettuce can "breathe." Unsealed, the lettuce will keep up to a week (provided you keep the paper towel moist). Sealed it will keep at most 24 hours. Salad greens should be torn, not cut, as a knife will darken the edges.

◇   ◇   ◇

Green Salad with Vinaigrette Sauce

The Spanish say it takes four men to make a perfect salad: a spendthrift to add the oil, a miser to dose out the vinegar, a wise man to parcel the salt, and a madman to do the mixing. I like a four to one ratio of oil to acid, mellowing the vinegar with lemon juice. Nor should you stint on the salt: the chief flaw in most homemade dressings is underseasoning.

Serves 4

> 1 large or 2 small heads Boston, butter, Bibb, green leaf, and/
> or red leaf lettuce
> basic Vinaigrette Sauce (see below)
> 1 tablespoon chopped fresh chives or other herbs

Wash and dry the lettuce as described on page 46, discarding any blemished leaves. Prepare the vinaigrette sauce in the salad bowl and place the lettuce on top. A few moments before serving, toss the salad and serve on chilled salad plates, with a sprinkling of chives for garnish.

VINAIGRETTE SAUCE

I make my vinaigrette sauce right in the salad bowl. The mustard helps the dressing emulsify. It is also important to whisk in the oil *gradually*. Squeeze the lemon through your fingers, as shown below, to catch the seeds.

>2 teaspoons red wine vinegar
>juice of ½ lemon (or to taste)
>1 scant teaspoon Dijon- or Meaux-style mustard
>¼ teaspoon salt
>fresh black pepper
>1 small clove garlic, minced (optional)
>4 tablespoons extra-virgin olive oil

Combine all the ingredients but the oil in the bottom of a salad bowl. Whisk until the individual grains of salt are completely dissolved. Vigorously whisk in the oil, little by little, to make a smooth emulsion.

Note: For spooning over fresh asparagus or cold poached seafood, vinaigrette can be prepared in the blender. (The food processor makes a poor emulsion.) Alternatively, the ingredients can be shaken together in a small sealed jar. Contrary to the practice of most chefs, I do not agree that vinaigrette may be made more than an hour ahead of time: it loses its fresh flavor.

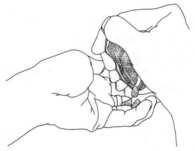

RASPBERRY WALNUT VINAIGRETTE

Raspberry vinegar is widely available, or you can make your own, as described on page 46. To toast walnuts, roast them on a piece of foil or a baking sheet in a hot (400°) oven or toaster oven for 10 minutes, or until well browned.

>1 tablespoon raspberry vinegar
>the juice of ½ lemon

½ teaspoon Dijon-style mustard
¼ teaspoon salt (or to taste)
   fresh black pepper
2 tablespoons chopped, toasted walnuts (optional)
4 tablespoons walnut oil, or 2 tablespoons each walnut oil and
   vegetable oil

Prepare as described above.

WATERCRESS AND BELGIAN ENDIVE WITH WALNUT DRESSING

This simple salad takes two minutes to make and goes well with omelettes, poached fish, or roast chicken. I don't even premix the dressing but simply sprinkle the oil, lemon juice, salt, and pepper directly on the greens.

Serves 4

2 heads Belgian endive
1 large or 2 small bunches watercress
3 tablespoons walnut oil
   juice of 1 lemon
   plenty of salt and fresh black pepper

Wash the endive and break it into leaves. Wash the watercress, twist off the coarse stems (the bottom two inches), and tear the remainder into two-inch sprigs. Combine these ingredients in a salad bowl. Just before serving add the oil, then lemon, then salt and pepper, and toss. Correct the seasoning and serve. For a pretty presentation, stand the endive leaves on end around the inside of the salad bowl.

STEVEN RAICHLEN'S CAESAR SALAD

Caesar salad is a dish dear to my heart, for it is the first "gourmet" recipe I ever prepared. The year was 1963, the place was Baltimore's Restaurant 3900 (since defunct), and a ten-year-old boy watched, spellbound, as a wizened waiter named Mr. Lewis mashed the garlic, chopped the anchovies, and squeezed the lemon juice to make Caesar salad. It was not long before the boy was at Mr. Lewis's side helping, then making the salad himself. Eventually he became a cooking teacher and the author of this book.
    I never bother to coddle the egg when making Caesar salad for myself,

but coddling the egg (boiling it for 2 minutes) will reassure squeamish guests when you prepare the salad at the tableside. (And you should: this is a dish that demands theatrics.) If you don't mention the presence of anchovies (and omit them as a garnish), most people—even the squeamish ones—won't even know that they are there. By the way, small heads of romaine tend to be less bitter than large ones.

Serves 4–6

- 2 small heads romaine lettuce
- 6 well-drained anchovy fillets, plus 8 to 12 fillets for garnish
- 1 small clove garlic, minced
    juice of ½ lemon (or to taste)
- 2 dashes Worcestershire sauce
- 1 teaspoon Dijon-style mustard
    a little salt and plenty of fresh black pepper
- 3 tablespoons extra-virgin olive oil
- 8–10 croûtes (see recipe on page 215) cut into 1-inch pieces
- 1 egg, coddled (boiled for 2 minutes) or raw
- 6 tablespoons freshly grated Romano cheese

1. Wash and dry the lettuce, discarding any blemished or tough outside leaves. This can be done ahead—store the lettuce leaves wrapped in damp paper towels inside an open plastic bag. Tear each leaf into two-inch pieces.

2. Just before serving, mash the six anchovy fillets with the garlic in the bottom of a wide salad bowl (or chop on a cutting board). Whisk in the lemon juice, Worcestershire sauce, mustard, salt, and pepper. Gradually whisk in the oil to make an emulsified dressing. Add the lettuce and croutons and gently toss to coat with dressing. Crack the egg on top and toss to blend. Sprinkle most of the cheese in and toss again. Divide the Caesar salad among chilled salad plates and garnish each with crossed anchovy fillets and a sprinkling of cheese. Serve at once. Fill your water goblets: there is no wine that can stand up to Caesar salad.

HOT GOAT CHEESE SALAD

I first tasted this salad in the Cévennes, a rocky highland in south-central France immortalized by Robert Louis Stevenson in his *Travels with a Donkey*. It's a clever way to combine the salad course and cheese course of a traditional French meal. Use a cylindrical-shaped goat cheese: montrachet if you like a mild cheese, or crotin de chavignol if you like something stronger. The cheese can either be broiled on a slice of French bread or breaded and pan-fried as described on page 67.

Serves 4

1 small head mild lettuce, like Boston or Bibb
1 bunch peppery greens, like arugula, mustard greens, or
    watercress
    Raspberry Walnut Vinaigrette (see page 48)
8 thin slices French bread
8 ½-inch slices goat cheese
4 tablespoons coarsely chopped walnuts

Wash and dry the greens. Prepare the dressing. Lightly toast the bread slices in a toaster oven (or under the broiler), top with goat cheese, and broil for 1–2 minutes, or until the cheese is hot and lightly browned. Meanwhile, toss the greens with the dressing. Mound the salad on one side of each salad plate and sprinkle with nuts. Place 2 hot goat cheese toasts on the other side. Serve at once.

SPINACH SALAD WITH MONKFISH AND GREEN PEPPERCORNS

In 1979 I had the good fortune to work with a gifted young chef in Brittany named Louis LeRoy. *Nouvelle cuisine* was all the rage and so were hot-cold salads like this one. Monkfish is discussed on page 133; feel free to substitute sea scallops or shrimp. (A full discussion of how to clean shrimp or scallops is found on pages 154 and 155.)

Green peppercorns are the pickled fruit of the pepper tree. Available canned or bottled at specialty shops, they have the flavor of pepper without the fiery bite. When dried, green peppercorns become black peppercorns; when they are peeled, then dried, they become white peppercorns.

Serves 4

¾ pound monkfish, or sea scallops, or shrimp
    salt and fresh black pepper
2 tablespoons extra-virgin olive oil
2 tablespoons green peppercorns, drained
12 ounces spinach, stems removed, washed, and dried
    Vinaigrette Sauce (see page 48)
2 tablespoons finely chopped shallots

1. Trim the grayish membrane off the monkfish and cut the fish across the grain into ¼-inch slices. Season with salt and pepper. Pour half the olive oil in a small frying pan, arrange the fish on top, and sprinkle with the remaining oil and the green peppercorns. Wash the spinach and make the dressing. The recipe can be prepared ahead to this stage.

2. Cook the monkfish, uncovered, in a preheated 400° oven for 6–8 minutes, or until the fish flakes easily. (Alternatively, the fish can be cooked on the stove over medium heat, but you'll have to turn the pieces.) Meanwhile, toss the spinach with the dressing. To serve, place a neat pile of spinach on each plate and arrange two or three peppered monkfish slices on top. Sprinkle with finely chopped shallots.

LESSON 6

Mayonnaise and Blender Dressings

—————◊—————

Techniques:
MAKING MAYONNAISE
TRIMMING AND COOKING ARTICHOKES

Master Recipes:
MAYONNAISE
BLENDER DRESSINGS

Variations:
FLAVORED MAYONNAISES
BLENDER SALAD DRESSINGS
ARTICHOKE SALAD WITH CURRY
   MAYONNAISE

◊ ◊ ◊

To most Americans the mere mention of the word "mayonnaise" summons visions of blue and white jars of Hellman's. (It's my favorite commercial brand.) The French have not forgotten how easy mayonnaise is to make from scratch; I have even watched housewives mix the ingredients with a fork. Homemade mayonnaise takes minutes to make and will keep in the refrigerator for two or three days.

This lesson focuses on how to make mayonnaise by hand, in a blender, and in a food processor. And while we have the blender handy, we'll also prepare a few creamy salad dressings. The finale is a stunning artichoke salad with curry mayonnaise—a synthesis of everything we have learned in the last two lessons.

Mayonnaise, like its cooked cousin hollandaise, is an emulsion; that is, a stable combination of two liquids that would normally remain separate. In the case of mayonnaise the liquids are vegetable oil and the water found in egg yolks. The secret of inextricably combining them lies in whisking them into minute particles, which are coated and stabilized by an emulsifying agent—lecithin—that is naturally found in egg yolks.

In practical terms, there are five cardinal rules for making mayonnaise:

—Have all ingredients at room temperature. To bring an egg that has just emerged from the refrigerator to room temperature, run it under hot water.

—Use a heavy glass or ceramic bowl with a rounded bottom inside, so that you will have both hands free to whisk and add the oil. Never use an aluminum bowl; it will turn the egg yolks green.

—Use a flavorless vegetable oil (unless you are making *aioli* (garlic mayonnaise). Olive oil disturbs the delicate balance of salt, mustard, and lemon juice.

—To bring back curdled mayonnaise, try whisking in a tablespoon of ice water. If this does not work, start with another egg yolk in another bowl, and whisk the curdled mayonnaise into this.

—Avoid making mayonnaise during a thunderstorm: the static electricity can interfere with the emulsification process.

◇　◇　◇

Basic Mayonnaise

Makes approximately 1 cup

1　large egg yolk
1　heaping teaspoon Dijon-style mustard
　　approximately ¼ teaspoon salt
1　cup flavorless vegetable oil
　　the juice of ½ lemon (or to taste), or an equal amount of
　　　　wine vinegar
　　fresh white pepper, cayenne pepper

Hand Method

1. Place the egg yolk, mustard, and salt in a heavy 4-cup bowl. Whisk these ingredients together until the individual grains of salt are dissolved.

Whisk in the oil in a *very* thin stream. When the sauce begins to thicken (after 3–4 tablespoons of oil), you can add the oil more quickly. Once all the oil has been added, the sauce should be as thick as pudding.

2. Whisk in the lemon juice, which will thin and lighten the sauce, followed by pepper, cayenne pepper, and, if needed, a little more salt. Correct the seasoning: mayonnaise should be very flavorful.

Blender Method

Place the yolk, mustard, and salt in a blender. Running the machine at low speed, add the oil in a thin stream, followed by the lemon juice and seasonings.

Food Processor Method

When making mayonnaise in a food processor, you must use more oil and a whole egg rather than an egg yolk.

Place 1 whole egg, the mustard, and the salt in the food processor, and run the machine for 1 minute. Add 1½ cups oil in a thin stream, followed by the lemon juice and seasonings.

◇   ◇   ◇

CUMIN-CAPER MAYONNAISE (a variation on tartar sauce): To 1 batch of basic mayonnaise add ½ teaspoon ground cumin, 1 tablespoon drained, finely chopped capers, 1 tablespoon drained, finely chopped *cornichons* (tiny sour French pickles), 1 tablespoon finely chopped green olives, and 3 finely chopped anchovy fillets. Serve with any kind of grilled or fried fish.

CURRY MAYONNAISE: To 1 batch of basic mayonnaise add 2–3 teaspoons good curry powder and a pinch of cayenne pepper.

HERB MAYONNAISE: Cook ¼ pound stemmed, washed spinach or watercress in rapidly boiling, salted water for 30 seconds. Rinse under cold water, drain, and wring dry. Very finely chop the spinach or watercress with 2 tablespoons fresh herbs, including basil, tarragon, oregano, and/or parsley. Make a batch of basic mayonnaise and whisk in the herb mixture. If desired, the sauce can be thinned with a little heavy cream. Serve herb mayonnaise with hearts of palm, steamed shellfish, or poached chicken breasts.

Blender Salad Dressings

The food processor has revolutionized cooking, but it will never completely replace that time-honored tool, the blender. Food processors simply aren't powerful enough to churn chunks of cheese, garlic, ginger, or even *tofu* (soybean curd) into smooth, creamy dressings. Each of the recipes below makes 1 cup dressing.

◇ ◇ ◇

UMEBOSHI PLUM DRESSING

Umeboshi are Japanese salted plums flavored with a basil-like herb called "beefsteak leaf." Their fruity tartness makes an intriguing dressing for salads. *Umeboshi* comes in paste form and as pitted, salted dried fruit; both are available at Japanese markets and health food stores.

> ¼ cup umeboshi plums, pitted, or 3 tablespoons plum paste
> 2 cloves garlic
> ⅓ cup sour cream
> ⅓ cup vegetable oil
> 2 tablespoons vinegar
> juice of ½ lemon
> fresh black pepper

Combine the ingredients in a blender and puree until smooth. Serve with a sturdy lettuce, like romaine, green leaf, and/or Belgian endive.

CREAMY TOFU DRESSING

High in protein, low in fat, *tofu* (soybean curd) has achieved worldwide popularity. Fresh tofu can be found at any Oriental grocery store; most supermarkets carry vacuum-packed bean curd. *Mirin* is a sweet Japanese rice wine; if unavailable, substitute white wine with a little sugar. Incidentally, this is one dressing that goes well with iceberg lettuce.

> 1 3-inch square tofu
> 1 clove garlic
> ½ inch fresh ginger root
> 2 tablespoons chopped scallion
> 1 tablespoon sesame oil

3 tablespoons soy sauce
2 tablespoons rice wine vinegar
2 tablespoons *mirin* (or white wine)
1 tablespoon sugar (2 tablespoons if using white wine instead
    of *mirin*)
¼ cup sour cream
¼ cup vegetable oil
    fresh black pepper and perhaps a whisper of salt

Combine all the ingredients in a blender and puree until smooth.

ROQUEFORT CHEESE DRESSING

Few people have ever tasted real Roquefort dressing. (Most is actually made with blue cheese.) Roquefort differs from all other blue cheeses in that it is made of sheep's milk. It is ripened in limestone caves. Roquefort cheese dressing goes well with Boston lettuce.

3 ounces imported Roquefort cheese
¼ cup vegetable oil
¼ cup sour cream
2 tablespoons wine vinegar
    juice of 1 lemon (or to taste)
    plenty of fresh black pepper, a little salt
    approximately 4 tablespoons cream

Combine the first six ingredients in a blender and puree until smooth. Whisk in the cream.

ARTICHOKE SALAD WITH CURRY MAYONNAISE

The artichoke is an edible thistle, but woe betide the neophyte who has not been warned how to eat one. I still remember my first artichoke. I was in a small neighborhood restaurant in Paris. For all that people touted French cuisine, this was the toughest vegetable I had ever tasted. The *patron* watched with amusement as I struggled to chew the whole leaves. He finally took pity on me and showed me the correct way to eat an artichoke. The leaves are plucked like the petals of a flower; the edible part is "nibbled" from the base of each leaf by pulling it through your front teeth. The "choke," or bristlelike core, is cut away and discarded, leaving the delectable heart at the center.

This recipe may seem involved, but it is nothing more than a series of simple steps that we have learned in the preceding lessons. For complete instructions on roasting peppers, see page 261. Alternatively, you can use jarred pimentos.

Serves 6

6 artichokes
½ lemon
salted water

FOR THE GARNISH:

3 heads Belgian endive
18 snow peas
1 large or 2 small red bell peppers
1 large or 2 small yellow peppers

FOR THE LIGHT VINAIGRETTE:

juice of ½ lemon
2 teaspoons red wine vinegar
salt and freshly ground black pepper
3 tablespoons extra-virgin olive oil
Curry Mayonnaise (see recipe on page 55)

1. To trim the artichokes, cut off the stem flush with the bottom. Cut off the top of the artichoke an inch below the crown. (Use a sharp, heavy knife because the leaves are very tough.) With a scissors snip off the barbed top of each leaf. Rub the cut ends with lemon to prevent them from blackening.

2. Cook the artichokes in at least 3 quarts of salted, rapidly boiling, acidulated (add a few drops lemon juice or vinegar) water for 25 minutes, or until the leaves pull off easily and the hearts can be pierced with a skewer. Do not overcook the artichokes, or they will fall apart.

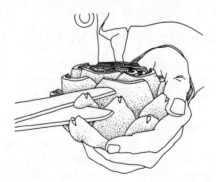

3. Drain the artichokes, refresh them under cold water, and drain the chokes upside down. You should also squeeze the chokes in the palm of your hand upside down to extract every last bit of water. Using a grapefruit

spoon, scoop out the center leaves and the bristlelike "choke," taking care not to pierce the heart. You should wind up with a 1½-inch cavity.

4. Break the endive into individual leaves. Snap the snow peas and blanch in rapidly boiling heavily salted water till crispy-tender. Refresh. Roast the peppers and peel, core, and slice them into ½-inch strips.

5. Prepare the light vinaigrette: whisk the ingredients together in a small bowl. Alternatively, the ingredients can be combined in a sealed jar and shaken.

6. To assemble the salad, place an artichoke in the center of each of six chilled dinner plates. Quickly toss the endive, snow peas, and red and yellow pepper strips in the vinaigrette and arrange them around the artichoke, like the spokes around a hub, alternating the colors. Place a generous spoonful of curry mayonnaise in the center of each artichoke (this is best done with a piping bag), and serve extra sauce on the side. Be sure to provide an empty bowl for the leaves.

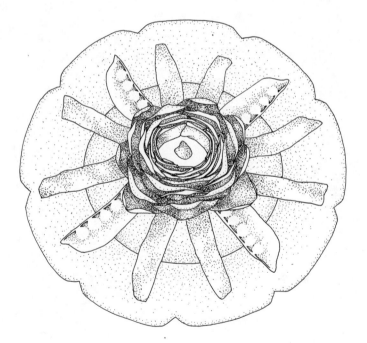

APPETIZERS

LESSON 7

Fritters and Tomato Sauce

◇

Techniques:
BREADING
BAKING FRITTERS

Master Recipe:
DÉLICES DE GRUYÈRE (CHEESE FRITTERS
    WITH TOMATO SAUCE)

Variation:
HOT GOAT CHEESE FRITTERS

◇   ◇   ◇

The fritter has a bum rap—think of the expression "to fritter one's time away." Nonetheless, these bite-sized snacks have been popular since Roman times. Our word "fritter" comes from the French *friture*—referring to both fried fare and the fryer in which it is cooked.

This lesson focuses on a long-time Bernerhof specialty—*délices de Gruyère* (pronounced "day-lease de gree-air")—Swiss cheese fritters. The filling for the *délices* is a sticky dough not unlike choux pastry (see Lesson 51). The dough is flavored with mustard, scallions, and gruyère cheese, then rolled into cork shapes, breaded, and fried. The délices are served with a quick tomato sauce (see below).

A NOTE ON MAKING FRITTERS

BREADING is one of the most universal cooking methods—used by the French to cook fish and the Viennese to make *Wiener schnitzel.* The procedure is simple: an ingredient is dipped first in flour, then in beaten egg, and finally in bread crumbs. When the breading is fried, it forms a crisp crust, leaving the filling moist and succulent. Breading has two advantages over batters: it can be done ahead of time and can be baked as well as fried—a boon to people wishing to limit their intake of fat. Here are some points to keep in mind when breading.

1. Use forks to dip the ingredients in the flour, egg, and bread crumbs. If you use your fingers, they will quickly become coated with crumbs.

2. Crumb-coated fritters can be pan-fried or baked in the oven. When pan-frying, use clarified butter or a half-and-half mixture of butter and veg-

etable oil: the oil has a higher burning point than butter and will keep it from burning.

3. Baking is an even better way to cook fritters. Lightly brown the crumb-coated fritters in butter, then bake them in the oven. This allows you to use less fat, and you can make the fritters ahead of time and bake them at the last minute.

4. Use fresh crumbs for breading; store-bought crumbs brown too much when fried. To make fresh bread crumbs, grind a firm, dense white bread in a food processor. Sieve if necessary to remove large pieces, and store excess crumbs in the freezer. Crumbs can also be made from stale bread, but the breading will not be as moist. For an interesting twist, try adding ground nuts to the bread crumbs.

5. If you wish to freeze fritters, first brown them lightly in butter. To heat, bake the frozen fritters, loosely covered with foil, in a 400° oven till crisp. Always blot fritters on paper towels to remove grease before serving.

◇ ◇ ◇

Délices de Gruyère

CHEESE FRITTERS WITH QUICK TOMATO SAUCE

These rich cheese croquettes have been a house specialty at the Bernerhof since the fifties, when Berne, Switzerland–born Claire Zumstein brought her wonderful Swiss recipes to New Hampshire's Mount Washington Valley. Gruyère is a cow's milk cheese made in France and Switzerland, distinguished from Emmenthaler ("Swiss") cheese by its small (pea-sized) holes, firm texture, and pungent taste. *Délices* can be made with any firm cheese, including cheddar.

Makes 20 fritters—enough to serve 6 as an appetizer

FOR THE FILLING:

    1 cup milk
    3 tablespoons butter, cut into small pieces
      salt, pepper, cayenne pepper, freshly grated nutmeg
    ⅔ cup flour
    5 ounces Gruyère cheese, grated
    4 tablespoons chopped scallions
    1 teaspoon Dijon-style mustard
    2 egg yolks

TO FINISH THE FRITTERS:

> 1 cup flour
> 1 egg, beaten
> 1 cup fresh bread crumbs
> 6 tablespoons clarified butter (see page 201), or 3 tablespoons
> butter and 3 tablespoons oil

1. Prepare the filling. Bring the milk to a boil in a large saucepan with the butter and seasonings. Remove the pan from the heat, sift in the flour, and stir the mixture with a wooden spoon over a medium heat for 1–2 minutes to obtain a paste the consistency of mashed potatoes. Remove pan from heat and beat in the cheese, scallions, mustard, and egg yolks. Spread the mixture in a flat pan, cover with plastic wrap, and chill for at least 3 hours, preferably overnight.

2. Prepare the fritters. Roll the chilled cheese mixture on a lightly floured surface to form long, ¾-inch-thick tubes. Cut each tube into 2½-inch lengths to make the individual croquettes. Have the flour, egg, and bread crumbs in shallow bowls. Dip each croquette in flour, then in egg, then finally in bread crumbs.

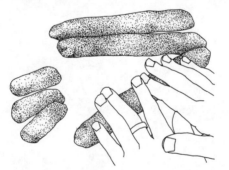

3. Heat the butter in a large frying pan over medium-high heat and brown the croquettes on all sides. Blot on paper towels. The fritters can be prepared up to 12 hours ahead to this stage, or they can be fully cooked and then frozen.

4. Just before serving, bake the croquettes in a preheated 400° oven for 10 minutes, or until crisp on the outside and hot and moist within.

Serving: Arrange three croquettes on a salad plate, ends joined at one end and spread out at the other. Place a spoonful of quick tomato sauce (see below) where the fritters meet, and garnish each plate with a sprig of parsley or dill. A Riesling from Alsace, California, or Washington State would make a good accompaniment.

◇　◇　◇

TO PEEL AND SEED TOMATOES

To Peel Tomatoes: Cut out the stem end with a sharp paring knife, and cut a small X on the bottom. Plunge the tomato in rapidly boiling water for 20–30 seconds, rinse it under cold water, then pull the skin off with your fingers.

To Seed Tomatoes: Cut them in half widthwise and hold them, cut side down, in the palm of your hand. Squeeze each half gently over a bowl or garbage disposal to wring out the seeds and watery juices.

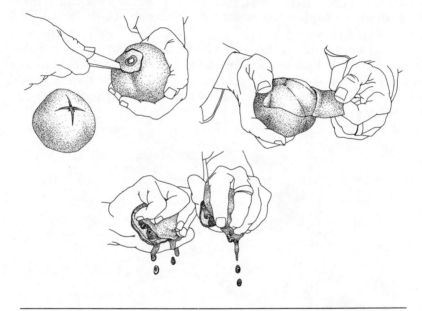

QUICK TOMATO SAUCE

This quick tomato sauce can be made with fresh tomatoes but only if they are very ripe. I usually use a good canned variety, like plum tomatoes from Italy.

Makes 2 cups

1 pound fresh *ripe* tomatoes, or 1 pound good-quality canned
    tomatoes
4 tablespoons extra-virgin olive oil

    1 onion, finely chopped
    1 green pepper, cored, seeded, finely chopped
1–2 cloves garlic, minced
    2 tablespoons chopped basil, oregano, or other fresh herb
      salt and fresh black pepper

1. Peel and seed the fresh tomatoes. If using canned tomatoes, seed them and drain. Finely chop the tomatoes.

2. Heat the olive oil in a saucepan. Sauté the onion and pepper over medium heat for 3 minutes or until soft. Add the garlic and cook for 30 seconds. Add the tomatoes, increase heat to high, and simmer for 2–3 minutes to evaporate some of the liquid. Stir in the fresh herb and salt and pepper to taste. The virtue of this sauce is its freshness. It should not take more than 10 minutes to make.

HOT GOAT CHEESE FRITTERS

I first tasted these hot goat cheese fritters in the southwest of France as part of a salad. But they go equally well atop grilled lamb chops or medallions of veal, or even by themselves as an appetizer. Literally dozens of goat cheeses are available in gourmet shops; for the best results select a soft, mild, log-shaped cheese, like a montrachet. (Don't worry about the black coating—edible ash—found on many goat cheeses.)

Makes approximately 12 fritters

    8 ounces montrachet, or other soft, mild goat cheese
    1 cup flour
    1 egg beaten with a pinch of salt
    1 cup fresh bread crumbs
    3 tablespoons butter
    3 tablespoons oil

1. Cut the cheese into ½-inch-thick slices. Using a fork, dip each slice first in flour (shake off excess), then in beaten egg, finally in the bread crumbs. Arrange on a dry plate. The breading can be done 2 hours ahead of time.

2. Heat the butter with the oil until foaming. (When the fat is the right temperature, dancing bubbles will form around a dipped slice of cheese.) Fry the cheese slices on one side for 30 seconds, or until golden brown, turn, and cook the other side the same way. The cheese can be lightly browned ahead of time in half as much fat and baked in a 400° oven. Blot on paper towels to remove excess fat before serving.

LESSON 8

Fondues and Dipping Sauces

◇

Technique:
TABLETOP COOKING

Master Recipe:
CHEESE FONDUE BERNERHOF

Variations:
CHEDDAR CHEESE FONDUE WITH STOUT
BAGNA CAUDA (HOT ANCHOVY DIP)
BURGUNDIAN BEEF FONDUE
DIPPING SAUCES

◇ ◇ ◇

Foods, like hemlines, go in and out of fashion. Consider the fondue. Ten years ago, any couple about to be wed could count on receiving at least three fondue sets among their presents. Today, the fondue is considered as corny as quiche, and tabletop cooking has gone the way of the waffle iron and crockpot.

The Taste of the Mountains Cooking School deplores this second-class status. Since our founding in 1980, we have welcomed students with an opening night fondue dinner. The reason is simple. Fondue is the perfect ice breaker, an ideal way for strangers to become friends as they share a common cooking pot. It is especially well suited to people who enjoy cooking, allowing each guest to customize the dish to taste. The universality of fondue—from Italian *bagna cauda* to Japanese *tempura* and Mongolian "firepot"—attests to its success as a method of cooking and as a way of bringing people together.

Fondues fall into one of two broad categories—dipping fondues and cooking fondues. The former consist of a highly flavored sauce (cheese in the case of *fondue savoyarde,* anchovy sauce in *bagna cauda*). The "dippers" range from lightly toasted bread cubes to sausages, vegetables, and even fruits. Cooking fondues consist of a hot liquid (oil in the case of *tempura* or beef fondue, stock in the case of Mongolian firepot) in which raw meat, poultry, and seafood are actually cooked. Both types demand visual artistry in arranging the dipping ingredients on the platter. And both types can, to a large extent, be prepared ahead.

For any fondue, you will need a fondue pot with an adjustable burner. Choose a set with a sturdy stand and a heavy pot for better heat conduction.

Following are four fondues designed to bring people together. On page 316 you will find a recipe for chocolate fondue for dessert.

◇　◇　◇

Cheese Fondue Bernerhof

Fondue began, so the story goes, as a piece of cheese that was too hard to eat. An enterprising Alpine cowherd (history neglects to say which one) melted it in a pot of boiling wine to make it palatable. Naturally, the cowherd had a clove of garlic, a flask of kirsch (cherry brandy), and bread for dipping. In time, his humble attempt to salvage stale cheese became the national dish of Switzerland!

Traditional Swiss fondue is made with Emmenthaler and Gruyère cheese, the former distinguished by its large holes and mild flavor, the latter by small holes and nutty bite. In the French Alps, Gruyère alone would be used. I have also made fine fondues with cheddar, or even smoked cheese. The wine should be quite acidic, like a Soave, Sauvignon Blanc, or inexpensive Chardonnay.

Serves 4

FOR THE FONDUE:

    1 clove garlic
    1 tablespoon butter
    1 cup acidic, dry white wine
    4 ounces Gruyère cheese, grated
    4 ounces Emmenthaler cheese, finely grated
    1 tablespoon flour
      salt, pepper, a pinch of cayenne pepper, freshly grated
        nutmeg
    1 tablespoon kirsch

FOR THE GARNISH:

    1 small loaf French bread, cut into 1-inch cubes
    1 small head each broccoli and cauliflower
    6 ounces fresh mushrooms, washed
    2 Granny Smith apples, cut into wedges
    ¼ pound pepperoni, salami, or other hard sausage, cut into
      ½-inch chunks

1. Have ready-measured all the ingredients for the fondue. The actual dip will be prepared at the last minute.

2. Meanwhile, toast the bread cubes in a preheated 400°F. oven till lightly browned. Place in a bread basket. Cut the cauliflower and broccoli into florets and cook in rapidly boiling, salted water until crispy-tender. Arrange these, the mushrooms, the apples, and sausage on a platter. (This can be done well ahead of time.)

3. Prepare the fondue itself. Rub the inside of a fondue pan, or heavy saucepan, with the cut clove of garlic, and smear it with butter. (The butter helps prevent the fondue from sticking to the bottom.) Add the wine and bring it to a boil. Meanwhile, mix the cheeses with the flour, and add them to the wine little by little, stirring with a wooden spoon. When the cheese is completely melted, stir in the seasonings, followed by the kirsch.

As soon as the fondue is cooked, serve it at once, using the bread, vegetables, apples, and sausage for dipping.

Tradition holds that if a lady drops her dipper in the fondue, she is obliged to kiss all the men at her table. A man who drops his dipper buys a round of drinks. The cheese that burns onto the bottom of the pan is considered the best part of the fondue; any that returns from the dining room is wolfishly devoured by the dishwashers. A Swiss or an Austrian wine, like a crisp Gruneveltleiner, would be delicious with Swiss fondue, but I wouldn't turn down a good California Chardonnay, either.

◇   ◇   ◇

CHEDDAR CHEESE FONDUE WITH STOUT: Prepare the fondue as described above, substituting Guinness stout for the wine, cheddar cheese for the Swiss cheese, and Dijon-style mustard for the kirsch. (If you don't like the bitter flavor of stout, use a milder beer.) Spooned onto toast points and browned under the broiler, this dish becomes a Welsh rarebit.

Leftover cheese fondue makes an excellent sauce for cooked vegetables.

BAGNA CAUDA

HOT ANCHOVY DIP

Bagna cauda means "hot bath" in Italian, and this warm anchovy dip offers welcome relief to palates grown weary on sour cream flavored with onion soup mix. It is so mild, it will be appreciated even by people with an avowed aversion to anchovies. (But don't tell them what's in it beforehand.)

Serves 8 as an appetizer

FOR THE BAGNA:

> 3 cups heavy cream
> 2 large cloves garlic, peeled
> 1 2-ounce can anchovies, drained
> 4 tablespoons butter
> fresh black pepper and cayenne pepper

FOR THE GARNISH:

> 2 carrots, peeled
> 1 cucumber, peeled, halved lengthwise, and seeded
> 2 red peppers, cored
> 1 bunch scallions, root end removed
> 24 *grissini* (slender Italian breadsticks) or sesame breadsticks

1. Place the cream, garlic, and anchovies in a heavy saucepan over a medium heat, and simmer for 20–30 minutes, stirring from time to time, until only half the liquid remains. Puree the reduced cream mixture in a blender. Return the mixture to a low heat and whisk in the butter and seasonings. NOTE: Once the butter is added, the sauce should not be allowed to boil.

2. Meanwhile, cut the vegetables into 3-inch-long strips, and stand them in cups or ramekins, with the breadsticks. Pour the *bagna cauda* into a chafing dish or fondue pot, surrounded by the garnish. Traditionally, the vegetables are dipped with one's fingers—if this feels too informal, provide toothpicks or bamboo skewers.

Serve a rich, dry Italian white wine with *bagna cauda*, like a Corvo Bianco from Sicily or a Verdicchio from the Adriatic coast. *Bagna cauda* also makes a wonderful sauce for grilled or poached fish.

BURGUNDIAN BEEF FONDUE

Burgundy is a region famed for its beef as well as its wine. Thus, Burgundian fondue features raw beef cooked at the table in a pot of hot oil. I find that peanut oil holds up best under heat. The oil can be reused two or three times if it is strained through a cheesecloth after each use. Beef fondue is customarily served with three or four dipping sauces, like the ones below, or the flavored mayonnaises on page 55.

Serves 4

> 1½ pounds beef tenderloin, trimmed and cut into ½-inch cubes
> 2–3 cups peanut oil
> lettuce leaves, tomato roses for garnish
> dipping sauces (see below)

1. Arrange the beef on a plate lined with a lettuce leaf. Just before serving, heat the oil to 375°F in the fondue pot. Thread the beef onto your dipping skewer and cook it to taste in the hot oil.

Never eat beef fondue directly off the dipping fork or you will burn your lips. Transfer the meat to a dinner fork. If, heaven forbid, the pot should fall over and set fire to the tablecloth, use salt or baking powder, *not* water, to extinguish the flames.

DIPPING SAUCES

Our thanks to Rick Spencer, chef of the Bernerhof, for these sauces, which can be made up to 24 hours ahead. Instructions for homemade mayonnaise are found on page 53. Alternatively, use a good commercial brand.

MUSTARD SAUCE: To ½ cup mayonnaise add 1 tablespoon grainy Meaux mustard.

ORANGE SAUCE: To ½ cup mayonnaise add 1 tablespoon orange marmalade, a generous splash of Grand Marnier, and the juice of ½ lemon.

CHINESE MAYONNAISE: To ½ cup mayonnaise add 2 teaspoons soy sauce, 2 teaspoons sherry, ¼ teaspoon hot chili oil, ½ teaspoon crushed Szechuan peppercorns, 1 small clove garlic (minced), ½ teaspoon grated lemon zest, and 1 tablespoon finely chopped parsley.

CAJUN MAYONNAISE

    1 egg yolk
    ½ cup Dijon-style mustard
    2 tablespoons imported paprika
    2 tablespoons ketchup
    2 tablespoons prepared horseradish
    2 tablespoons Worcestershire sauce
    1 teaspoon Pickapepper sauce or Tabasco sauce
    1 teaspoon sugar
    1 cup vegetable oil

2 tablespoons parsley
¼ cup finely chopped onion
¼ cup very finely chopped celery
    salt and freshly ground black pepper

Place the first eight ingredients in a bowl and whisk them together thoroughly. Gradually whisk in the oil, followed by the remaining ingredients, then the salt and pepper to taste. Alternatively, the ingredients can be combined in a food processor.

LESSON 9

Soufflés

◇

Techniques:
MAKING SOUFFLÉS
DOUBLE-BUTTERING
BEATING EGG WHITES
FOLDING

Master Recipe:
CLASSIC CHEESE SOUFFLÉ

Variations:
CHEDDAR SOUFFLÉ WITH SCALLIONS
GOAT CHEESE SOUFFLÉ
GARLIC SOUFFLÉ
CRAB SOUFFLÉ PIE

◇   ◇   ◇

When I studied cooking in Paris, I was fortunate enough to have chefs who believed that even the most difficult recipes were nothing more than a series of simple, straightforward steps—that cooking should be not intimidating but fun. I have tried to make this the philosophy of the Taste of the Mountains Cooking School. And no dish is in greater need of demystification than that bane of all fledgling cooks—the soufflé.

A soufflé is really nothing more than white sauce leavened with egg whites. The sauce is not particularly delicate: if anything, it resembles library paste. The tricky part is the egg whites, which are stiffly beaten and gently folded into the base mixture. When a soufflé is baked, the air bubbles in the whites expand, causing the characteristic (or at least hoped for) puff. (The word "soufflé" comes from the French *souffler*, "to breathe" or "breathe into.") Soufflés are quick and easy to make—I often whip one up when besieged by unexpected guests. They are a great way to use up leftovers, and when properly prepared, they can even be assembled ahead of time.

Below are step-by-step instructions for even the rawest beginner on how to make a soufflé. If you are already an accomplished soufflé-maker, you can skip directly to the recipes on page 76.

HOW TO MAKE A SOUFFLÉ

Most people are less concerned with what makes a soufflé rise than with what makes it fall. There are lots of potential stumbling blocks.

THE SOUFFLÉ DISH: It must be the right shape—wider than tall—and just large enough to hold all the soufflé mixture. Soufflés can also be baked in a charlotte mold (a metal mold with outwardly sloping sides) or a skillet or on a baking sheet.

BUTTERING THE DISH: Many a soufflé has fallen victim to a poorly buttered soufflé dish. If the soufflé mixture sticks to the sides or top of the dish, it will not puff. To grease a soufflé dish, we use a technique called double-buttering—the dish is brushed once with melted butter, chilled in the freezer, then buttered a second time. (The freezing enables the second coat of butter to adhere to the first.) Use a pastry brush; you just can't apply a smooth, even coat with your fingers. For further "lubrication," we sprinkle the inside of the dish with bread crumbs, ground nuts, or grated cheese (or sugar or cookie crumbs in the case of sweet soufflés); this "lubricant" has the added virtue of giving the soufflé a buttery crust.

THE BASE MIXTURE: The base mixture should be very thick, hot to the touch, and highly seasoned. The thickness gives the soufflé body. The heat cooks the egg whites slightly, helping to stabilize the soufflé. Assertive seasoning is important, because the air in the egg whites dilutes the flavor.

THE EGG WHITES: The single most crucial factor for successful soufflés is beating the egg whites. In the old days, whites were beaten by hand in a copper bowl, and you usually pooped out before you incorporated enough air. Since the advent of such excellent mixers as the Kenwood and Kitchen-Aid, the tendency is to overbeat the whites, reducing their ability to leaven. On page 298 you will find complete instructions for beating egg whites. Read them before you start.

LIGHTENING THE BASE MIXTURE: We now have a thick, hot, well-flavored base mixture and snowy, stiffly beaten egg whites. The next step is to combine them as gently as possible, so as not to deflate the air bubbles. Using a whisk, stir a quarter of the whites into the hot base mixture to lighten it—get the vigorous whisking out of your system, as the next step requires the utmost delicacy.

FOLDING: Pour the lightened base mixture over the remaining egg whites, and, using a wide rubber spatula, fold them together. To fold, start the spatula at the far side of the bowl, and bring it toward you through the center. When you reach the close side of the bowl, lift and twist the spatula slightly and begin turning the far side of the bowl toward you. This turn of the bowl will mix the ingredients. Work as gently as possible, and do not twist the handle of the spatula in your holding hand. "Cut through the center, lift, and turn, cut through the center, lift, and turn . . ."—this is the correct motion. Practice with a bowlful of dried beans or rice until you master it. If you are using a dry flavoring, like grated cheese, sprinkle it in as you fold. Fold just till the ingredients are mixed. Poor or excessive folding is another major reason that soufflés fail to rise.

MOLDING THE SOUFFLÉ: Gently spoon the soufflé mixture into the prepared dish. Smooth the top, and if you fancy, make a design with a moistened spatula. Now, run your thumbs around the inside of the dish, clearing ½ inch of soufflé mixture from the edge. This allows the soufflé to rise without obstruction. There is no need for the waxed-paper collar recommended by many cookbooks. If you have followed steps 1–5, your soufflé mixture should be sturdy enough to survive up to a four-hour delay in the refrigerator.

BAKING AND SERVING THE SOUFFLÉ: Clean any spills from the outside of the soufflé dish before you bake it (the dish will be impossible to clean when it is hot). Bake the soufflé in a preheated 400° oven for 20 minutes or until cooked to taste. The French like their soufflés less cooked than we do—the gooey center acts as a sauce for the crusty outside. Do not open the oven door needlessly during baking; the cold air can deflate the most stalwart soufflés. Serve your masterpiece as soon as it is baked: guests wait for soufflés, not the other way around.

Now that we know all the pitfalls, let's try some specific recipes.

◇   ◇   ◇

Classic Cheese Soufflé

Cheese soufflé can be made with almost any cheese—Gruyère, cheddar, Parmesan, even goat cheese. I cannot think of a more heartwarming supper than cheese soufflé with French or garlic bread and a green salad (see Lesson 5).

Serves 2 hungry people as an entrée or 4 as an appetizer

3 tablespoons butter, plus butter for the dish
3 tablespoons flour
1 cup milk
4 egg yolks
  salt, fresh black pepper, cayenne pepper, freshly grated
    nutmeg
1 heaping teaspoon Dijon-style mustard

  7 egg whites
    pinch of salt
    pinch of cream of tartar
  1 cup freshly grated cheese (I like a half-and-half mixture of
      Gruyère and Parmesan)
  ⅓ cup lightly toasted bread crumbs or additional Parmesan for
      lining the soufflé dish

  1 5-cup soufflé dish, double-buttered and lined with bread
      crumbs

1. Melt the butter in a 1-quart saucepan over high heat. Whisk in the flour, and cook for 2 minutes without browning. Add the milk in one fell swoop off the heat, return pan to heat, and boil the sauce, whisking vigorously, for 3 minutes. Remove the pan from the heat, and whisk in the yolks, one by one. The mixture should thicken; if it doesn't, cook it just to a gentle simmer. Whisk in the seasonings and mustard—the mixture should be highly seasoned.

2. Meanwhile, beat the egg whites to stiff peaks (see page 298 for instructions), adding a pinch each of salt and cream of tartar after 20 seconds. Whisk ¼ of the whites into the *hot* base mixture to lighten it. Fold the base mixture back into the remaining whites as gently as possible, sprinkling in the grated cheese as you fold. Gently spoon the soufflé mixture into the prepared dish, and smooth the top with a wet metal spatula. Run your thumbs around the inside of the dish to clear ½-inch soufflé mixture from the edge. If you have beaten and folded your whites properly, the soufflé can be prepared up to 4 hours ahead of time and refrigerated.

3. Bake the soufflé in a preheated 400° oven for 20 minutes, or until cooked to taste. Serve at once. A light red wine, like a Chiroubles or St. Amour from the Beaujolais district, would be lovely.

◇   ◇   ◇

CHEDDAR SOUFFLÉ WITH SCALLIONS: Substitute an imported English cheddar for the Gruyère and Parmesan; line the soufflé dish with ground walnuts instead of bread crumbs. Fold in 3 tablespoons finely chopped scallion greens with the cheese.

GOAT CHEESE SOUFFLÉ: Substitute a hard, full-flavored goat cheese, like *Crottin de Chavignol*, for the cheddar above. Fold ⅓ cup lightly toasted walnut pieces into the soufflé mixture with the grated cheese.

GARLIC SOUFFLÉ

This unusual garlic soufflé makes an exotic side dish for beef or lamb. I like to bake it in a skillet instead of a soufflé dish, and serve it in wedges, like pie. Garlic (which comes from the Anglo-Saxon words for "spear" and "leek"—an apt description of its green shoots) loses its jarring pungency when simmered in milk. A soufflé of shallots or spring onions would be prepared the same way.

Serves 6 as a side dish

2 heads (approximately 16 cloves) fresh garlic
2 cups milk
3 tablespoons butter
3 tablespoons flour
4 egg yolks
   salt, fresh black pepper, cayenne pepper, freshly grated
     nutmeg
6 egg whites
   pinch of cream of tartar
   pinch of salt
½ cup freshly grated Parmesan cheese

1 8-inch cast-iron skillet (or 1 5-cup soufflé dish or 6
   ramekins), double-buttered, sprinkled with bread crumbs

1. Peel the garlic. (To peel garlic, smash each clove lightly with the side of a knife or the heel of your palm and pull away the dry outer skin.) Gently simmer the garlic in the milk for 20 minutes, or until the cloves are soft. Drain and reserve 1 cup of milk. Puree the garlic in a food processor and return it to the milk.

2. Make a roux with the butter and flour. Add the milk and garlic to make a thick white sauce. Whisk in the yolks one by one off the heat. The mixture should thicken slightly. If it doesn't, cook it over a low flame till it does. Add the spices—the mixture should be very highly seasoned.

3. Meanwhile, beat the egg whites to stiff peaks (see page 298 for instructions), adding the salt and cream of tartar after 20 seconds. Stir ¼ of the whites into the *hot* base mixture; then gently fold the base mixture into the remaining whites, sprinkling in the cheese. Bake the garlic soufflé in a preheated 400° oven for 15–20 minutes or until cooked to taste. To serve garlic soufflé, cut it in wedges, and serve like pie.

CRAB SOUFFLÉ PIE

I like to make this elegant appetizer with sweet Maine crab, which we receive fresh from Portland. Depending on where you live, you could use Dungeness crab from the Pacific, blue crab from the Chesapeake Bay, stone crab claws from Florida, or even Alaskan king crab. (Try to avoid frozen crab, however, as it is watery.) Soufflés with dense flavorings, like crab, don't tend to rise much. For this reason, we bake this one in a skillet and serve it in wedges, like pie.

Serves 4–6

8 ounces fresh crab meat
3 tablespoons butter
3 tablespoons finely chopped shallots
1 teaspoon imported paprika
3 tablespoons flour
1 cup milk
2 tablespoons sherry
4 egg yolks
1 heaping teaspoon Dijon-style mustard
  salt, pepper, cayenne pepper, freshly grated nutmeg
7 egg whites
  pinch of salt
  cream of tartar

1 8-inch cast-iron skillet, double-buttered, lined with bread
  crumbs

1. Pick through the crab meat, removing any pieces of shell.
2. Melt the butter in a 1-quart saucepan over medium heat and sauté the shallots and paprika for 30 seconds or until the shallots are soft. Add the flour, cook for 1 minute, then add the milk and sherry in one fell swoop off the heat. Return the mixture to the heat and boil for 3 minutes, whisking vigorously. Remove the pan from the heat, and whisk in the yolks one by one. The mixture should thicken slightly; if it doesn't, bring it to a gentle simmer. Stir in the crab meat, mustard, and seasonings. The mixture should be highly seasoned.
3. Beat the whites to stiff peaks (see page 298 for instructions), adding a pinch each of salt and cream of tartar after 20 seconds. Stir ¼ of the whites into the *hot* base mixture, then gently fold it into the remaining whites. Spoon the mixture into the prepared frying pan, mounding the mixture toward the center.
4. Bake the soufflé in a preheated 400° oven for 15–20 minutes or until cooked to taste.

Serving: Cut the soufflé into wedges on plates spread with the parsley sauce on page 190 or the butter sauce on page 141. A flinty Chablis or Pouilly-Fuissé would be a perfect beverage.

LESSON 10

Pasta Sauces and Pestos

◇

Techniques:
SELECTING PASTA
COOKING PASTA
PESTO

Master Recipe:
PESTO

Variations:
PARSLEY-MINT PESTO
GOAT CHEESE PESTO
SPAGHETTI CARBONARA
LINGUINE WITH BRANDIED WILD
    MUSHROOM SAUCE
FETTUCCINE WITH GORGONZOLA AND
    PECANS

◇   ◇   ◇

It used to be that to enjoy fresh egg pasta, you had to make it yourself. The pasta revolution of the seventies has made it possible to buy excellent fresh egg noodles almost anywhere.

Fresh egg pasta differs from dried packaged pasta in that the flour is mixed with eggs instead of water. Egg pasta is traditionally associated with the north of Italy, an area whose relative affluence made it possible to use eggs as a subsidiary ingredient. Dried pasta evolved in the poorer south of Italy, where eggs were a luxury to be served as a separate course. Eggs make a softer pasta, consequently one that is easy to roll and cut at home. Dried pasta, made with water and Durham wheat (a harder grain), requires industrial presses to form the various shapes. This is the reason that extruder-type pasta machines work so poorly at home, for they are designed to be used with the hard, water-based doughs of the south. When egg pasta is forced through an extruder, the noodles stick together.

Fresh egg pasta is neither better nor worse than dried pasta, just different. Similarly, no one shape is better than another. Each has a specific function: spaghetti for thin butter and cream sauces; *fusilli* (pasta squiggles) for sauces with sliced vegetables (they catch in the springlike coils); *conchiglie* (shells) for meat sauces (the meat lodges in the hollows); *rigatoni* (large tubes) for stuffing and baking; and so on.

There are, however, good and bad brands of fresh egg pasta and dried pasta. When buying the former, avoid noodles that are sticky and knotted together. Finding a good dried pasta is a matter of trial and error. A bad brand will go from undercooked to overcooked in a matter of seconds. A good brand will take a full minute or two to go from too hard to too soft. You are usually safe with an imported brand from Italy or Greece; top Italian brands include Del Verde and De Cecco. One pound of fresh egg pasta will serve 4–5 as an appetizer, 3 as an entrée; one pound dried serves 5–6 as an appetizer, 4 as an entrée.

When cooking either kind of pasta, use at least 4 quarts of water per pound of pasta. Too little water produces starchy pasta. The water should be rapidly boiling and lightly salted; add a teaspoon of oil to keep the individual noodles from sticking together. Properly cooked pasta will be slightly chewy; the Italians aptly describe this with the expression *al dente*, literally, "to the tooth." Fresh egg pasta will usually be cooked by the time the water returns to a rapid boil. Dried pasta takes longer, typically 6–8 minutes. Unless you are making a cold pasta salad, there is no reason to rinse cooked pasta. Just toss it with the sauce and serve it.

Below are four quick sauces appropriate for dried or fresh egg pasta.

PESTO

Born in Genoa on the Ligurian Coast, this pungent herb sauce has taken America by storm. (Curiously, another Genoese product did the same thing 500 years ago: Christopher Columbus!) Traditional pesto is a pungent condiment made with basil, garlic, olive oil, pine nuts, and grated cheese. The basil should be fresh; the olive oil, extra-virgin (cold-pressed from the first picking); the traditional cheese is Romano, which, like Roquefort, is made of sheep's milk.

I regard pesto as a process, not a specific recipe. Any fresh herb— oregano, mint, even parsley—can be substituted for the basil. Walnuts, hazelnuts, even pecans (for an American touch) can be substituted for the pine nuts. Similarly, walnut oil can be used in place of olive oil; Parmesan or even goat cheese, in place of Romano. To any recipe, traditional or otherwise, I always add fresh lemon juice to balance the richness of the oil and cheese.

Traditionally, pesto is served on pasta, but its uses are endless. Housewives in the south of France invigorate their vegetable soups by adding a spoonful of *pistou*—the French version of pesto. Pesto can be spread on broiled fish, baked in hollowed-out tomatoes, or even painted on a rack of lamb before roasting. One could well make a dessert pesto using sweet ingredients (mint, honey in place of oil, ricotta cheese in place of Romano) for baking inside filo dough or pastry.

In the old days, pestos were laboriously pounded in a mortar with a pestle. The food processor has shortened the preparation time to seconds. To assure a smooth, even consistency, puree the dry ingredients before you add the wet ones. Unless otherwise stated, each of the following recipes makes 1½ cups.

◇　◇　◇

Traditional Basil Pesto

Our word "basil" comes from the Greek *basilikos,* meaning "kingly," and in ancient times the first of the crop would be harvested by the local ruler with a golden sickle. Recognizable by its broad green leaves, basil has a fragrant smell and almost licoricy flavor. If you can't find fresh basil, move on to the parsley pesto below.

Serves 4–6

> 1 cup loosely packed fresh basil leaves (about 2 bunches,
> washed and stems removed)
> ¼ cup pine nuts or walnuts, shelled
> 2 cloves garlic (or as much as you can stand)
> 4 tablespoons Romano cheese, grated or broken into small
> pieces (for a milder pesto use half-and-half Parmesan and
> Romano)
> ¼ cup extra-virgin olive oil
> juice of ½ lemon (or to taste)
> a little salt and plenty of fresh black pepper

Place the basil, pine nuts or walnuts, garlic, and cheese in a food processor and churn in spurts until the mixture is reduced to a fine puree. Gradually churn in the remaining ingredients, adding salt and pepper to taste. (You won't need much salt, as the cheese is already quite salty.) The pesto is ready to use, or it can be stored for up to 2 weeks in the refrigerator. It can be frozen almost indefinitely. I make a big batch of pesto in the fall, freeze it in small containers, and parcel it out throughout the winter.

Serving: When serving pesto with pasta, many people like to add a few tablespoons boiling pasta water to the pesto to temper the flavor of raw garlic. Place the cooked pasta in a bowl, spoon the pesto on top, and toss until well mixed. One cup pesto will coat 1 pound of fresh pasta. When using pesto to flavor soups, add it at the last minute. Pesto should not be boiled or simmered, or it will lose its bright green color and freshness.

If necessary, heat the pasta with the pesto for a few seconds in the pan in which the pasta was cooked.

Note: Pesto can also be made in a blender, but you will need more liquid. To the recipes above add ¼ cup chicken stock or water. Run the blender at low speed and continuously scrape the ingredients down with a spatula until reduced to a smooth paste.

◇   ◇   ◇

PARSLEY-MINT PESTO: Flat-leaf parsley has more flavor than the curly leaf. According to Ovid, mint is named for the nymph, Mentha, who had an affair with Pluto. Persephone surprised the pair and angrily threw the maiden to the ground to trample her. To this day, we crush the leaves of fresh mint to fully release the flavor.

Follow the recipe above, substituting a large bunch of fresh flat-leaf parsley or equal parts parsley and fresh mint. (Discard the coarse stems.) This pesto is excellent brushed on roast rack of lamb (see page 193) or baked in hollowed-out tomatoes.

GOAT CHEESE PESTO: This recipe combines the piquancy of goat cheese with the nutty richness of walnut oil. Use a soft, mild goat cheese like montrachet, lingot, or bucheron. Walnut oil spoils very quickly and should be stored in the refrigerator once opened.

Prepare the basil pesto recipe above, substituting ¼ pound goat cheese for the Romano and ¼ cup walnut oil for the olive oil. To make rack of lamb with goat cheese pesto, see pages 193–96.

SPAGHETTI CARBONARA

Flavored with bacon and eggs, this pasta dish was supposedly invented during World War II to honor American soldiers stationed in Italy. *Pancetta* is Italian-style bacon—dry-cured rolled pork belly, which resembles prosciutto in flavor. *Pancetta* has a unique flavor and it is worth trying to track down. If it is unavailable, use regular bacon.

Serves 3–4

> ½ pound *pancetta* or bacon, cut into ⅛-inch slivers
> 6–8 tablespoons softened butter
> 2 eggs, beaten
> ½ cup freshly grated Parmesan cheese, plus cheese for sprinkling
> fresh black pepper, plus perhaps a little salt
> 1 pound fresh spaghetti or fettuccine

1. Render the bacon in a cast-iron frying pan. The pieces should be lightly browned but not too crisp. Transfer the bacon with 3–4 tablespoons fat to a large bowl. Stir in the remaining ingredients.

2. Cook the pasta of your choice. Drain it quickly and toss it with the ingredients in the bowl. (The heat of the pasta should cook the eggs. If the sauce looks too thin, place it, pasta and all, in a saucepan, and stir it over high heat until cooked to taste.) Sprinkle each portion with a little extra cheese before serving. I would serve an Amarone—a robust red wine from the north of Italy, traditionally made with partially dried grapes.

LINGUINE WITH BRANDIED WILD MUSHROOM SAUCE

This sauce is inspired by a dish I have never tasted. I saw it on the menu of a restaurant in Philadelphia called Victor's. Victor's is an opera lover's paradise, boasting innumerable paintings and photographs of opera singers, a 50,000-volume record collection, and waiters and waitresses who frequently break into song. *Porcini* are wild mushrooms ("boletus" in English) commonly sold dried by the ounce in Italian or gourmet grocery stores. Here is how I would imagine Victor's wild mushroom sauce for pasta.

Serves 3–4

1 pound dried or fresh linguine

FOR THE SAUCE:

3 ounces (⅓ cup) dried *porcini* mushrooms (or other wild mushrooms)
¾ cup boiling water
¼ cup cognac
1 cup heavy cream
4 tablespoons butter
4 tablespoons fresh parsley
6 tablespoons freshly grated Parmesan cheese, plus 4 tablespoons for sprinkling
salt and fresh black pepper

1. Soften the *porcini* in a small bowl in the boiling water for 20 minutes. Remove the mushrooms and wash thoroughly in several waters (see page 253). Strain the mushroom liquid into a wide saucepan. Bring this liquid to a boil and reduce to ¼ cup. Add the cognac and reduce the mixture by half. Add the mushrooms, and cream, and boil until ¾ cup liquid remains. Whisk in the butter. When it is melted, whisk in the parsley, 6 tablespoons grated cheese, and salt and pepper to taste.

2. Cook the pasta in at least 4 quarts rapidly boiling, lightly salted water. When the pasta is *al dente,* drain it, and toss with the sauce. Sprinkle the remaining cheese on top of each serving.

FETTUCCINE WITH GORGONZOLA AND PECANS

Gorgonzola is Italy's answer to Roquefort, an odiferous blue cheese that will curl your toes (but not your stomach!). Its pungency is mellowed by the other cheeses and cream.

Serves 3–4

1 pound fresh fettuccine

FOR THE SAUCE:

1 cup heavy cream
3 ounces Gorgonzola cheese, crumbled
¼ cup grated fresh mozzarella cheese
¼ cup grated fresh Parmesan cheese, plus some for sprinkling
6 tablespoons butter
½ cup pecans
salt and fresh black pepper

1. Bring the cream to a boil in a large saucepan and cook till reduced by half. Whisk in the Gorgonzola and simmer gently till melted. Working over the lowest possible heat, whisk in the remaining ingredients, and season to taste.
2. Cook the pasta in at least 4 quarts rapidly boiling, lightly salted water. When the pasta is *al dente,* drain it and toss with the sauce. Sprinkle more Parmesan cheese on top of each serving.

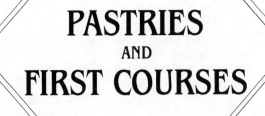

PASTRIES
AND
FIRST COURSES

LESSON 11

Crêpes and Blintzes

◇

Techniques:
MAKING CRÊPES
MAKING BLINTZES

Master Recipes:
BASIC CRÊPES
BLINTZES

Variations:
GOAT CHEESE BLINTZES
SMOKED SALMON BLINTZES

◇ ◇ ◇

Every nation has its version of pancakes: Russian *blini*, Jewish blintzes, American flapjacks. But the most famous of all is the crêpe. Crêpes once took the place of bread in western France, and Breton crêpe-makers still ply their trade at countless street-corner stalls around Paris.

The French bring to their "pancakes" all the whimsy that superstition can muster. If you flip a crêpe on New Year's Day while holding a coin in your hand, they believe, you will have money throughout the year. Not even Napoleon was above such superstition when he flipped crêpes at Candlemas in 1812. Four of the pancakes landed safely back in the pan, while the fifth, to the emperor's mortification, tumbled to the floor. The day Moscow went up in flames, reports French food historian Robert Courtine, Napoleon turned to one of his commanders and said: "There is my fifth crêpe!"

The crêpe is a sort of culinary *tabula rasa:* it can be spread with jam or butter and sugar, lavished with cream sauce, even filled and baked with soufflés. Crêpes serve equally well as appetizers, entrées, and desserts; the Austrians cut them into slivers to make crêpe noodle soup. This lesson starts with a basic crêpe recipe and ends with two of my favorite blintz recipes.

◇ ◇ ◇

◇

TO SEASON CAST IRON

Crêpes should be cooked in a well-seasoned pan. (The traditional crêpe pan has low, sloping sides.) Crêpe pans are usually made of cast iron or carbon steel, both of which are slightly porous. When a pan is seasoned, the minute holes in the metal fill with oil, creating a nonstick surface. Cast iron spreads heat evenly—a boon for making crêpes and pan-frying.

To season a new pan, wash it thoroughly to remove any machine oil, then wipe it dry over a low heat. Sprinkle ¼ inch salt over the bottom of the pan and add vegetable oil to cover. Bake the pan in a 300° oven for 2–3 hours. The idea here is to bake the oil into the microscopic pores in the iron. Let pan cool and discard the oil and salt. Wipe the pan out with a paper towel: the salt serves as an abrasive.

Never cook an acid, such as wine, in cast iron: it will strip away the seasoning. Soap is equally deleterious; when possible, wipe the pan clean with paper towels. If you have to wash a cast iron pan, do so with water and a plastic scrubber, and dry the pan promptly over high heat. If the pan should develop spots where food sticks, go over them with a paper towel smeared with butter and salt.

Crêpes

When I was at cooking school, the supreme test of a student was to see how many crêpe pans he or she could have going at once. Four pans are the mark of an expert; two are not too hard to manage and certainly reduce the cooking time. There is no need to let the batter rest.

Makes 12–14 6-inch crêpes

    1 cup flour
1½ cups milk
      scant ½ teaspoon salt
      scant ½ teaspoon sugar (this helps the crêpes brown)
    3 eggs, beaten
    4 tablespoons melted butter (melt it in the crêpe pan to avoid
        dirtying extra pots)

    2 or more 6-inch crêpe pans

1. Place the flour in a bowl, and make a depression in the center. Whisk in most of the milk to obtain a smooth paste. Whisk in the salt, sugar, and eggs, and strain the batter. Then whisk in the melted butter. The batter should be the consistency of heavy cream; as it stands, it will thicken. Use the reserved milk to thin the batter as necessary.

2. Wipe out the pans and heat them over a medium flame. When the pans are the right temperature, a few drops of water sprinkled on them will evaporate in 5 seconds. Off the heat, in one fell swoop, add approximately 3 tablespoons batter. (It should hiss as it hits the pan.) Gently swirl the pan to coat the bottom with batter, pouring off any excess: the crêpe should be as thin as possible.

3. Cook the crêpe over medium-high flame for 30 seconds or until beads of butter "sweat" through to the top. Turn it with a spatula or your fingers (or you can try flipping it), and cook the other side for 15 seconds. A perfect crêpe will be lacy and golden brown on one side; spotted like a leopard skin on the other. Stack the crêpes one on top of another. They can be made 24 hours ahead and refrigerated, but they don't take well to freezing.

Note: The key to successful crêpes lies in heating the pan to the correct temperature. If the pan is too cool, the crêpes will be starchy and thick. If the pan is too hot, hundreds of tiny holes will appear. If the crêpe sticks, rub the trouble spot with a paper towel smeared with butter and salt. (The salt acts as an abrasive, the butter, a lubricant.) Don't worry if your first few crêpes come out badly. (Mine usually do.) Just keep adding as little batter as possible and slowly swirling the pan, and soon your crêpes will look like those made by a street vendor on the Boulevard St. Michel.

◇ ◇ ◇

PALATSCHINKENSUPPE *(Crêpe Noodle Soup):* Prepare the chicken soup on page 25. Fold each crêpe in three like a business letter, and cut widthwise into ⅛-inch slivers. Unfolded, these will make noodles. Serve 2 crêpes per person.

FOUR QUICK DESSERT CRÊPES: Spread hot crêpes with:
—butter and sugar (or cinnamon sugar)
—your favorite jam
—*crème de marron* (sweetened chestnut puree, available at gourmet shops) and a splash of rum
—the chocolate fondue on page 316 of this book

Blintzes

Blintzes stir nostalgia in nice Jewish boys, the way *madeleines* (shell-shaped cookies; see page 325) spurred Proust to a remembrance of things past. There are probably as many variations as there are Jewish grandmothers. A purist might omit the vanilla, cinnamon, and raisins in the following recipe. A traditional Jewish grandmother might balk at the goat cheese and smoked salmon blintzes listed as variations. Farmer's cheese and pot cheese (available at delicatessens and cheese shops) are drier and firmer than cottage cheese. If you must use cottage cheese, drain it in a strainer first.

Serves 4

> ¾ pound farmer's cheese, pot cheese, or drained small-curd cottage cheese
> 1–2 tablespoons sugar
> pinch of salt
> juice and grated zest of 1 lemon
> ½ teaspoon vanilla (optional)
> ⅛ teaspoon cinnamon (optional)
> ¼ cup sultanas (yellow raisins), or black raisins, softened in hot water, then drained (very optional)
> 1 egg
> 1 batch crêpes (see above)
> 6 tablespoons butter for frying
> sour cream, cinnamon sugar (optional) for serving

1. Combine the first 8 ingredients in a bowl and beat with a spoon to a smooth paste. Place one heaping tablespoon in the center of each crêpe. (The crêpe should be turned dark side up, so the light side will be on the outside.) Fold the first inch of the left and right sides of the crêpe toward the center. Now fold the bottom section up and the top section down like a business letter—you should wind up with what looks like an egg roll. The blintzes can be fried right away, but they will hold together better if they are refrigerated for 2–4 hours before cooking.

2. Just before serving, melt the butter in one large or two small skillets over medium heat. When the butter foams, add the blintzes, seam side down, and fry for three to four minutes or until golden brown. Invert and fry the tops. Serve at once with sour cream and cinnamon sugar.

GOAT CHEESE BLINTZES

These tangy blintzes are unlike anything my grandmother ever made. Use a soft, mild chèvre, like lingot, montrachet, or a domestic goat cheese.

Serves 4

6 ounces mild goat cheese
½ pound farmer's cheese, pot cheese, or drained small-curd
    cottage cheese
  freshly ground black pepper and perhaps a whisper of salt
2 tablespoons fresh chopped chives or scallions
1 egg
1 batch crêpes
6 tablespoons butter for frying
  sour cream for serving

In a bowl combine the first 5 ingredients. Fill and fry the blintzes as described above. Goat cheese blintzes would be lovely for a brunch or light luncheon. Serve a Sancerre or a Pouilly-Fumé.

SMOKED SALMON BLINTZES

Use smoked or Nova Scotia salmon for the filling: lox would be too salty.

Serves 4

¾ pound pot cheese
2 tablespoons fresh dill, minced
1 egg
  freshly ground pepper
¼ pound smoked salmon, finely chopped
1 batch crêpes
6 tablespoons butter for frying

In a bowl combine the first 5 ingredients. Fill and fry blintzes as described above. Serve smoked salmon blintzes with a well-chilled Chardonnay.

LESSON 12

Working with Filo Dough

———————◇———————

Technique:
WORKING WITH FILO

Master Recipe:
FILO DOUGH TRIANGLES

Variations:
ROQUEFORT-LEEK FILLING
THREE-CHEESE FILLING WITH PEPPERONI
CRAB FILLING
CURRIED LAMB FILLING

◇ ◇ ◇

For literally a thousand years, bakers have known the secret of layering dough with butter to make pastries that shatter into countless delectable flakes at the first bite. But this effect has been achieved by two radically different means. In Western Europe (especially France), a simple dough made from flour and water is wrapped around a solid block of butter, then repeatedly rolled and folded. What results is puff pastry.

In the Near East a similar effect is achieved with much less labor. The cook starts with *filo* (pronounced "fee-lo")—a flour-water dough stretched into sheets that are literally thin as paper. The individual leaves (*filo* means "leaf" in Greek) are brushed with melted butter and layered. When filo is baked, the butter bubbles, leavening and crisping the individual sheets. Puff pastry requires cool surroundings, prodigious dexterity with a rolling pin, and at least 2 hours from start to finish. Filo pastries can be assembled by anyone, any time of the year, in a matter of minutes.

Filo is widely available frozen. (Look for the characteristic long, slender box.) In cities with large Greek or Armenian communities, you can usually buy fresh filo.

NOTES ON WORKING WITH FILO

1. Filo comes in 1-pound packages and there are approximately twenty 12-×-20-inch sheets to a pound. It is best to use fresh filo, but frozen will work fine if you thaw it for 24 hours in the refrigerator. (Quick thawing at room temperature will cause the individual leaves to stick together.)

2. To work with filo, you will need a natural-bristled pastry brush, a sharp knife, a large cutting board, a couple of dish towels, melted butter, and fillings. Open filo only when you are ready to use it—that is, once your fillings have been prepared.

3. The chief problem with filo is that it dries out *very* quickly. As soon as you open the package, unfold the bundle of sheets and lay them flat on a dry work surface. Work with one sheet of dough at a time, keeping the rest covered with a clean, ever-so-slightly damp dish towel. Avoid working in direct sunlight or near heat, and try to work quickly.

4. To transfer the filo to a cutting board, take hold of the top sheet at one end, and gently lift it from the pile. If a sheet sticks to the one below it, shake it gently to free it. Don't worry too much if two sheets stick together; simply brush them with a little more butter. Feel free to patch any tears or holes with pieces from another sheet.

5. Use unsalted butter, and have it melted and slightly cooled before you start. (Purists used clarified butter—see instructions on page 201.) Brush each sheet of filo *lightly* but thoroughly before laying another on top of it. A pound of filo will require approximately 3 sticks of butter.

6. When making individual pastries, lay the sheets of filo on the cutting board—two sheets are sufficient for most pastries. For extra crunch in filo triangles and strudels, sprinkle bread crumbs or poppy or sesame seeds between the layers. The pastry will rise better if the top is lightly scored—use the tip of a sharp paring knife, but do not cut all the way through to the filling.

7. Once assembled, filo pastries can be refrigerated up to 4 hours before baking. They can also be frozen: freeze them on a baking sheet, then transfer to plastic bag when hard. Do not thaw the pastries before baking. Leftover dough should be tightly sealed, first in plastic, then in foil. When properly stored, open dough will keep up to 10 days in the refrigerator.

8. Filo dough, like puff pastry, should be baked in a hot oven (400°F.). (The quicker the butter bubbles, the flakier the pastry will be.) It should be cooked until well browned. (Like most pastries, it tastes better slightly overcooked than undercooked.) Let filo pastries cool for 5 minutes before serving. To reheat filo pastries, place on baking sheets and bake in a 400° oven for 10 minutes, or until crisp.

◇   ◇   ◇

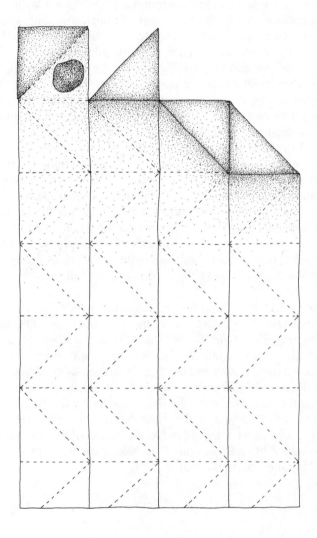

Filo Dough Triangles

Filo dough triangles are popular with caterers because they are simple to make, infinitely varied, and easily eaten at cocktail parties.

(Two boxes of filo will make 80–90 three-inch triangles)

> 2 pounds filo dough (available in any Greek or Near East market)
> 1–1½ pounds unsalted butter, melted and slightly cooled
> 3 batches of any of the fillings below

1. Spread a sheet of filo on a dry work surface, narrow edge toward you, keeping the remainder covered with a slightly damp dishcloth. Brush the filo with butter, place a second sheet on top, and brush it with butter as well. Cut the rectangle lengthwise into 4 even strips.

2. Place a spoonful of filling in the center of each strip, 1 inch below the top. Fold the left-hand corner over the filling, as pictured. Continue folding the strip like a flag to make a 3-inch triangle.

3. Work in this manner until all the filo and fillings are used up. Lightly score the tops of the triangles with a sharp knife, without cutting through to the filling. The triangles can be prepared up to 4 hours ahead to this stage and can be refrigerated or frozen. Just before serving, bake the triangles in a preheated 400° oven for 20–25 minutes, or until browned and crisp. Cool slightly on a cake rack before serving.

Note: People will want to know what the various triangles are filled with. To distinguish one filling from another, I sprinkle one triangle with sesame seeds, one with poppy seeds, and leave the last one plain.

ROQUEFORT-LEEK FILLING

Fills 24–30 triangles

> 2 leeks, washed and finely chopped (about ½ cup)
> 3 tablespoons butter
> 2 ounces Roquefort cheese, crumbled
> ⅔ cup ricotta cheese
> 1 egg yolk
> fresh black pepper and perhaps a little salt

Sauté the leek in the butter until soft and translucent. Stir in the remaining ingredients, and season to taste.

THREE-CHEESE FILLING WITH PEPPERONI

Fills 24–30 triangles

½ cup ricotta cheese
3 tablespoons grated mozzarella cheese
3 tablespoons freshly grated Parmesan cheese
¼ cup very finely chopped pepperoni
1 egg yolk
  fresh black pepper and perhaps a little salt

Combine the ingredients and season to taste.

CRAB FILLING

Fills 24–30 triangles

8 ounces fresh crab meat
3 tablespoons butter
3 tablespoons very finely chopped shallots
1 tablespoon sherry
1 tablespoon Dijon-style mustard
  salt and fresh black pepper

Pick through the crab to remove any pieces of shell. Melt the butter in a frying pan, and lightly sauté the shallots over medium heat for 1 minute or until soft but not browned. Add the crab and sherry, and sauté for 30 seconds. Stir in the mustard and seasonings, and let the mixture cool before wrapping it with the filo.

CURRIED LAMB FILLING

This filling can be made with scraps from trimming the rack of lamb on page 194.

Fills 24–30 triangles

- 8 ounces lean, boneless lamb
- 3 tablespoons butter
- 1 small onion, finely chopped (about ½ cup)
- 1 clove garlic, minced
- 1–2 teaspoons curry powder
- ¼ teaspoon ground coriander
  salt, fresh black pepper, pinch of cayenne pepper

Chop the lamb into a ¼–inch pieces. Melt 2 tablespoons butter in a small frying pan and brown the lamb over medium-high heat. Transfer the lamb to a bowl and sauté the onion, garlic, curry, and coriander for 2–3 minutes, or until soft. Stir in the lamb and season to taste with salt, pepper, and cayenne. The filling can be prepared up to 24 hours ahead of time.

LESSON 13

Basic Pie Dough

◇

Techniques:

MAKING PIE DOUGH BY HAND

MAKING PIE DOUGH BY MACHINE

ROLLING DOUGH

LINING A TART PAN

BLIND-BAKING

Master Recipe:

BASIC PIE DOUGH

◇　◇　◇

For reasons unclear to me, most people consider making pie dough inordinately difficult. If I had a dollar for every student who said, "Oh, I never try pie pastry at home!," I would be a wealthy fellow. Yet our grandmothers could make a home-made crust quicker than it takes to say "Table Talk." The advent of the food processor has rendered the procedure practically instantaneous and failproof.

There are almost as many different kinds of pie doughs as there are cooks to make them. The traditional American formula is flour, water, and lard (or shortening). In Eastern Europe the pastry is enriched with sour cream and butter. At the Taste of the Mountains, we use a dough based on French *pâte brisé,* literally "broken" or "flaky" pastry. Whatever the recipe, the crust should crumble into buttery dust at the first bite.

Our pie dough differs from most in that it is made with cream in place of water. (Cream makes a flakier crust.) There are three secrets to success:

—the ingredients must be well chilled;

—they should be combined as quickly as possible;

—the dough should be handled as little as possible.

These measures are taken to minimize the negative effects of gluten.

Gluten is a stringlike protein found in most flours, and it is developed by heat and by kneading. Its elasticity is ideal for yeasted doughs, which must expand to hold swelling air bubbles. However, gluten is the bane of rolled doughs, like pie dough and puff pastry, causing them to shrink when rolled out or baked.

In order to minimize this shrinkage, it is best to make pie pastry with pastry flour or a mixture of all-purpose flour and cake flour. Pastry flour—available at baker's supply shops—is a low-gluten flour milled from soft wheat. (Whole wheat pastry flour is *not* the same thing.) Alternatively, you can use what I call "Steve's Special Flour," made by cutting two parts glutinous all-purpose flour with one part low-gluten cake flour, like Swans Down or Soft As Silk.

STEVE'S SPECIAL FLOUR

2 parts all-purpose flour
1 part cake flour

Combine the flours and mix thoroughly with a whisk. I always keep a large batch of *special flour* on hand. You can also use special flour in sauces and stews.

Now you are ready to tackle the pie dough itself.

◇   ◇   ◇

Basic Pie Dough

SPECIAL FLOUR	1 cup	1½ cups	2 cups
SALT	½ scant tsp.	¾ scant tsp.	1 scant tsp.
BUTTER, WELL CHILLED	4 tb.	6 tb.	8 tb.
EGGS	1 yolk	2 yolks	2 yolks
HEAVY CREAM	2–3 tb.	3–4 tb.	4–5 tb.
YIELD	1 8-inch tart	1 10-inch tart	1 12-inch tart

Machine Method

Food processor pie dough is equal to—indeed superior to—dough made by hand. It is quicker, too: the dough can be made in 1 minute.

1. Combine the special flour with the salt; then cut the butter (it should be cold) into ½-inch cubes. Add the butter to the flour mixture in a food processor fitted with a chopping blade. Run the machine for 30 seconds or until the butter is completely cut up and the mixture sandy and even-textured: it will feel like cornmeal.

2. Add the yolks and cream, and run the machine in 10-second spurts *just until* the dough comes together into a compact mass (1–2 minutes). If

necessary, add a little more cream. Gather the dough into a ball and chill it for at least 30 minutes.

Hand Method

1. Sift the flour onto a pastry marble or flat work surface. Using the bottom of your measuring cup, make a 4-inch "well" (depression) in the center. Soften the butter by pounding it with a rolling pin (it should remain cold), and break it into ½-inch pieces in the center of the well. Add the salt, egg, and most of the cream. Using your fingertips, work the ingredients in the center into a paste, incorporating the flour little by little. Now, using your fingertips, or a plastic pastry scraper, work the dough into largish crumbs. If the crumbs are dry, add more cream.

2. The ingredients are actually mixed not by kneading (which would develop the elasticity in the dough) but by a smearing process called *fraisage*. Take a little of the dough under the heel of your palm and smear it across the work surface. Your arm should move about 10 inches and the wet ingredients should be smoothly mixed with the dry ones. Repeat this smearing motion, until all of the dough is at the other end of your work surface. Gather it up with a pastry scraper and repeat the process once or twice or until the dough is completely smooth. Gather it up and roll it into a ball on a lightly floured work surface. The dough should feel soft but not squishy, and it should flunk the "Pillsbury doughboy" test: press your thumb in lightly; the mark or indentation should remain and *not* bounce back. Chill immediately.

Once the dough has been chilled for 30 minutes, it is ready to be rolled. It can be prepared up to 3 days ahead of time and stored in the refrigerator. (Cold dough must be pounded with the rolling pin to soften it before rolling.) Pie dough can also be frozen and thawed overnight in the refrigerator before using. But because it can be prepared so quickly, I usually prepare it the same day I intend to use it.

ROLLING THE DOUGH

1. Lightly flour your work surface. (To do this, put a pinch of flour in the palm of your hand and "throw" it across the surface as though you were skimming a stone.) It is important not to use too much flour for rolling, or the crust will become starchy.

2. Using the rolling pin, pound the dough into the shape you wish to end up with. In other words, for a round tart pan, pound the dough into a disk. To line a series of small tartlet pans, pound the dough into a square, which will be rolled into a rectangle. Flatten the dough, tapping with the side of the rolling pin, turning it frequently to ensure an even thickness.

3. You are now ready to start rolling. Place the pin at the edge closest to you, roll 4 inches forward, and roll the pin back to its starting point. Lift

the pin and starting where the first roll ended make another 4-inch roll back and forth. Continue this way until you reach the end. This will feel some-what jerky to begin with, but gradually the motion will become smooth.

4. When you are finished rolling in one direction, turn the dough 90 degrees and continue rolling. Flour your rolling pin and work surface as necessary. It is important to turn the dough, not your rolling pin or your torso: this gives you more control and prevents the dough from sticking. Now turn the dough 45 degrees and roll, then another 90 degrees and roll. You should wind up with a circle about 2 inches larger than the tart pan you wish to line. Dough should be rolled to a thickness of ³⁄₁₆-inch for large tarts; ⅛-inch for tiny tartlets.

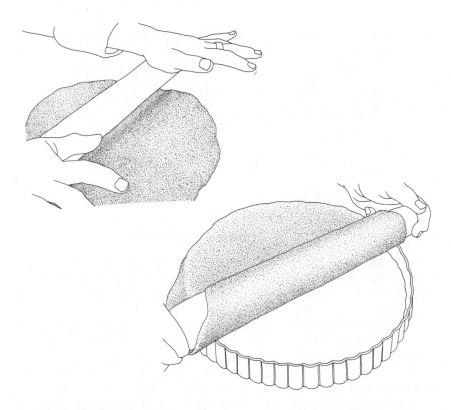

Transferring the Dough

To transfer the dough to the tart pan, roll it up loosely on the pin, and unroll it over the pan. (Alternatively, you can fold the dough in half, then in quarters, then unfold it over the pan.) I bake all my pies in the French tart pans (distinguished by their low, fluted sides and removable bottoms). Such pans are shallow, so the filling cooks completely; the fluted sides produce an attractive tart.

Lining the Pan

Lifting the edges, gently press the dough into the corners of the pan. It is important to press, not stretch the dough into the corners, or the sides shrink during baking. Next, fold the top of the dough back toward the center of the pan, then over the edge to make a ½-inch lip. Now, roll the pin over the edge of the pan to cut away excess dough. Grasping the side of the pan between your thumb and forefinger, press the dough into the side of the pan. The crust should rise ⅛ inch above the metal. (This will compensate for shrinkage during baking.) Prick the bottom of the crust all over with a fork (this prevents it from rising as it cooks) and chill it for 5 minutes in the freezer. You are now ready for baking.

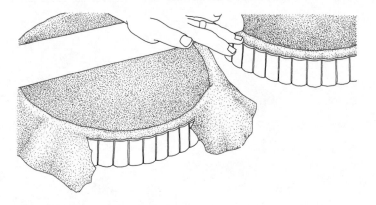

BAKING THE CRUST

The chief problem with most pie crusts is that they are soggy on the bottom. This is particularly true of quiches and other pies in which the filling is baked at the same time as the crust. There are three ways to avoid soggy crusts:

—by cooking, or "blind-baking," the pie shell before adding the fillings;

—by lining the crust with a moisture-absorbing mixture, like almond frangipane (see page 303);

—by baking the pie on the floor of the oven or on a preheated baking sheet so that the heat quickly reaches the bottom crust.

Blind-baking is essential for tarts and pies with uncooked fillings, and it will produce a crisper, flakier crust for any pie or quiche.

To Blind-Bake a Crust

Line it with aluminum foil (or parchment paper), pressing the foil firmly into the corners. Fill the lined crust with dried beans, peas, cherry pits, or rice. (This maintains the shape of the crust and prevents the sides from shrinking during baking.) Place the crust in a preheated 400° oven for 15

minutes or until the edge is firm. Remove the beans and foil; then paint the crust with egg glaze (see below). (This prevents the filling from leaking through the fork holes.) Bake the crust for an additional 5–10 minutes, or until the bottom is completely dried out and cooked. If the edges begin to brown, protect them with strips of foil or the ring from another tart pan. It is better to overbake the crust slightly than to underbake it. Let the crust cool and examine it for cracks. These can be plugged with a scrap of raw dough. You are now ready to add the various fillings.

EGG GLAZE

Crusts are painted with egg glaze to prevent them from becoming soggy. Elsewhere in this book, egg glaze is used as an adhesive (to glue pieces of dough together) and as a sort of shellac (to give the finished pastry an attractive sheen).

1 egg
¼ teaspoon salt

Beat the egg thoroughly with the salt. (The salt helps thin the white.) Let stand for 15 minutes before using. If you wish to use the egg glaze right away, pour it through a strainer. Egg glaze will keep for up to 3 days in the refrigerator. It actually improves with age.

LESSON 14

Savory Tarts

◇

Technique:
MAKING SAVORY PIES

Master Recipe:
ALSATIAN ONION TART

Variations:
ROQUEFORT-LEEK TART
MUSHROOM TART

◇   ◇   ◇

In the last lesson we learned how to make and blind-bake a pie shell. This lesson focuses on some individual savory fillings.

The first is an onion-caraway tart traditionally served in Alsace. The onions are baked in a custard—a mixture of milk (and/or cream) and eggs (and/or yolks). My basic formula for a custard is 2 eggs and 1 yolk for every cup of milk. For a richer custard, you can use exclusively egg yolks (2 yolks equal 1 whole egg) and heavy cream.

When a custard is cooked, the proteins in the eggs harden, thickening the filling. Custards are best cooked at a moderate temperature (350°F.) because prolonged high heat causes the water to separate from the solids. To test the filling for doneness, gently jab the side of the pan: if the filling wiggles or ripples, it is not cooked. You can also insert a skewer or the tip of a paring knife: the point will come out clean when the custard is set.

The second tart is flavored with sautéed leeks and Roquefort cheese. Its filling is a white sauce enriched with whole eggs, which puff when the tart is baked. The third tart features a fresh mushroom filling. As this one is already cooked, the tart need only be warmed in the oven. Whatever your filling, take care not to spill it over the crust into the tart pan. When this happens, it makes the crust soggy and often difficult to remove from the pan. If the filling settles during baking, you can always add more.

Start baking any tart directly on the floor of the oven. (This direct blast of heat on the bottom helps prevent a soggy crust.) After 10–15 minutes, transfer the tart to a higher rack. If you have an electric oven, place the tart on a preheated baking sheet.

Each of the following tarts is baked in a French tart pan. When placing the pan in and out of the oven, hold it by the sides, not the movable bottom.

To unmold the finished tart, set the pan atop a jar or canister. The rim should fall to the work surface. (If it doesn't, give it a gentle pull.)

Transfer the tart to a cake rack and let it cool for 2 minutes. Carefully loosen the bottom of the pan from the tart with a slender knife or metal spatula, and gently pull it out. If the crust looks pale or soggy on the bottom, return the tart on a cake rack to the oven and bake it for five more minutes. Sometimes, this is the only way to completely cook the bottom. Let cool slightly, then slide the pan bottom back under the tart before attempting to transfer it back to a platter.

And now, three recipes for savory tarts. If you are a newcomer to pie making, read the previous lesson before attempting them.

◇ ◇ ◇

Alsatian Onion Tart

Alsace is the easternmost province of France, and its cuisine (not to mention its fruity white wines and Teutonic dialect) has as much in common with neighboring Germany as with the rest of France. This onion tart would make an excellent centerpiece for brunch or a light lunch or dinner. *Kümmel* is a caraway-flavored liqueur.

Serves 8–10

4–5 yellow onions (about 3 cups thinly sliced)
  4 tablespoons butter
  1 clove garlic, minced
  1 tablespoon *kümmel* (optional)
  1 teaspoon caraway seeds
    salt, fresh black pepper, cayenne pepper, freshly grated
      nutmeg
  1 egg
  1 egg yolk
 ⅔ cup milk or cream
  1 prebaked 12-inch pie shell (see recipe on page 101)

1. Cut the onions into thin slices. Melt the butter in a large skillet and cook the onions and garlic over medium heat, stirring from time to time, for 8–10 minutes or until the onions are soft and limp and beginning to brown. Stir in the *kümmel,* caraway seeds, and seasonings, and simmer for 20 seconds; the mixture should be highly seasoned. Let cool slightly.

2. Spoon the onion mixture into the blind-baked pie shell. Beat the egg and egg yolk with the milk to make a custard and carefully pour it over the onions. Add the custard to within ⅛-inch of the lowest side of the crust, taking care not to spill it over the edge, or the crust will be soggy (not to mention impossible to remove from the pan). Add more custard as necessary during baking.

3. Bake the tart in a preheated 350° oven for 25 minutes, or until the custard is set. Remove the tart from the oven, let cool slightly; then unmold and cool the tart on a cake rack. If the bottom is soggy, bake the unmolded tart on the cake rack for 5 more minutes, or until crisp and brown. Serve warm.

The natural sweetness of the onions calls for a wine with some sweetness, like an Alsatian Sylvaner, Riesling, or Gewürztraminer or a California Chenin Blanc.

ROQUEFORT-LEEK TART

Roquefort is the world's greatest blue cheese (with all due respect to Gorgonzola and Stilton), and all of the world's Roquefort comes from a tiny town in the southwest highlands of France. The town of Roquefort-sur-Soulzon sits high on a limestone bluff that is honeycombed with caves. The cheese owes its uniqueness to two factors: it is made with sheep milk (not cow, as is blue cheese), and it is ripened in the cool, damp atmosphere of the limestone caverns. The following recipe was inspired by a house specialty of the Hôtel de Roquefort.

Serves 8–10

    3–4 leeks (enough to yield 2 cups chopped)
      3 tablespoons butter
      2 tablespoons flour
      1 cup milk
      3 ounces Roquefort cheese, crumbled with a fork
      2 eggs, beaten
        fresh black pepper, freshly grated nutmeg, perhaps a little
          salt
      1 prebaked 12-inch pie shell (page 101)

1. Trim, wash, and finely chop the leeks. Melt the butter in a large saucepan. Add the leeks, and cook over medium heat for 4–5 minutes, or until the leeks are soft. Stir in the flour and cook for 1 minute. Stir in the milk, bring to boil, reduce heat, and simmer for 3 minutes. Remove pan from heat. Beat in the Roquefort cheese, followed by the eggs. Add the seasonings. Roquefort is quite salty, so salt may not be needed.

2. Spoon the mixture into the tart shell, and bake for 25 minutes, or until golden brown and set. Cool tart slightly on a cake rack and unmold. (If necessary, cook it on the cake rack in a hot oven for five minutes more to dry out the bottom.) Serve the tart warm, with a gutsy red wine, like a Gigondas or Hermitage from the Côtes de Rhône.

MUSHROOM TART

Serves 8

This fragrant filling is based on a *duxelles* (finely chopped mushroom forcemeat). For a full discussion of *duxelles,* see page 258.

> 12 ounces fresh mushrooms
>   juice of ½ lemon (or to taste)
> 3 tablespoons butter
> 3 tablespoons minced shallots
> ¼ cup finely chopped parsley or fresh dill
> 2 tablespoons flour
> ½ cup heavy cream
> ½ cup sour cream, plus ½ cup for garnish (optional)
>   salt, fresh black pepper, cayenne pepper, freshly grated
>   nutmeg
> 1 10-inch prebaked pie shell

1. Prepare the *duxelles:* wash and finely chop the mushrooms as described on pages 253–54. Sprinkle the mushrooms with lemon juice to prevent them from discoloring. Melt the butter in a large frying pan and add the mushrooms, shallots, and parsley or dill. Cook the mixture over high heat, stirring from time to time, for 5 minutes or until all the liquid has evaporated and the volume is well reduced. Stir in the flour and cook the mixture for 1 minute. Stir in the cream and sour cream and simmer for 3 minutes. Add the seasonings—the mixture should be quite spicy. The filling can be prepared ahead to this stage.

2. Spoon the filling into the pie shell, and warm in a hot oven for 5–10 minutes.

Just before serving, using a piping bag fitted with a ¼-inch star tip, decorate the top with rosettes or a lattice of sour cream. (See page 278 for instructions on piping.)

VARIATIONS: The *duxelles* can be prepared with fresh or dried wild mushrooms combined with or instead of domestic ones. (See page 254 for proportions.)

Quick Yeast Dough

◇

Technique:
WORKING WITH YEAST

Master Recipe:
QUICK YEAST DOUGH

Variations:
SIX-ONION SMOKED-CHEESE PIE
PISSALADIÈRE NIÇOISE

◇   ◇   ◇

The pizza is as Italian as the Leaning Tower of Pisa. Or is it? Yeast dough pies are made all over Europe, topped with whatever cheeses or vegetables are popular in a particular region. Traditional Italian pizza has nothing on a *pissaladière niçoise* (onion-olive-tomato pie from Nice) or *flamiche* (a glorious leek pie topped with redolent Maroilles cheese from the north of France). In this lesson we will learn to make a simple but rich yeast dough that can be used for a wide range of savory pies.

Yeast is a single-celled microscopic organism that turns grain into beer, grapes into wine, and flour into bread dough. The process is simple: the yeast eats the sugar (fructose in the case of grapes; simple starches in the case of grain and flour), giving off alcohol and carbon dioxide as by-products. In wine and beer making, it is the alcohol that is important; in the case of yeast doughs it is the carbon dioxide. As the yeast "eats" the sugar, it emits tiny bubbles of carbon dioxide throughout the dough. When the dough is baked, these bubbles expand, causing the dough to rise. Because the rising process is organic rather than chemical (as in the case of baking powder and baking soda), yeast doughs are unsurpassed in their flavor and moistness.

◇

Yeast comes in two forms—cake and dried. The former has the advantage of dissolving instantly, but its perishability limits its shelf life. Dried yeast has a prolonged shelf life, but it takes longer (up to 15 minutes) to dissolve. One envelope dried yeast (1 scant tablespoon bulk) has the same leavening power as a 0.6-ounce cake of compressed yeast.

Dried yeast or refrigerated cake yeast is in a state of suspended animation. To activate it we must (1) rehydrate it by adding a little water, (2) feed it by adding a little sugar, and (3) make it comfortable by providing warm surroundings. (People share the same need for food and warmth!)

Yeast works best at a temperature of 95–110°F.; at lower temperatures the generation of carbon dioxide is slower, and the yeast, as it were, goes to sleep. Too much heat, however, (over 120°) kills yeast, which explains why dough stops rising midway through baking. Never add boiling water to yeast for this reason.

To activate yeast, mix it with a little sugar and warm water and let it stand for 3–5 minutes. When the mixture foams, the yeast is ready. Activating, or "proofing" the yeast in this way, has two advantages: it speeds up the rising process, and it assures you that the yeast is healthy. (This is particularly useful when using perishable cake yeast. If the yeast fails to foam, discard it and buy a fresh batch.

◇ ◇ ◇

Quick Yeast Dough

The following yeast dough can be made by hand, in the food processor, or in a machine fitted with a dough hook. It will take 5–10 minutes to make, and another 1–1½ hours to rise. For convenience, it can be prepared the day before and refrigerated.

If you are like me, you will probably start the dough at the last minute. To speed up the rising process, warm all the liquid ingredients (run the eggs under hot water) before kneading, and place the finished dough in its oiled bowl in a larger bowl filled with warm (body temperature) water. Turn the dough a couple of times as it rises—you'll find you can reduce the leavening time to 30–40 minutes.

To tell when a yeast dough is cooked, tap it: it should sound "hollow."

Makes enough dough to line a 12-inch tart pan

2–2¼ cups unbleached all-purpose flour
⅔ cake compressed yeast or ⅔ envelope dried yeast, or 2 teaspoons bulk dried yeast
2 tablespoons warm water
1 tablespoon sugar
2 eggs
1 tablespoon vegetable oil, plus oil for the bowl
1 scant teaspoon salt

Hand Method

1. Place the flour on a work surface and using the bottom of a measuring cup, make a 6-inch "well" (depression) in the center. Use your fingertips to make a small (1-inch) well in the wall of flour. (See illustration below.) Place the yeast, the water, and the sugar in the small well and stir lightly with your fingertips. Let stand for 3–5 minutes or until the yeast is dissolved and the mixture foams.

2. Add the eggs, oil, and salt to the big well. Mix well with your fingertips. Gradually work in the yeast mixture and the flour. Knead the dough for 5 minutes or until smooth, adding flour as necessary; the dough should be soft but not sticky.

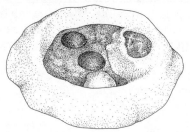

Food Processor Method

Activate the yeast with the sugar and water in a small bowl. When the mixture foams, place it with the eggs, oil, and salt in a processor fitted with a chopping or pastry blade. Run the machine until the ingredients are mixed. Add the flour and run the machine in short bursts for 2 minutes, or until the dough forms a smooth pliable ball. If necessary, knead it for a few minutes on a lightly floured surface.

Mixer Method

(This method is for a heavy-duty mixer, such as a KitchenAid or Kenwood, fitted with a dough hook.)

Activate the yeast with the sugar and water in the bowl of the mixer. When it foams, add the eggs, oil, and salt, and beat to mix. Add the flour, and beat at low speed until the dough is smooth and pliable.

RISING, PUNCHING DOWN, AND ROLLING THE DOUGH

1. Place the dough in an oiled bowl, turn the dough once or twice to coat with oil, and loosely cover with plastic wrap. Let the dough rise in a warm, draft-free place for 1–1½ hours or until doubled in bulk.

2. Punch down the dough. Do not let it rise more than doubled in bulk, or it will take on a sour, "beery" flavor—the result of excessive alcohol and carbon dioxide. If you wish to refrigerate or freeze the dough, wrap it in a ziplock or plastic bag. (Unlike plastic wrap, a bag will not burst if the dough

expands.) If the dough expands too much in the refrigerator, punch it down a second time. Thaw frozen dough in the refrigerator the night before you plan to use it.

SIX-ONION
SMOKED-CHEESE PIE

This robust appetizer or brunch dish takes its inspiration from the *flamiche* of northeast France—an onion-leek pie garnished with a malodorous cheese called *Maroilles.* Our version calls for a smoked cheese, like smoked mozzarella or Bruder Basil. It is currently in vogue to give dishes alpha-numeric names—like three-chocolate cake, five-peppercorn steak, or six-onion smoked-cheese pie. (No doubt fallout from the burgeoning computer sciences!).

Serves 8

  1 batch quick yeast dough (from preceding recipe)

FOR THE FILLING:
- 2 yellow onions, peeled
- 1 red onion, peeled
- 4 large shallots, trimmed and washed
- 2 cloves garlic, peeled
- 3 leeks, trimmed and washed
- 1 bunch scallions, trimmed and washed
- 3 tablespoons butter
- 2 tablespoons chopped fresh parsley and other herbs
- ⅓ cup heavy cream (or more as needed)
- salt, fresh black pepper, cayenne pepper
- 6 ounces smoked mozzarella, or other smoked cheese, cut into 8–10 slices

1. Prepare the dough as described above. It should have risen once and been punched down. Roll it out and use it to line a 12-inch French tart pan.
2. Meanwhile, finely chop the first 6 ingredients. (Detailed instructions on chopping are found on pages 28–30.) Cook the vegetables in the butter in a large skillet over a medium heat for 4 to 5 minutes, or until soft. Add the herbs, the cream, and the seasonings, and gently simmer for 5 minutes or until the cream is completely absorbed by the onions. The mixture should be highly seasoned.
3. Let the filling cool slightly and spoon it into the crust. Arrange the cheese slices on top around the edge of the tart, leaving the center open. Let the tart stand in a warm place for 30 minutes before baking. Bake the six-onion smoked-cheese pie in a preheated 400° oven for 40–50 minutes or until the crust is browned and sounds hollow when tapped. (If the edge

of the crust browns too fast, protect it with a piece of foil.) Cool slightly before serving. A fruity white wine from Alsace, like a Riesling or Gewürztraminer, would be a perfect beverage.

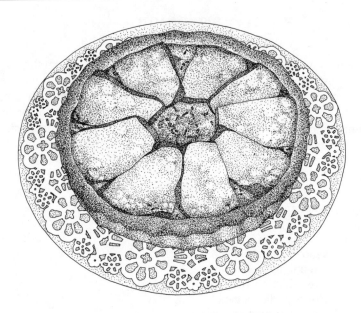

PISSALADIÈRE NIÇOISE
FRENCH "PIZZA"

Pissaladière is a sort of French pizza, served all up and down the Côte d'Azur. It originated in Nice—whence the name. In this version, sautéed onions take the place of the traditional tomato sauce; thinly sliced tomatoes replace the melted cheese. Like any respectable Italian pizza, this one boasts olives and anchovies. Because of the high salt content in the anchovies and olives, *pissaladière* makes an excellent dish for summer. For the best results use ripe tomatoes, fresh herbs, extra-virgin olive oil, and full-flavored olives, like tangy Greek *calamata*.

1 batch simple yeast dough from above

FOR THE FILLING:

4 tablespoons extra-virgin olive oil, plus 2 tablespoons for sprinkling
4 onions, thinly sliced (about 2 cups)
1 bay leaf, crumbled
pinch of thyme

2 tablespoons chopped fresh herbs, including basil, oregano,
   marjoram, and parsley
  a little salt, plenty of fresh black pepper, cayenne pepper
3 large, ripe tomatoes
2 2-ounce cans anchovy fillets, drained
1 cup imported black olives

1. Prepare the dough as described in the master recipe, letting it rise once and punching it down. Roll it out and use it to line a 12-inch French tart pan.

2. Meanwhile, heat the olive oil in a large skillet and add the onions, bay leaf, thyme, and the chopped herbs. Sauté over medium heat for 3 minutes, then increase heat to high. Cook the onions for 6–8 minutes, or until most of the liquid has evaporated and the onions just begin to brown. (The idea here is to cook out all the water, which would make the crust soggy, and to concentrate the flavor of the onions.) Season the mixture with salt (but not too much: the anchovies are quite salty), pepper, and cayenne pepper and let cool slightly.

3. Cut the tomatoes into thin, widthwise slices. Cut the anchovies in half lengthwise. Cut the olives in halves or thirds, so as to avoid the pits. Spoon the onion mixture into the crust. Arrange a single layer of tomato slices on top to completely cover the onions. Arrange half the anchovies in parallel rows 1 inch apart. Turn the *pissaladière* 60 degrees and arrange the remaining anchovies in parallel rows to form a neat lattice. (A diamond-shaped lattice is more aesthetically pleasing than a square one.) Place an olive slice in the center of each diamond formed by the lattice. Sprinkle the top with a few drops of olive oil.

4. Let the dough rise for 30 minutes before baking. Bake the *pissala-dière* in a preheated 400° oven for 40–50 minutes, or until the crust is browned and sounds hollow when tapped. Let stand 5 minutes before serving. Serve with a salad, a light fruit mousse, and a rosé from Provence, Languedoc, or even Portugual.

Note: To keep from crying when chopping onions, put a slice of bread in your mouth. The bread will absorb the fumes.

LESSON 16

Brioche

◇   ◇   ◇

arie Antoinette did not say, "Let them eat cake." When told that the starving peasants had no more bread, she actually replied "Let them eat brioche." It's easy to see how the absence of this buttery pastry could lead to a revolution!

Brioche is to regular bread what hollandaise is to white sauce. Start with a yeast dough made with whole eggs instead of water. Now imagine the finest butter you would spread on toast mixed directly into the dough, and you will have a good picture of brioche. The French have the right idea in their colloquial speech, calling a "potbelly" a brioche.

Brioche is delectable by itself, and it is the perfect pastry for baking foods *en croûte* ("in a crust"). For while puff pastry becomes soggy when used as a wrapping, brioche forms a firm, crisp crust. It can be made by hand or by machine; it is best made the day before; and it is one dough that does not suffer from freezing.

In this lesson we learn first how to make brioche by hand, then in a heavy-duty mixer. This recipe cannot be made in the food processor.

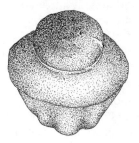

Brioche

4 cups all-purpose flour
1 0.6-ounce cake yeast, or 1 envelope dried yeast, or
   1 tablespoon bulk dried yeast
4 tablespoons warm milk
⅓ cup sugar
   approximately 6 large eggs, warmed in hot water
2½ teaspoons salt
1 pound unsalted butter, at room temperature
   oil for oiling the bowl
1 egg beaten with a pinch of salt for glaze

Hand Method

1. Sift the flour onto a pastry marble or work surface. Use the bottom of a measuring cup to make a well (depression) in the center of the flour. Make a smaller well alongside the center well, and in it place the yeast, warm milk, and half the sugar. Gently stir the ingredients in the small well with your fingertips and let stand until the yeast is completely dissolved and the mixture begins to foam.

2. Beat the eggs and add them to the center well with the remaining sugar and the salt. Mix with your fingertips, gradually incorporating the flour into the other ingredients. The dough should be wet and sticky; add additional eggs if necessary.

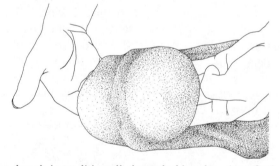

3. Brioche dough is traditionally kneaded by slapping. Gather the dough into an oblong with a pastry scraper. Lift it by the narrow end farthest away from you, swing it away from you in the air, and slap it firmly against the pastry marble. Flip the end you are holding over the rest of the dough to form another oblong. Lift this by the narrow end, swing it, slap it, and flip it. Repeat for 4–5 minutes or until the dough is smooth and shiny; when it's ready it will look like chamois cloth.

4. Unwrap the butter and pound it with your fist until it is as soft as the dough. Place it on top of the dough. Cut the butter and dough in half

vertically with a knife, a pastry scraper, or your hands. Place one half on top of the other and cut the butter and dough in half again. Continue cutting until the butter is completely blended with the dough. It will take about 20 cuts. Slap the dough a few more times to make it perfectly smooth. Breathe a sigh of relief: the hard part is over.

Note: Slapping brioche dough and incorporating the butter requires lots of practice. If you are anything like me, the first time you do it, you are apt to wind up with dough in your hair, on the walls, and on the ceiling. Resist the temptation to stiffen the dough by adding flour; soft, sticky dough yields a moist, delicate brioche.

Machine Method

You will need a heavy-duty mixer, like a KitchenAid or Kenmore, fitted with a paddle or dough hook.

1. Combine the yeast with the warm milk and half the sugar in the mixing bowl. When the mixture foams, add the eggs, remaining sugar, and the salt and beat at medium speed. When the egg mixture is smooth, reduce speed to low, and gradually beat in the flour. Beat for 8–10 minutes or until the dough is smooth and elastic. It may be necessary to add another egg: brioche dough should be quite sticky. It will almost certainly be necessary to stop the machine 2 or 3 times and scrape down any dough that rides up the hook.

2. When the dough is smooth, soften the butter by pounding it with your fist, and add it little by little to the brioche dough. Continue beating until the dough is smooth and homogeneous.

Note: As you can see, making brioche is much easier by machine than by hand. I find the process of slapping brioche dough by hand satisfying and cathartic, but outside class I always use a machine.

LEAVENING, SHAPING, AND BAKING BRIOCHE

Gather the dough into a ball and place in an oiled bowl. Turn it to oil the top and cover loosely with plastic wrap and a dishcloth. Place it in a draft-free area of the kitchen (not too warm a spot, or the butter will melt out of the dough). Let the dough rise for 1½ hours or until doubled in bulk. Punch it down, cover tightly, and refrigerate for at least 3 hours, preferably overnight. (NOTE: You will probably have to punch the dough a second time in the refrigerator. For a lighter brioche, let the dough rise a second time and then punch it down.) You are now ready to shape and bake the brioche. If you prefer, you can freeze the dough, and come back to it in a few days or weeks. Thaw dough in the refrigerator overnight.

◇　◇　◇

BRIOCHE À TÊTE

The classic shape for this butter-rich dough is *brioche à tête*—"brioche with a head," literally. The dough is baked in a fluted mold with outwardly sloping sides.

One batch of dough will make 3 5-inch breads or 2 loaves

1 batch brioche dough (leavened, pinched down, and chilled
   at least 3 hours
   butter (for the mold)
1 egg beaten with a pinch of salt to make glaze

3 5-inch brioche molds

1. Thickly brush the molds with butter. Pinch off enough dough to form a 4-inch ball. Roll it into a smooth sphere. Place the ball in the mold. Dip your finger in flour, and make a deep depression in the center of the dough. Pinch off a smaller portion of dough and roll it into a 2-inch pear shape. Brush the inside of the large ball with egg glaze and set the pear shape, pointy end down, in the center. Continue making breads until all the dough is used up.

2. Using scissors, make vertical cuts between the big and little balls at 90-degree intervals. (This will help the bread rise evenly.) Loosely cover breads with a cloth and let them rise for 1–1½ hours or until swelled by 50 percent and quite soft to the touch. Preheat the oven to 400° F.

3. Brush the top of each brioche with egg glaze (see page 105), taking care not to drip any on the mold. Glaze the brioches a second time, and place in oven. Bake the breads for 30–40 minutes or until firm and golden brown. If the surface browns before the dough is completely cooked, cover it loosely with foil to prevent it from burning. When brioche is done, it will sound hollow when tapped. Turn the breads onto a cake rack to cool for at least 15 minutes. Brioche can be served any time in the next 12 hours, but it tastes best hot out of the oven.

Note: Brioche can also be baked like bread in regular loaf pans.

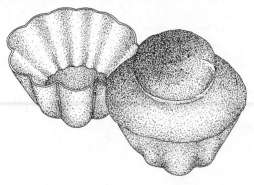

BRIE CHEESE IN BRIOCHE

Brie or Camembert baked in brioche is lovely for a brunch or buffet. Brie in brioche should be baked at least 6 hours before serving, so the cheese has a chance to resolidify. The dough can be quickly warmed at the last minute.

One 10-inch Brie will serve 8–12 people

¾ batch of brioche dough, leavened, punched down, and
    chilled at least 3 hours
1 whole 10-inch Brie cheese, or 2 whole Camemberts, or a
    soft-ripened cheese of your choice
1 egg beaten with a pinch of salt to make a glaze

1. Pinch off ⅓ of the dough and roll it into an 11-inch circle. (Work quickly when rolling the dough and use plenty of flour.) Fold the circle in half and transfer it to an inverted baking sheet. (It is easier to slide the cooked Brie off the back side of the baking sheet than over the edges.) Brush the circle with egg glaze, set the cheese on top, and brush the sides and top of the cheese with glaze. Press the overlap of the circle against the sides of the cheese, and brush the outside with glaze.

2. Roll ⅔ of the remaining dough into a 12-inch circle, and drape the circle over the cheese, pressing the edges against the sides. Brush the dough-wrapped cheese with glaze.

3. Roll out the remaining dough to a thickness of ³⁄₁₆-inch and cut it into whatever shapes you fancy. I like to use a fluted ravioli cutter to cut ½-inch strips, which I lay on the top in a lattice. Alternatively, you can use cookie cutters to cut triangles, half moons, or other shapes. Cover the decorated pastry with a clean dishcloth and let it rise until the dough is soft and puffed, about 1 hour. Do not let it rise too much, however, or the top will crack.

4. Brush the dough twice with egg glaze. Bake Brie in brioche in a preheated 400° oven for 40 minutes or until the crust is firm and golden brown and sounds hollow when tapped. Transfer the Brie in brioche to a cake rack and cool at least 2 hours before serving. If you serve it right away, the cheese will come gushing out like sauce.

FISH
AND
SEAFOOD

LESSON 17

Pan-Fried Fish

◇

Techniques:
BREADING FISH
PAN-FRYING FISH

Master Recipe:
CRISP RED SNAPPER WITH SESAME OIL
   AND GINGER

Variations:
FILLET OF SOLE WITH BROWN BUTTER AND
   CAPERS
TROUT WITH ROQUEFORT SAUCE

◇ ◇ ◇

Like thousands of the Baby Boom generation, I grew up on a frozen, breaded seafood substance called fish sticks. Hardly the fare to turn a child into a fish lover! It wasn't till I visited London for the first time and ate fish and chips from a cone of rolled newspaper that I developed a lasting love of seafood.

Frying is one of the best methods for cooking fish, particularly delicate white fish, like cod or haddock. The crisp coating gives backbone to a fragile white fish that would crumble if poached or baked. A batter or crumb coating seals in the moisture of any fish, making this method ideal for inherently dry species like trout or sole.

Fish can be fried in one of three ways. The most simple is to dip it in milk, then seasoned flour, then pan-fry it in melted butter. The French favor a method called *à l'anglaise* ("English-style"): dipping the fish first in flour, then in beaten egg, finally in bread crumbs. When pan-fried, this coating forms a crisp crust. The third method, the one actually used by the English, is batter frying: the eggs and flour are combined to make a wet batter, in which the fish is dipped prior to being deep-fat-fried.

From the home kitchen, I prefer pan-frying, deep fat being dangerous and messy. The best tool is a well-seasoned cast-iron skillet (see page 90 for instructions on seasoning a pan). We use clarified butter (see page 201) or a half-and-half mixture of butter and oil for frying, as together both are less likely to burn. Thin pieces of fish (up to ¼ inch) can be fried all the way through in the pan; to cook thicker pieces of fish, we lightly brown the pieces on all sides in butter, then finish cooking the fish (in the frying pan) in a preheated 400° oven.

◇ ◇ ◇

Crisp Red Snapper with
Sesame Oil and Ginger

In this dish, the skin is left on the fish, which makes the outside very crisp and the inside moist and tender. The ginger, sesame oil, and hot chili oil lend an Oriental accent. (Both oils are sold at any Oriental grocery store. Be sure to use imported Japanese sesame oil: the domestic oils sold at health food stores do not have the proper flavor.) A special thanks to Jasper White, owner of the restaurant Jasper in Boston, who inspired this recipe.

Serves 4

4 thin red snapper or yellowtail snapper fillets (6–8 ounces each), skin on

FOR DIPPING THE FISH:

1 cup milk
1 tablespoon soy sauce
2 teaspoons sesame oil
  salt and fresh black pepper
½ teaspoon Szechuan peppercorns, crushed
  approximately ½ cup seasoned flour

TO FINISH THE DISH:

½ cup snow peas
1 sweet red pepper, cored and seeded
2 inches fresh ginger root
1 bunch enoki mushrooms (optional; see page 255)
6 tablespoons sesame oil
½ teaspoon hot chili oil
  juice of ½ lemon (or to taste)
¼ cup thinly sliced scallions

1. Run your fingers along the snapper, feeling for bones. Remove any bones with a tweezers or needle-nose pliers. Combine the milk, soy sauce, and sesame oil in a shallow bowl and beat with a fork. Combine the salt, peppers, and flour in another shallow bowl.

2. Cut the snow peas and pepper into a fine julienne (see page 139). Peel the ginger, cut it lengthwise in julienne, and blanch these strips in boiling water for 1 minute. Cut the enoki mushrooms off at the roots.

3. Dip each fish fillet, first in milk mixture, then in flour, then in milk

again, then in flour. Heat 3 tablespoons sesame oil in a large frying pan. Cook the fish, skin side down, over medium flame for 2–3 minutes, or until the skin is golden brown. Turn the fish and continue cooking for 2–3 minutes, or until the fish flakes when pressed. Drain the fillets on paper towels and transfer to warm plates or a platter. Keep the fillets warm without covering.

4. Meanwhile, heat another frying pan, almost to smoking. Add the remaining sesame oil, and hot chili oil, then the snow peas, peppers, ginger, scallions, and lemon juice. Cook the vegetables for 30–40 seconds and spoon them over the fish. Garnish with enoki mushrooms. This fine dish calls for a big, oaky California Chardonnay, like an Acacia, Ggritch Hills, or Chateau St. Jean.

Note: Before the actual cooking, have all your ingredients chopped and ready and the plates or platter warmed.

FILLET OF SOLE WITH
BROWN BUTTER AND CAPERS

This preparation resembles trout *grenobloise* ("cooked in the style of Grenoble"). Any delicate white fish can be substituted for the sole.

Serves 4

4 large or 8 small fillets of sole (about 1½ pounds)

FOR DIPPING:

seasoned flour (see below)
1 cup milk

TO FINISH THE DISH:

5 tablespoons butter
4 tablespoons chopped parsley
2–3 tablespoons capers, drained
2 or 3 anchovy fillets, chopped, or 2 strips fried bacon, crumbled
(optional)
juice of 1 lemon (or to taste)
lemon wedges

1. Trim any bones off the sole fillets, cutting large fillets in two. If any fillets are more than ¼ inch thick, pound them between two pieces of moistened parchment or waxed paper with the side of a cleaver. Combine the flour with the seasonings and herbs in a shallow bowl. Dip the fish in the milk, then the seasoned flour, shaking off the excess.

2. Melt the butter in a large frying pan over medium-high heat and cook the fillets for 1 minute per side, or until the fish flakes easily when pressed. Arrange the fillets on a platter or warm dinner plates. Increase the heat to high and continue cooking the butter until it becomes brown. Add the remaining ingredients to the butter and cook for 10 seconds. Pour the butter over the fish. Serve with the lemon wedges. A California Chardonnay would go nicely.

TO CUT LEMON WEDGES

As a restaurant critic, one of my pet peeves is a badly cut lemon wedge. To cut proper lemon wedges, slice ¼ inch off each end of the lemon. Now, cut the lemon lengthwise into six wedges. Cut ⅛ inch off the narrow edge of each wedge and remove the seeds. Note how the ends of the wedges are blunted to give your fingers a place to squeeze.

SEASONED FLOUR

Here is a nice seasoned flour for pan-frying. Szechuan peppercorns (not peppercorns, really, but the reddish-brown berry of a small shrub) have a pungent, slightly sweet flavor. The spices can be ground in a coffee grinder or blender. Feel free to vary the proportions to suit your taste.

    1 cup flour
    ½ teaspoon salt
    ¼ teaspoon white pepper
    ¼ teaspoon fresh black pepper
    ¼ teaspoon ground Szechuan peppercorns
    ¼ teaspoon ground oregano
    ¼ teaspoon ground thyme
    ⅛ teaspoon ground coriander

Combine all the ingredients.

TROUT WITH ROQUEFORT SAUCE

This dish was inspired by one I tasted in the Tarn Gorge—France's version of the Grand Canyon. The river was so clear, you could watch your dinner swimming; the nearby town of Roquefort supplied the cheese for the sauce. Any mild fish could be substituted for the trout, and to save time, you could omit the vegetable garnish. Instead of using bread crumbs for coating, we use ground nuts.

Serves 8

>   4 large (12-ounce) brook trout
>   salt and pepper
>   1 cup flour
>   2 eggs, beaten
>   1½ cups slivered almonds, ground (but not too finely) in a food
>   processor
>   6 tablespoons clarified butter

FOR THE SAUCE:

>   1 cup dry white wine
>   3 tablespoons finely chopped shallots
>   2 cups heavy or whipping cream
>   2–3 ounces genuine Roquefort cheese, crumbled
>   fresh black pepper and perhaps salt
>   4 tablespoons chopped fresh chives

FOR THE GARNISH:

>   32 fiddlehead ferns (about ¾ pound), picked and cleaned, or
>   asparagus tips
>   1 pound (5–6 medium) carrots
>   salt
>   sugar
>   3 tablespoons butter
>   1 lemon, thinly sliced for garnish
>   8 whole, unblanched almonds

1. Prepare the trout. Fillet the fish, and pressing the skin between the knife and the cutting board, remove the skin. Using a needle-nose pliers, remove any bones from the trout fillets, and fold them in half. Season the fillets with salt and pepper, and dip them first in the flour, then in the eggs, then in the almonds. (The trout can be prepared up to an hour ahead of time this way and kept on a plate.)

2. Meanwhile, prepare the sauce. Place the wine and shallots in a saucepan, and boil until only ¼ cup wine remains. Add the cream, and continue simmering (you will have to stir it from time to time to keep it from boiling over) until reduced by half. Whisk in the Roquefort cheese over a low heat; the sauce should simmer gently, not boil. Season with pepper and perhaps a little salt (remember, the cheese is already quite salty). Whisk in the chives.

3. Meanwhile, prepare the garnish. Cook the fiddlehead ferns in rapidly boiling salted water for 1 minute or until crispy-tender. Refresh them under

cold water. "Turn" (see page 234 for instruction and illustration) the carrots
—that is, cut them into olive shapes with a paring knife (you should wind
up with 32 pieces). Cook the carrots in water to cover with salt, a pinch of
sugar, and 1 tablespoon butter. As the water evaporates, the carrots should
become glazed. At the last minute, reheat the fiddleheads in the remaining
butter.

4. Just before serving, heat the butter, and fry the trout fillets over a
medium heat for 3 minutes per side, or until the coating is golden brown
and the center of the fish is cooked. Alternatively, the fillets can be lightly
browned in butter, then baked in a 400° oven for 10 minutes.

5. To assemble the dish, spoon the sauce onto 8 warm dinner plates
and sprinkle the sauce with the chives. Set a cooked trout fillet on top.
Surround each fillet with four carrots and four fiddleheads, alternating colors, and top the fish with a lemon slice surmounted by an almond. Serve
at once.

L E S S O N   1 8

Braised Fish

◇

Technique:

BRAISING FISH

Master Recipe:

ORIENTAL-STYLE BLUEFISH

Variations:

BASS PROVENÇALE

MONKFISH WITH MUSSELS AND SAFFRON
  SAUCE

◇   ◇   ◇

If I were to pick a single method for cooking fish, it would surely be braising. Braising has all the advantages and none of the drawbacks of deep frying, poaching, and baking. As in baking, the fish is cooked in the oven; the timing is not as split-second as with frying or grilling, so you can turn your attention to the rest of the dinner. As in poaching, the fish is cooked in liquid to cover, which maximizes tenderness and moistness. For these reasons, braising is the easiest, most reliable way to cook fish.

To braise fish, a shallow roasting pan is lined with aromatic herbs and vegetables. (Try to use a pan that is just large enough to hold the fish.) The fish is cut into uniform pieces, seasoned, then arranged on top of the vegetables. A suitable liquid (cream, wine, fish stock, soy sauce, etc.) is added to moisten the fish, followed by more aromatic vegetables and seasonings. The pan is loosely covered with buttered foil. Any braised fish dish can be prepared ahead to this stage.

Just before serving, the fish is baked in the oven. (To speed up the cooking process, you can bring the pan juices to a boil on the stove. To do this, use a metal roasting pan rather than a glass one.) To test for doneness, press the fish with your index finger: it should crumble into firm flakes. The fish can be served directly in its poaching liquid, or the liquid can be reduced or thickened to make a sauce.

The braising pan can be set up well ahead of time, and the fish put into the oven the moment you sit down to dinner. Never braise fish in an aluminum or cast-iron pan, as the wine or lemon juice may react with the metal. The following recipes illustrate the principle of braising fish. Feel free to come up with your own variations.

◇   ◇   ◇

Oriental-Style Bluefish

Many people shy away from bluefish because of its forthright flavor. The Oriental ingredients in this recipe—ginger, soy sauce, sesame oil—help cut the inherent oiliness of the fish. *Mirin* is a Japanese sweetened rice wine; substitute white wine sweetened with sugar. This recipe uses a technique called "dry-braising": relatively little liquid is used, so that the fish cooks in its own steam.

Serves 4

1½ pounds skinless bluefish fillets
    salt and plenty of fresh black pepper
  3 tablespoons sesame oil
  3 tablespoons chopped scallions
  2 teaspoons fresh finely chopped ginger
  2 cloves garlic, minced
  3 tablespoons toasted sesame seeds (see box below)
  3 tablespoons soy sauce
  3 tablespoons *mirin* or white wine sweetened with sugar
    juice of ½ lemon

1. Run your fingers over the bluefish, feeling for bones. Remove any you find with a tweezers or needle-nose pliers. Cut the bluefish into 4-inch pieces and season with salt and pepper.

2. Spread a small roasting pan with half of the flavorings. Arrange the fish on top, and sprinkle it with the remaining flavorings. The dish can be prepared ahead to this stage. Braise the bluefish for 15–20 minutes or until it flakes easily when pressed. Spoon the pan juices over for serving. There are many possibilities for beverages: tea, beer, or a Gewürztraminer from Alsace or California.

◇

To toast sesame seeds, place them in a dry frying pan over a medium heat, and roast them, stirring constantly until the hulls are lightly browned. They burn quickly, so pay attention to their color.

BASS PROVENÇALE
(BRAISED WITH GARLIC, OLIVES, AND TOMATOES)

Provence is a province in southern France, renowned for its olives, garlic, and juicy sun-ripened tomatoes. Niçoise olives (from the town of Nice) are tiny ones that look like raisins; feel free to use dry-cured olives, Greek *calamatas,* or even pitted, canned olives. Any fleshy white fish, like halibut or snapper, could be substituted for the bass.

Serves 4

       1½ pounds skinless bass fillets
           salt and plenty of fresh black pepper
        4 tablespoons extra-virgin olive oil
        1 onion, diced
      2–3 cloves garlic, minced
        3 *ripe* tomatoes, peeled, seeded, and chopped (see page 66)
        ½ cup *Niçoise* olives
        4 tablespoons chopped fresh herbs, including parsley,
           oregano, and basil
      2–3 tablespoons dry white vermouth

1. Run your fingers along the bass feeling for bones, and pull out any you find with a tweezers or pliers. Cut the fish into 4-inch pieces and salt and pepper them.

2. Heat the olive oil in a small frying pan over medium heat and sauté the onion for 3 minutes or until soft. Add the garlic and sauté for 30 seconds. Add the tomatoes, increase heat to high, and cook for 2 minutes to evaporate some of the tomato liquid. Stir in the olives and herbs.

3. Spread a small metal roasting pan with half the tomato mixture. Arrange the fish on top, and spread with the remaining tomato mixture. Pour the vermouth on top. Cover the pan with oiled foil or parchment paper. The recipe can be prepared up to 6 hours ahead to this stage.

4. Bring the liquid in the pan to a boil on the stove and bake the bass in a preheated 400° oven for 20 minutes, or until the fish flakes when pressed. Serve the bass with the vegetables and pan juices spooned on top.

A tart, dry white wine, like Muscadet or Fumé Blanc, would go well with this dish.

MONKFISH WITH MUSSELS AND SAFFRON SAUCE

Few foods mark the progress of the American palate like that unlovely sea creature, the monkfish. Twenty years ago, American fishermen threw it away or else shipped it to France. (Ironically, French restaurants bold enough to serve it in those days re-imported it from Paris.) Today, monkfish commands high prices in fashionable shops but can be had for a few dollars a pound at a fishmonger in a humble neighborhood. Its firm white flesh—likened to that of lobster—has made it popular with contemporary chefs. Instructions for cleaning mussels are found on page 148. Notes on butter sauces are found on page 140.

Serves 6

2 pounds monkfish
salt and freshly ground black pepper
butter for the baking dish
½ cup dry white wine
3 tablespoons finely chopped shallots

TO COOK THE MUSSELS:

2 pounds mussels
½ cup dry white wine
3 tablespoons minced shallots

FOR THE SAUCE:

1½ sticks cold, unsalted butter
3 tablespoons finely chopped shallots
generous pinch (⅛ teaspoon) saffron
½ cup heavy cream
fresh pepper and cayenne

1. Trim the purplish membrane off the monkfish and cut the fish into diagonal ½-inch slices. Sprinkle with salt and pepper. Lightly butter a baking dish just large enough to hold the fish and sprinkle the bottom with the finely chopped shallots. Arrange the slices on top. Sprinkle the wine over the fish, and cover the pan with buttered foil or parchment paper. The fish can be prepared up to 12 hours ahead to this stage.

2. Thirty minutes before you plan to serve it, place the fish in a preheated 400° oven, and cook for 20–25 minutes or until the flesh flakes easily when pressed. Strain the pan juices and reserve. Keep the fish covered and in a warm spot.

3. Meanwhile, scrub the mussels, reserve the mussel broth, and remove the threads, discarding any with cracked shells or shells that fail to close when tapped. In a large pot bring the wine to a boil with the shallots. Add the mussels and steam, covered, over high heat for 5 minutes, or until the shells open. Remove the mussels from the shells, reserving a dozen or so shells for garnish, and remove the beards and any threads from the shellfish. Cover the mussels and keep them warm. Strain the juices and reserve, leaving any sandy dregs in the pot.

4. To prepare the sauce, melt 3 tablespoons butter in a 1-quart sauce-pan over medium heat and cook the remaining shallots for 1 minute, or until soft but not browned. Add the pan juices from the fish and bring to a boil. Add the reserved mussel juices and saffron, and boil until only ¼ cup liquid remains. Add the cream and boil until the mixture is reduced by half. Whisk in the remaining butter in ½-inch pieces. Do not let the sauce boil after all the butter has been added, or it will curdle. Correct the seasoning with pepper and cayenne: it should already be sufficiently salty. Stir the shelled mussels into the sauce.

5. To serve the monkfish with mussels and saffron sauce, arrange the pieces of monkfish in a serving dish or on a bed of rice pilaf (see recipe on page 267) and spoon the sauce over. Place a few mussels back in their shells and use them for garnish. Steamed kale (see recipe on page 232) would make a colorful accompaniment. I can think of no better wine than a fine California Chardonnay, or a Meursault, or a Montrachet from Bur-gundy.

LESSON 19

Papillote Cooking

————————◇————————

Techniques:

MAKING PAPILLOTES

JULIENNING

MAKING BUTTER SAUCES

Master Recipe:

PAPILLOTES OF SALMON WITH JULIENNED
  VEGETABLES

Variations:

PAPILLOTES OF SOLE, SNAPPER, OR
  SWORDFISH

PAPILLOTE OF HALIBUT WITH BACON AND
  SUN-DRIED TOMATOES

◇   ◇   ◇

A *papillote* (pronounced "pah-pee-yote") is many things in French: a curling paper, a candy wrapper, a cutlet frill. But above all, it is a cooking method well suited to seafood and delicate meats and poultry.

The method involves baking the food in tightly sealed paper or a foil bag. (The term comes from the Latin *papilio,* "butterfly.") Papillote cooking has three distinct advantages: the ingredients can be assembled well ahead of time and baked at the last minute; the bag seals in moisture and flavor; and few dishes make a more spectacular impression than a papillote hot out of the oven, the bag puffed like a balloon.

In the old days, papillotes were made of parchment paper, which was pretty to look at but difficult to seal. Today's chefs favor a high-tech look, using squares of aluminum foil to form the bags. Papillotes are not difficult to make, but be sure to seal the edges as tightly as possible. Serve papillotes as soon as they emerge from the oven.

◇   ◇   ◇

Papillotes of Salmon with
Julienned Vegetables

This dish was a specialty of Louis LeRoy, a Breton chef with whom I trained in 1979. Its lavish use of vegetables is typical of *nouvelle cuisine,* the "new" cooking style that swept France in the seventies. Complete instructions on "julienning" vegetables (cutting them into matchstick-like slivers) are given on page 139.

Serves 4

1½ pounds skinless salmon fillets, or other fish (see below)

FOR THE VEGETABLE GARNISH:

1 medium-sized turnip or parsnip
2 small or 1 large leek
2 carrots
¼ pound mushrooms
12 snow peas
12 small green beans
¼ cup shucked fresh peas (optional)
6 ounces fresh spinach
salt, pepper
4 tablespoons melted butter or extra-virgin olive oil
2 tablespoons each chopped fresh chives and parsley
4 generous sprigs dill, tarragon, chervil, or other fresh herb
4 tablespoons dry white vermouth
White Butter Sauce (see recipe on page 141)

4 12-x-24-inch sheets aluminum foil

1. Run your fingers over the salmon fillets, feeling for bones. Pull out any bones with tweezers or pliers. Cut the fish on the diagonal into ¼-inch slices.

2. Julienne the turnip or parsnip and leeks. Cut the carrots either into julienne or into carrot flowers as shown on page 234. Wash the mushrooms, remove sandy stems, and cut in thin slices. Snap and string the snow peas and string beans. Shuck the peas. Remove stems from spinach, wash it thoroughly in several waters, and cut the leaves into ½-inch ribbons.

3. Bring 2 quarts salted water to a boil. Cook the turnip or parsnip, leeks, carrots, snow peas, green beans, and fresh peas, successively, in rapidly boiling water for 30–60 seconds, or until each is crispy-tender. Use a slotted spoon or skimmer to remove the vegetables—do not overcook them. Refresh each vegetable under cold water. The vegetables can be prepared ahead of time.

4. Spread a sheet of foil, shiny side down, on your work surface. (The shiny side will be on the outside of the finished papillote.) Lightly brush it with butter or oil. Place a quarter of the spinach in a small mound in the center of the foil. Arrange a few of the salmon slices on the spinach and season with plenty of salt and pepper. Dot these lightly with butter and sprinkle with some of the chopped herbs. Arrange a quarter of each vegetable on top of the fish—work with a light hand—the vegetables should

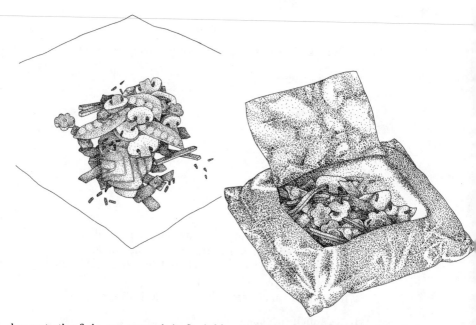

decorate the fish, not entomb it. Sprinkle on more salt and pepper, chopped herbs, melted butter, 1 tablespoon vermouth, and finally a sprig of dill.

5. Fold the top half of the foil over the bottom and bring the edges together. Close the bag by folding over each edge, ¼-inch at a time, 3–4 times in all to make a hermetic seal. Make the folds as neat and tight as you can: the papillote will not puff if any of the steam can escape. The papillotes can be prepared up to 2 hours ahead of time to this stage and cooked at the last minute.

6. Just before serving, bake the papillotes in a preheated 400° oven for 10–12 minutes, or until the foil bags are puffed like balloons. Try not to open the oven; if you must, open it quickly and just a crack. (The cold air will make the bags collapse.) Papillotes are like soufflés: guests may wait for them, but they wait for no one. Serve at once.

Serving: At the restaurant where I learned to make these, the maitre d' would set the spectacularly puffed papillote in front of the guest and slice it open with a sharp knife, lifting the lid toward the guest's nose so that the latter could enjoy the aroma. After this, the waiter would slide the fish onto warm dinner plates, to be enjoyed minus the foil, and spoon the White Butter Sauce on top. Have your guests serve themselves the same way.

Many wines go well with salmon: a California Chardonnay, a French Chablis, or a Macon from the south of Burgundy.

VARIATIONS: The recipe above can be prepared with a multitude of fishes, especially sole, red snapper, and swordfish steaks. (Slice the latter across the grain into ¼-inch steaks.) You can also vary the herbs and vegetables.

A *julienne* is a vegetable or other ingredient cut in matchstick-like slivers.

To Julienne Round Vegetables Like Potatoes or Turnips:

1. Cut a thin slice off the bottom. (This keeps the vegetable from rolling around on the cutting board.)

2. Cut the vegetable into vertical slices, each ⅛-inch thick. Lay the slices on top of one another and cut them into vertical slices, each ⅛-inch thick, again. You should wind up with slivers the size of matchsticks.

Lay the slices one on top of another and again cut them into lengthwise slices.

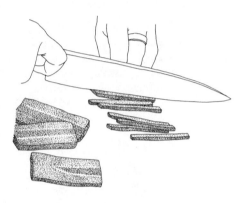

To Julienne Elongated Vegetables Like Carrots or Parsnips:

1. Cut them into 2-inch pieces. Cut a thin slice off a rounded side. This will serve as a base for the vegetable and will hold it steady. Holding the knife blade vertical, cut the vegetable lengthwise into slices, each ⅛-inch thick.

To Julienne Leeks:

Discard the dark-green leaves. Cut the leeks in half lengthwise, leaving the root end intact. Wash the leeks thoroughly under cold running water (see page 29). Lay the leeks, cut side down, on the cutting board. Cut each one into 2-inch lengths. Cut each piece, lengthwise, into ⅛-inch slices.

PAPILLOTE OF HALIBUT WITH
BACON AND SUN-DRIED TOMATOES

Sun-dried tomatoes are the most fashionable ingredient to come out of Italy in the last decade. A specialty of Liguria (the Italian Riviera), they are quite literally made by salting vine-ripened tomatoes and drying them in the sun. The tomatoes are then packed in olive oil. (The cheaper brands are dried in fruit driers. To prepare them place in a bowl with boiling water to cover for 20 minutes, then drain and toss with olive oil). The oil-packed tomatoes can be used directly from the jar. Sun-dried tomatoes have an intense flavor not unlike that of prosciutto. They are expensive, but a little of them goes a long way.

Serves 1

1 halibut steak (6 ounces, about ¾ inch thick)
  salt and fresh black pepper
3 strips bacon or pancetta
1 leek, washed and julienned
3 tablespoons sour cream
3 oil-cured sun-dried tomatoes

1 12-x-24-inch sheet of foil, shiny side down, bottom half
  lightly buttered

1. Lightly sprinkle the fish with salt and pepper. Sauté the bacon or pancetta in a small skillet to render the fat. Drain the strips on a paper towel and cut into ¼-inch slivers. Discard all but 2 tablespoons fat and lightly brown the fish on both sides. Transfer the fish to a plate. Add the chopped leek to the pan and cook it over medium heat for 2 minutes or until soft.
2. Arrange the leek in the center of the bottom half of the foil. Place the fish on the leek and top with the sour cream, sun-dried tomatoes, and bacon or pancetta. Bake in a preheated 400° oven for 15 minutes.

◇   ◇   ◇

BUTTER SAUCES

The French have a saying: *Plus ça change, plus c'est la même chose.* ("The more things change, the more they remain the same.") So it is with sauces. When *nouvelle cuisine* revolutionized classical French cooking in the early seventies, the first heads to fall were starch-thickened sauces. In their stead came a host of "reduction" sauces, epitomized by a rich, buttery concoction called *beurre blanc.*

The principle was simple: in the old days, sauces were made by thickening a well-flavored liquid, like broth or fish stock, with flour or cornstarch. The new approach was to "reduce" that liquid; that is, boil it down to an intensely flavored glaze, then to give it body by beating in butter. The new sauces, perhaps, have more finesse than the old ones; they certainly contain more calories! Thus, to think that the *nouvelle cuisine* is dietetic or low in calories is a gross misconception, although the portions have certainly dwindled in size.

The rallying sauce of the new chefs was *beurre blanc* (pronounced "burr blahnk"), literally, "white butter" sauce. *Beurre blanc* is made by boiling down dry white wine with shallots (and sometimes vinegar) to a quarter of its original volume, then whisking in pieces of cold butter. The sauce is an emulsion, like mayonnaise or hollandaise; in this case the acidic reduction emulsifies the butter. (For this reason it is important to use an acidic wine.)

Actually, *beurre blanc* is about as "new" as a grandmother's *coq au vin.* The sauce has long been a specialty of the Loire Valley, where it is made with the excellent butter from Echiré and acidic Loire wines, like Gros Plant or Muscadet. It is the traditional accompaniment of pike and pickerel fished from the tributaries of the Loire.

Beurre blanc is popular with contemporary chefs because it is easy to make and flavorful and lends itself to almost endless variations. Red wine or red vinegar can be used instead of white to make a *beurre rouge;* fish stock or mussel broth in addition to the wine makes an excellent sauce for fish. A saffron *beurre blanc* is delicious (add a pinch to the boiling wine); so is one flavored with caviar or pureed roasted red peppers.

BEURRE BLANC

(WHITE BUTTER SAUCE)

Beurre blanc is not difficult to make, but it is fairly temperamental. The addition of heavy cream helps stabilize the sauce. A shallot is a small member of the onion family, whose delicate flavor suggests spring onions and garlic. Excess chopped shallots, by the way, can be stored in white wine to cover.

Makes 1 cup sauce

¾ cup dry white wine (a very acidic one like Muscadet or
    Sauvignon Blanc)
¼ cup white wine vinegar
4 tablespoons very finely chopped shallots
¼ cup heavy cream
12 tablespoons (1½ sticks) well-chilled, unsalted butter, cut
    into ½-inch pieces
    salt, fresh white pepper, cayenne pepper

1. Bring the wine, vinegar, and shallots to a boil in a heavy saucepan. (Do not use aluminum or cast iron as they react with the acidic ingredients.) Rapidly boil the mixture until only ⅓ cup liquid remains. Add the cream and continue boiling until only 5–6 tablespoons liquid remain.

2. Add the butter, piece by piece, whisking vigorously. The first pieces of butter should be almost melted before you add the next. The sauce should boil while you are adding the butter. Do not let it boil for more than 10 seconds once all the butter is in. Remove the pan from the heat and whisk in salt, pepper, and cayenne pepper to taste. The sauce should be highly seasoned. If you would like it a little more piquant, add a few drops of lemon juice or vinegar. Serve this sauce with any poached, baked, or grilled fish.

Note: Keep *beurre blanc* hot in a warm spot on your stove, or over a pan of hot, but not boiling, water. Do not attempt to heat the sauce directly on the heat or it will curdle. (It is not a sauce that is meant to be served piping hot.) If the sauce starts to separate, whisk in some cold heavy cream. If the sauce curdles completely, try whisking it into 4 tablespoons boiling cream.

L E S S O N   2 0

Salmon Coulibiac

◇

Technique:
BAKING EN CROÛTE
(in a crust)

Master Recipe:
SALMON COULIBIAC

◇   ◇   ◇

Few dishes are more spectacular than *coulibiac* (pronounced "kool-ee-bee-ack"), a layered loaf of salmon, mushrooms, rice pilaf, and herbed hard-cooked eggs, baked in a fancifully decorated crust. A dish of Russian origin, coulibiac entered the French repertoire in the nineteenth century, when Russian aristocrats vacationed in Paris. The name of the dish comes from German *Kohlgebaeck*—choux pastry—but today we use buttery brioche.

Coulibiac looks complicated, but in fact it is built on a series of simple steps we have learned in other lessons. Detailed instructions on preparing rice pilaf are found on page 267, mushroom *duxelles* on page 258, crêpes on page 90, and brioche on page 118. The crêpes are optional; they do help absorb any moisture from the fish, thereby keeping the crust nice and crisp. The individual components can be prepared as much as 48 hours ahead of time (the brioche *should* be made the night before). Coulibiac makes a spectacular buffet showpiece.

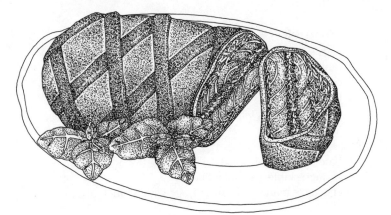

Salmon Coulibiac

Serves 10–12

FOR THE BRIOCHE DOUGH:

>   4 cups all-purpose flour
>   4 tablespoons warm milk
>   1 0.6-ounce cake yeast, or 1 envelope dried yeast, or
>   1 tablespoon bulk dried yeast
>   ⅓ cup sugar
>   approximately 6 eggs, warmed in hot water, beaten
>   2½ teaspoons salt
>   3 sticks unsalted butter, at room temperature

FOR THE RICE PILAF:

>   1 onion, finely chopped (about ½ cup)
>   2 tablespoons butter
>   ⅔ cup long-grained rice
>   1 cup water
>   *bouquet garni*
>   salt and fresh black pepper

FOR THE MUSHROOM DUXELLES:

>   12 ounces mushrooms, washed, stems removed, finely chopped
>   juice of ½ lemon
>   2 shallots, minced (2–3 tablespoons)
>   2 tablespoons butter
>   3 teaspoons fresh chopped parsley
>   salt, pepper, cayenne pepper, fresh nutmeg, a pinch of
>   thyme

FOR THE HERBED HARD-COOKED EGG MIXTURE:

>   2 eggs
>   2 tablespoons butter
>   2 shallots, minced (2–3 tablespoons)
>   3 tablespoons fresh chopped dill
>   salt, fresh black pepper, cayenne pepper

TO FINISH THE COULIBIAC:

>   1 batch crêpes (optional)
>   2 10-inch skinless salmon fillets
>   egg glaze made by beating 1 egg with a pinch of salt

1. Prepare brioche dough the night before as described on page 118. Let it rise till doubled in bulk, punch it down, and refrigerate for at least 6 hours. If it continues to rise in the refrigerator, punch it down again.

2. Prepare the rice pilaf: sauté the onion in the butter in a small frying pan at medium heat for 2–3 minutes or until soft. Add the rice and sauté for 1 minute or until rice is coated with butter and shiny. Stir in the water, add the *bouquet garni,* salt, and pepper. Bring the rice to a boil, cover the pan tightly, and bake it in a preheated 400° oven for 18 minutes. Fluff the rice with a fork and transfer it to a shallow bowl to cool.

3. Prepare the mushroom duxelles: sprinkle the chopped mushrooms with lemon juice to prevent them from discoloring. Sauté the minced shallots in butter in a small frying pan for 1 minute or until soft. Add the mushrooms and parsley, and increase the heat to high. Cook the duxelles, stirring from time to time, until all the liquid from the mushrooms has evaporated. Season the mixture with the salt, peppers, nutmeg, and thyme. Transfer the duxelles to a shallow bowl to cool.

4. Prepare the herbed, hard-cooked egg mixture: place the eggs in cold, lightly salted water and bring to a boil. Reduce heat and simmer the eggs for exactly 11 minutes. Rinse under cold water and shell the eggs at once. NOTE: Cooking the eggs for longer than 11 minutes will result in a green ring around the yolk. It is easier to shell the eggs when the insides are still warm. Melt the butter in a small frying pan and sauté the shallots for 2 minutes or until soft. Coarsely chop the eggs and combine with the shallots, dill, salt, black pepper, and a little cayenne pepper. Transfer to a shallow bowl to cool.

5. If using crêpes, prepare them as described on page 90. Cool.

6. Lay the salmon flat on a cutting board and run your fingers along it, feeling for bones. Remove bones with tweezers or needle-nose pliers. Steps 1 through 6 can be done up to 48 hours ahead of time.

7. Assemble the coulibiac. Pinch off ⅓ of the brioche dough and roll it on a lightly floured work surface to form a 12-x-8-inch rectangle. Place the rectangle on a greased, inverted baking sheet. (It is easier to slide the baked coulibiac off the back of the sheet than over the edges.) Lay 3 crêpes on top. Spread half the rice pilaf on top of the crêpes in a neat rectangle, lay a salmon filet on top, spread with half the mushroom duxelles and all the egg mixture. Spread the remaining mushroom duxelles on top of the egg mixture, lay the second salmon fillet on top and spread with remaining pilaf. Cover the top and sides with crêpes.

8. Pinch off ⅔ of the remaining dough and roll it out to form a 14-x-18-inch rectangle. Roll this widthwise up on the rolling pin, and unroll it over the coulibiac. Brush the underside of the lower crust with egg glaze and fold it up under the upper crust. Trim off the excess dough—you should end up with what looks like a giant loaf of bread.

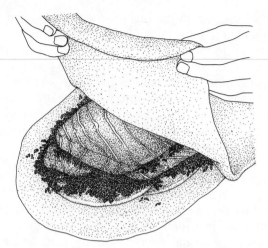

9. Roll out the remaining dough, and cut it into ½-inch strips, using a fluted pastry wheel. Brush the crust with egg glaze and lay the strips on top to form a lattice. The coulibiac can be prepared up to 2 hours ahead to this stage, but it should be allowed to rise for at least 30 minutes. Cover loosely with plastic wrap and refrigerate until baking.

10. Baking and serving the coulibiac: preheat the oven to 425°F. Brush the coulibiac one final time with egg glaze. Cut a ¼-inch hole in the center of the top crust. Roll a 2-inch square of aluminum foil around a chopstick, and oil it lightly. Insert the foil tube in the hole and slip out the chopstick: the tube provides an escape valve for steam. Bake the coulibiac for 15 minutes, reduce heat to 375°F. and bake 50 minutes more, or until an inserted skewer comes out very hot to the touch. If the crust starts browning too much, cover the coulibiac with a tent of foil.

The classic way to serve coulibiac is to cut the loaf in half lengthwise, then widthwise into 3-inch pieces. I prefer to cut coulibiac like a loaf of bread—into 1-inch slices, supporting each with a spatula for serving. (This method yields an attractive cross section.) The traditional sauces for coulibiac are hollandaise (see page 197), white butter sauce (see page 141), and warmed sour cream with chopped dill. When you've gone to this much trouble, the appropriate beverage is champagne.

VARIATION: Coulibiac can also be made with bluefish or halibut.

L E S S O N 2 1

Clams and Mussels

◇

Technique:

SCRUBBING, STEAMING, AND BEARDING
MUSSELS

Master Recipe:

MUSSELS MARINIÈRE (steamed in
wine)

Variations:

MUSSELS WITH ESCARGOT BUTTER
MUSSELS WITH ALMOND-PERNOD BUTTER
PORTUGUESE-STYLE STEAMERS

◇   ◇   ◇

"**H**appy as a clam," goes the saying. A clam at high tide? Or a clam on the half-shell, freshly steamed, or in chowder? I don't know how the clam feels (actually, it probably doesn't feel much, being on a low rung of the evolutionary ladder), but I feel happy whenever I eat a clam or one of its black-shelled cousins, mussels.

Clams fall into two broad categories: soft-shells and hard-shells. Soft-shells, also called "steamers" (after the best method for cooking them) and "piss" clams (because they squirt a stream of water at you when you try to catch them), have a thin, elongated shell, which fails to close completely. For this reason, soft-shells are usually gritty and must be purged of sand before eating (see page 148).

Hard-shell clams have firm, rounded shells that form a hermetic seal when closed. (Our word clam comes from the Anglo-Saxon *clamm*, "bond" or "fetter," literally, a concept of closeness or union reflected in the Japanese custom of serving clam broth at a wedding.) Littlenecks, cherrystones, and quahaugs (pronounced "co-hog") are different-sized members of the same species. The first (named for Littleneck Bay on Long Island) is the smallest (up to 2 inches across); the second (named for Cherrystone Creek in Virginia) should not exceed 2½ inches across; quahaugs (chowder clams) are anything larger. Littlenecks and cherrystones are delicious raw on the half shell; quahaugs should always be cooked (see chowder recipes in Lesson 4).

As for mussels, once disdained, and still relatively unappreciated, they richly reward the cook patient enough to prepare them. Their briny succulence makes them one of the tastiest of all shellfish, and their low price (as little as 3 pounds for $1 in Boston) will please even the most budget-minded gourmet.

Mussels are among nature's most prolific creatures, lending themselves readily to "cultivation" on pilings and ropes hung from rafts. They are distinguished by jet-black shells and a flesh that ranges in hue from tan to lurid orange. They are abundant on both coasts, and most of the time they are safe to gather and eat. Do not gather mussels during periods of "red tide"—an invasion of microorganisms that turn the water a reddish color, and that, although harmless to the shellfish themselves, can be fatal to humans. Consult your local seashore officials.

Below are recipes for mussels *marinière* (steamed in wine), shellfish with escargot butter, mussels with almond-Pernod butter, and Portuguese-style steamers.

PREPARING MUSSELS FOR COOKING

1. Pick through the mussels, discarding any with cracked or broken shells. Tap any mussels with gapped or open shells. If the shell fails to close within 30 seconds, the animal is dead, and should be discarded.

2. Scrub the mussels with a stiff brush, using the back of an old paring knife to pry off any barnacles. Find the tuft of black threads where the two shells meet: pinch these threads between your thumb and the back of a knife and firmly pull them out.

3. The first step in any mussel recipe is to steam the shellfish in wine and herbs—a delicacy in its own right, which the French call *moules marinière*, "mariner-style mussels" (see below). If you plan to use steamed mussels in another dish, you can omit the herbs.

4. For fancier dishes, we remove the mussels from the shells and "beard" (defringe) them. The beard is a lacy fringe running around the perimeter of the animal. Simply pull it off. At the same time, check the inside of the mussel, at the base of the siphon, for any threads that may have escaped your prying fingers.

TO PURGE SHELLFISH OF SAND

Steamers and mussels are sometimes gritty, particularly when gathered during stormy weather. To remove the sand, the shellfish are purged in salted water with cornmeal. To make salt water, dissolve 3 tablespoons salt in 2 quarts cold water. Arrange the shellfish in a shallow pan or in the sink with salt water just to cover and sprinkle with ½ cup cornmeal. Let stand for 3 hours. The shellfish will ingest the cornmeal and expel the grains of sand.

Mussels Marinière

Imagine for a moment that you are in a waterfront cafe in the French coastal town of Dieppe. Ask for the house specialty, and you would receive a huge bowl of the tiny, tender local mussels steamed in wine and herbs. You would pry one mussel from its shell with your fingers, and use the empty set of shells as tongs to pick out the others. When you had finished, you would use a half mussel shell as a spoon to lap up the broth. You would chew French bread and sip the local cider. By the time you finished, you would think you had died and gone to heaven.

Serves 6 as an appetizer and 3 as an entrée

     3 pounds mussels
 ½–1 cup dry white wine
     4 tablespoons finely chopped shallots
     4 tablespoons finely chopped parsley
     1 2-inch sprig fresh rosemary
     2 cloves garlic, peeled
     ½ tablespoon coarsely crushed black peppercorns
     2 bay leaves
        generous pinch thyme

1. Scrub the mussels as described above and remove the threads.
2. Add ¼ inch wine to a pot large enough to hold all the mussels. Add the flavorings and bring the mixture to a rolling boil. Add the mussels, tightly cover the pot, and cook over high heat for 4–5 minutes, or until the shells open. Be sure to shake the pot from time to time or stir the mussels to give the ones on the bottom room to open.

Serving: Transfer the mussels to a bowl with a slotted spoon. Carefully pour the broth over them, leaving the last ¼ cup in the pot. (It is apt to be full of sand.) Serve the steamed mussels as soon as the shells open, with crusty French bread and hard cider or a dry white wine like Muscadet. Be sure to provide a bowl for the empty shells.

Note: Steamers can be prepared the same way.

MUSSELS WITH CREAM AND SAFFRON: Follow the recipe above, adding ¼ cup heavy cream and a generous pinch of saffron. When the mussels are opened, transfer them to a serving bowl and boil down the broth until only half of it remains. Pour the sauce over the mussels, leaving the last ¼ cup (if it is gritty) in the pot.

MUSSELS WITH ESCARGOT BUTTER

I started making this dish back in my student days, when I simply couldn't afford escargots. Today I would be hard-pressed to say which I preferred: snails or mussels. Escargot butter also makes excellent garlic bread.

Serves 8 as an appetizer

    3 pounds mussels
 ½–1 cup dry white wine
       flavorings from master recipe (optional)

FOR THE ESCARGOT (GARLIC-PARSLEY) BUTTER:

 1½ sticks unsalted butter, at room temperature
 2–3 cloves garlic, minced
    4 tablespoons fresh parsley, chopped
       a few drops fresh lemon juice
       salt, freshly ground black pepper, cayenne pepper

    1 cup kosher salt to line platter

1. Scrub the mussels as described above, removing the threads. Steam them till the shells just open as described in the master recipe. Let cool.

2. Meanwhile, prepare the escargot butter. Cream the butter, whisking in flavorings and seasonings to taste.

3. Remove the mussels from the shells and reserve half of the shells (the prettiest ones). Arrange the shells on an ovenproof platter spread with ¼ inch kosher salt (this prevents the shells from tipping). Beard the mussels (that is, pull off the lacy fringe running around the outside of each) and place 1 or 2 mussels in each shell. Top each mussel with a spoonful of escargot butter. The mussels can be prepared to this stage up to 24 hours ahead of time.

4. Just before serving, cook the mussels in a preheated 450° oven for 5 minutes, or until the shellfish are hot and the butter bubbly. Serve at once, with plenty of crusty French bread for mopping up the sauce.

Note: Feel free to substitute other herbs for the parsley (fresh tarragon would be delicious). This recipe can be prepared with littlenecks or cherrystones in place of mussels.

MUSSELS WITH ALMOND-PERNOD BUTTER

Pernod is an anise-flavored aperitif popular in France. Its licoricy taste makes a perfect accompaniment to mussels.

Serves 8 as an appetizer

3 pounds mussels, cooked and shelled as described above

FOR THE PERNOD BUTTER:

1½ sticks unsalted butter
2 cloves garlic, minced
4 tablespoons fresh chopped parsley
4 tablespoons finely chopped toasted almonds
   juice of ½ lemon
   juice of ½ orange
2 teaspoons Pernod or other anise-flavored aperitif
   salt, fresh black pepper, cayenne pepper

Prepare the mussels as described in the previous recipe, substituting the Pernod butter for the escargot butter.

PORTUGUESE-STYLE STEAMERS

In the nineteenth century, Massachusetts was the world's chief supplier of whale oil (used for lighting). The whaling ships would leave Nantucket, New Bedford, and Provincetown with skeleton crews, stopping in the Azores to take on cheap labor. In time, the Portuguese settled in New England, bringing with them a taste for assertive seasonings. *Linguica* is a spicy pork sausage; substitute *chourico* (another spicy Portuguese sausage) or Italian hot sausage. If using uncooked sausage, sauté it.

Serves 4 as an appetizer

3 pounds steamers
3 tablespoons olive oil
½ cup diced linguica or chourico sausage
4 strips bacon, cut into ¼-inch slivers
1 onion, diced (approximately ⅓ cup)
1 clove garlic, peeled and finely chopped
2 teaspoons imported paprika
2 tomatoes, peeled, seeded, coarsely chopped (see instructions on page 66)
3 tablespoons finely chopped fresh parsley
¼ cup dry white wine

1. Thoroughly scrub the steamers. If they are sandy, purge them, following the instructions below.

2. Heat the olive oil in a large saucepan and sauté the linguica or chourico, bacon, and onion for 3–4 minutes, or until the latter are soft and translucent. Pour off all but 3 tablespoons fat.

3. Add the remaining ingredients, minus the clams and wine, and cook for 3 minutes over high heat. Add the wine and bring it to a boil. Add the clams, tightly cover the pan, and steam for 3–4 minutes or until the shells open wide.

Serving: Serve the Portuguese-style steamers at once, providing crusty bread for dipping and a bowl for the empty shells. A dry Portuguese wine, like Minho Verde, would go well. Before eating steamers, pull off and discard the black membrane covering the "neck," or "siphon," of the clam.

Note: Mussels can be prepared the same way.

LESSON 22

Seafood Crêpes and Seafood Salad

◇

Techniques:

CLEANING SHRIMP, SCALLOPS, AND SQUID

MAKING VELOUTÉ SAUCE

ASSEMBLING CRÊPES

Master Recipes:

SEAFOOD CRÊPES

CURRIED SEAFOOD SALAD

◇ ◇ ◇

I first tasted these seafood crêpes at the Normandy home of Anne Willan, founder of La Varenne cooking school in Paris. The shrimp had been live and kicking; the scallops, still in the shell. The mussels from the town of Dieppe nearby were the sweetest I have ever tasted. The dish was a real sensation.

Seafood crêpes are what I consider a perfect dish for a cooking class. Students learn how to clean and cook all the major species of shellfish, prepare crêpes, and make a velouté sauce. There is plenty of work to keep people busy. (If you are the sort of host who likes to put your company to work, this dish is ideal.) Once assembled, the crêpes can be held for several hours and heated just before serving.

In a restaurant, this and other fish dishes would be made with fresh fish stock. Bottled clam broth produces excellent results—it is quite salty, however, so we cut back on the salt in the final sauce. (Purists will find a recipe for fish stock on page 25.)

The shellfish is poached in the clam broth, which intensifies its flavor. The poaching liquid is, in turn, used to make the sauce. The sauce is called a *velouté* (from the French *velours,* "velvet") and it is thickened with a roux. Velouté sauce is similar to basic white sauce except that we use stock instead of milk.

The methods for cleaning and poaching shellfish described below hold for a wide variety of seafood. The seafood filling for the crêpes can be served in patty shells, on toast points, or on a bed of pasta; and the sauce can be flavored with curry powder or saffron. We end the lesson with a recipe for curried seafood salad.

CLEANING AND TRIMMING SHELLFISH

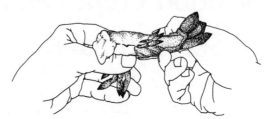

To Shell Shrimp:
If you are right-handed, hold the shrimp in your left hand and pinch the legs between the thumb and index finger of your right hand. Peel off the shell as you would the peel from around a tangerine.

To Devein Shrimp:
There are two ways to remove the vein. With small shrimp, insert the tine of a fork in the back of the shrimp just below the vein. Slowly extract the vein by pulling the fork away from the shrimp. The advantage of this method is that it leaves the shrimp body intact, but it does not work well with frozen shrimp. By the way, I prefer small shrimp to large shrimp.

The second way to remove the vein is to "butterfly" the shrimp. Lay the shrimp flat on the cutting board. Cut a V-shaped groove along the back of the shrimp and remove the vein in a single piece. Butterflying is well-suited to large shrimp. For the following recipe, cut large shrimp in half lengthwise.

To Clean Squid:

Squid is tasty, cheap, and nutritious. It can also be disconcerting to anyone who is squeamish or who has watched too many Captain Nemo movies. To clean squid, pull the tentacles away from the body, and cut them off just before the eyes. Discard the eye section and the attached viscera. Lay the body on a cutting board, scrape it from tail

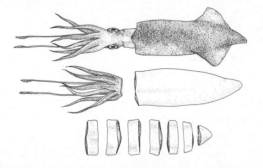

to head with the blunt edge of knife, then reach in with a spoon or your fingers and pull out the viscera. Gently peel the reddish membrane off the body and tentacles, and rinse the squid inside and out. Cut the body into ½-inch rings. Cut the tentacle section into 2 or 3 pieces.

To "Circumcise" Scallops:

Scallops have a small, opaque, thumbnail-shaped muscle on the side, which is tough and chewy. Sometimes this muscle falls off when the scallop is shucked; if it is still there, pull it off and discard. I call this "circumcising" a scallop. Cut large scallops in quarters, medium-sized ones in half; leave bay scallops as they are.

Seafood Crêpes

Feel free to use more or less of a particular shellfish to suit your taste.

Makes 10–12 crepes, serving 4–6 as an entree

1 batch crêpe batter (see recipe on page 90)

FOR THE FILLING:

½ pound shrimp
½ pound scallops
¾ pound fresh squid (½ pound cleaned)
½ pound cooked crab or lobster
¾ pound fresh mushrooms
   salt, pepper, a few drops lemon juice

TO POACH THE SEAFOOD AND FINISH THE SAUCE:

2 cups fish stock (see recipe on page 25) or bottled clam
   broth
4 tablespoons butter
4 tablespoons flour
½ cup heavy cream
   juice of ½ lemon (or to taste)
   salt, freshly ground black pepper, cayenne pepper
   freshly grated nutmeg
   butter for the baking dish

1. Make the crêpes, following the recipe on page 90.

2. Clean and trim the shrimp, scallops, and squid, as described on pages 154 and 155. Pick through the crab or lobster, discarding any bits of shell. Cut the shellfish into ½-inch pieces.

3. Wash and stem the mushrooms and cook them in ¼ inch of water with the salt, pepper, and lemon juice in a covered pan over high heat for 3 minutes. Drain.

4. You are now ready to poach the shellfish. Bring the fish stock or clam broth to a boil in a large saucepan and reduce heat to a gentle simmer. Poach each shellfish separately (each cooks at a slightly different rate) just until firm, then transfer it to a colander over a bowl to cool and drain. The shrimp will take approximately 45 seconds (when cooked they will turn pink); the scallops, 30 seconds; the squid, 30 seconds. The crab or lobster need not be poached. Err on the side of undercooking; remember, shellfish is at its most tender raw. Add the liquid from the bowl to the poaching liquid and boil it until only 1½ cups remain.

5. Prepare the sauce. Melt the butter in a heavy saucepan. Whisk in the flour to make a roux (see below for method). Remove the pan from the heat and strain the poaching liquid into the roux. Add the cream. Return the

sauce to the heat and bring it to a boil, whisking vigorously. Simmer the sauce for 3 minutes. Add the lemon juice and seasonings: the sauce should be highly seasoned. Stir in the seafood and adjust the seasoning.

6. Assemble the crêpes. Lay a crêpe on a plate, dark side down, and place a spoonful of seafood filling in the center. Roll the crêpe into a log shape. Arrange the crêpes, seam side down, in a buttered baking dish. Continue rolling the crêpes until all are used. Spoon any leftover filling on top. The seafood crêpes can be prepared up to 24 hours ahead to this stage. If you are making the crêpes ahead, cool them to room temperature before refrigerating. If the crêpes are in a glass dish, be sure to let it warm to room temperature before baking.

7. Bake the crêpes in a preheated 375° oven for 20 minutes or until thoroughly heated.

Serving: Accompany the crêpe with a bright green vegetable, like the steamed kale on page 232. Shellfish demands a crisp acidic wine, like Muscadet from the Loire Valley or a California Sauvignon Blanc.

ROUX AND FLOUR-THICKENED SAUCES

1. Use a heavy pan to avoid scorching. Use equal parts butter and flour. Melt the butter first, and then whisk in the flour. A whisk, not a wooden spoon, is the proper tool for making any sauce.

2. Cook the roux over medium heat for 2–3 minutes to remove the raw taste of the flour and increase its absorptive properties. When destined for a light-colored liquid, like milk or fish stock, the roux is cooked without browning. When a dark liquid, like veal stock, is added, the roux is cooked until the flour browns. In Cajun cooking, the roux is cooked very dark—almost black. Indeed, this is the cornerstone of Louisiana cooking.

3. The best way to avoid lumps is to add the liquid in one fell swoop off the heat. The pan is then returned to the heat and vigorously whisked. The sauce reaches the optimum thickness the moment it comes to a boil. It should, however, be simmered for at least 3 minutes, whisking often, to cook out the starchy taste.

4. To prevent a skin from forming on the surface of a starch-thickened sauce, spread the top with butter. To do this, impale a piece of butter on a fork and run it lightly over the surface of the sauce.

Curried Seafood Salad

This spicy salad calls for the same combination of shellfish, cleaned and poached as described above. Instead of cream sauce, however, we use homemade curried mayonnaise. (Feel free to use other flavorings.) For a full discussion of making mayonnaise, see Lesson 6.

Serves 4–6

FOR THE SHELLFISH:

- ½ pound shrimp
- ½ pound scallops
- ¾ pound fresh squid (½ pound cleaned)
- ½ pound cooked crab or lobster
- 1 cup clam broth, fish stock, or equal parts dry white wine and water

TO FINISH THE SALAD:

- Curry Mayonnaise (see page 55)
- 1 head Boston lettuce
- 1 bunch fresh coriander leaves for garnish

1. Clean the various shellfish and poach in gently simmering clam broth as described above. Remove the fish from the pan, cool the broth slightly, return the shellfish to the pan, and cool completely in the broth. (Cooling shellfish in broth helps preserve moistness.)

2. Prepare the curry mayonnaise.

3. Drain the shellfish and mix with the curry mayonnaise. Correct the seasoning: the mixture should be quite spicy.

Serving: Line chilled salad plates with lettuce leaves and mound the seafood salad on top. Sprinkle each salad with fresh coriander leaves. You'll need a gutsy wine to stand up to the curry: try an Alsatian Gewürztraminer or a Riesling from the Pacific Northwest.

LESSON 23

Fish Stews

◇

Technique:
BUILDING FISH SOUPS

Master Recipe:
NEW ENGLAND BOUILLABAISSE

Variations:
CALDIERADA (PORTUGUESE FISH STEW)
SOUPE DE PÊCHEUR À L'ÎLE DE HOUAT
(FISHERMAN'S SOUP FROM THE ISLE
OF HOUAT)

◇   ◇   ◇

Epicures are a pompous lot, and nothing brings out their pedantry like bouillabaisse. "It doesn't exist outside Marseilles," declare some; "It can't contain potatoes or lobster," protest others. To my thinking, such niggling is pointless.

There is no denying that *bouillabaisse* is a Mediterranean fish stew that originated in the ancient port of Marseilles. (So did the French national anthem, by the way, which was named for the Marseillaise patriots who sang it on their march to Paris during the French Revolution.) The name of this illustrious soup comes from words *bouia abaisso,* which in the local dialect mean "boil and reduce." Thus, the secret to a good bouillabaisse lies in rapidly boiling the broth to concentrate the flavor and emulsify the olive oil.

Purists argue that an authentic Marseillaise bouillabaisse owes its unique flavor to such weird Mediterranean sea creatures as *rascasse* (hog fish), *grondin* (grunter), *murène* (murney eel), and St. Pierre (John Dory fish). This is true to some extent, but the curious combination of three Mediterranean land flavors—saffron, orange, and anise—contribute equally to the bouillabaisse's distinction. Use fresh fish, and plenty of it, and you'll wind up with a soup that would do a French fishwife proud.

Bouillabaisse is only part of the fish stew picture. Every land has a version: Spanish *zarzuella,* Italian *zuppa de pesce,* Belgian *waterzooi,* etc. Below are recipes for a New England bouillabaisse, a spicy Portuguese seafood stew called *caldierada,* and an unusual curried fish soup from a tiny island in Brittany.

◇   ◇   ◇

New England Bouillabaisse

In the beginning, bouillabaisse was not a dish of gastronomic pretention, but a way to use up leftovers. And far from requiring hours of preparation, it can—indeed, should—be thrown together in 20 minutes. It is more important to choose fresh fish than it is to choose a particular species of fish. Let regional and seasonal availability be your guide.

Fennel is a bulbous celerylike vegetable with a licorice flavor. If it is unavailable, use 2 teaspoons fennel or anise seed or extra Pernod. Pernod —the national aperitif of France—is an anise-flavored liqueur. Bouillabaisse is traditionally served with a slice of fried bread spread with garlicky *rouille* (red pepper or "rust" sauce—see recipe on page 264).

Serves 8–10

FOR THE FISH:

    2 pounds firm fish, such as monkfish, halibut, hake, bass, red snapper, porgy, and/or mullet
    1 pound flimsy fish, such as whiting, flounder, cod, and/or sole
    1 pound shellfish, such as shrimp or scallops
    1 or more pounds crustacean, such as crab and/or lobster
    2 pounds bivalves, such as littlenecks, steamers, and/or mussels

FOR THE BROTH:

    ⅓ cup extra-virgin olive oil
    2 onions, finely chopped (about ⅔ cup)
    2 leeks, washed, green leaves discarded, finely chopped (about ⅔ cup)
    1 small bulb fennel, finely chopped (about ⅔ cup—if unavailable substitute 2 teaspoons anise or fennel seed)
    3 cloves garlic, minced
    4 large ripe tomatoes, peeled, seeded, and coarsely chopped, or 1 16-ounce can imported plum tomatoes, drained, seeded, and chopped
    3 strips orange peel (reserve the orange for juice)
    ¼ teaspoon saffron
    2 bay leaves, crumbled
    generous pinch of thyme, scant pinch of cayenne pepper
    1 generous teaspoon each dried oregano, basil, marjoram
    ½ cup dry white wine
    8 cups fish stock, or 6 cups clam broth and 2 cups water
    ¼ cup chopped fresh parsley
    2 tablespoons Pernod or Anisette (or to taste)
    juice of 1 orange (or to taste)
    salt and fresh black pepper

FOR SERVING:

> croûtes (fried bread slices; see page 215)
> rust sauce (see page 264)

1. Prepare the seafood. Skin the fish and cut it into 2-inch pieces. Shell and devein the shrimp. "Circumcise" the scallops. If you are feeling macho, cut the live crab or lobster into 3-inch pieces (if not you can add them whole, and cut them up later). Scrub the bivalves (if using steamers, be sure to "purge" them ahead of time). If the mussels are dirty, steam them open in a little dry white wine, remove beards, and strain the broth and reserve. (Leave a few mussels in the shells for color.)

2. Heat the olive oil in a large heavy pot over medium heat and add the onions, leeks, fennel, and garlic. Sauté for 3–4 minutes or until the vegetables are soft and translucent. Add the tomatoes, orange peel, and spices, increase heat to high, and cook for 3 minutes, or until most of the liquid from the tomatoes has evaporated. Add the white wine and bring to a boil. Add the fish stock (or clam broth and water) and simmer for 5 minutes. The recipe can be prepared ahead to this stage.

3. Add the lobster and crab if using them, and bring the bouillabaisse to a boil. Add the bivalves and bring to a boil. Next add the firmer fish, like monkfish and halibut, followed by the flimsy fish and, last of all, the shellfish. The idea here is to add the seafood which takes the longest time to cook first. The whole process should take no longer than 20 minutes. The broth should boil violently at the end: the bubbling emulsifies the olive oil. Add the parsley, Pernod, orange juice, and salt and pepper to taste. The broth should be fragrant with saffron, a little sour with orange juice, a little sweet from the Pernod. Add more of these ingredients as needed.

Serving: Ladle the bouillabaisse into shallow bowls. Float a croûte on top and spoon the *rouille* sauce over it. A Frenchman would eat the fish and broth separately, but I like them together.

There are many wines that would go well: a Gaillac (dry, white, slightly effervescent wine from the southwest of France), a white Chateauneuf-du-Pape, or a steely Chardonnay from the Sonoma Valley.

CALDIERADA
PORTUGUESE FISH STEW

Caldierada is the national fish stew of Portugal. Portuguese seamen brought this dish to New England in the early 1800s, when they flocked here to join the whaling boats that sailed from Nantucket. Chourico and linguica are spicy Portuguese sausages—in their absence substitute bacon. Use the freshest fish you can find.

Serves 6

½ pound shrimp
½ pound scallops
1 pound firm white fish, such as monkfish, hake, or halibut
1 cooked chourico or linguica sausage, or 4 strips bacon,
    diced (about ½ cup)
3 tablespoons olive oil
1 onion, finely chopped (about ¾ cup)
2 leeks, washed, green leaves discarded, finely chopped
3 cloves garlic, peeled and minced
½ teaspoon ground cumin
½ teaspoon ground coriander
1 bay leaf, crumbled
  generous pinch thyme
  generous pinch saffron
4 large ripe tomatoes, peeled, seeded, and finely chopped
    (about 1 cup), or 1 16-ounce can imported plum
    tomatoes, seeded, drained, and chopped
1 cup dry white wine
4 cups fish stock or clam broth
  approximately 1 cup water
2 potatoes, peeled and cut in half lengthwise, then in ¼-inch
    slices
1 tablespoon red wine vinegar
½ cup finely chopped fresh parsley
  salt and fresh black pepper

Prepare the *caldierada* as you would the bouillabaisse above. Sauté the sausage with the vegetables. Add the potatoes with the liquids, and simmer for 5–10 minutes or until half-cooked before you add the fish. Add the vinegar in place of the Pernod: the soup should be quite piquant.

SOUPE DE PÊCHEUR
À L'ÎLE DE HOUAT

FISHERMAN'S SOUP FROM THE ISLE OF HOUAT

This tiny island (it's so small there are no roads or cars) lies south of the Breton mainland. Its 500 year-round inhabitants are a sturdy breed of fishermen and, more recently, marine biologists, who run one of the world's largest lobster hatcheries there. This particular soup is the specialty of one Madame LeRoux, who uses conger eel, cat shark and gurnard (and whatever else her fisherman husband lands with the day's catch), plus fresh fennel, which grows wild on the island. The saffron and curry powder recall the cooking of nearby Nantes, once the capital of the French spice trade. Mme. LeRoux purees her soup in a food mill, but it is perfectly good whole. (The food processor is not recommended for pureeing, as it will produce an odd texture.) "It's very fragile, so whatever I don't sell that day, I throw out," says Mme. LeRoux.

Serves 6–8

> 4 tablespoons olive oil
> 1 onion, diced
> 2 leeks, diced
> 1 small bulb fresh fennel, diced, or 1 teaspoon dried fennel
> 2 cloves garlic, smashed
> 4 tomatoes, peeled, seeded, and chopped
> 1 teaspoon curry powder
> generous pinch saffron
> 1 large potato, diced
> 2½–3 pounds mixed boneless white fish (e.g., sole, cod, halibut, snapper, porgy, red fish, monkfish)
> *bouquet garni*
> 2 tablespoons tomato paste
> 6 cups fish stock, or 4 cups bottled clam broth plus 2 cups water
> salt, pepper, cayenne pepper

1. Heat the olive oil in a large soup pot, and sauté the onion, leeks, fennel, and garlic over medium heat for 5 minutes, or until tender. Add the tomatoes, curry, and saffron, increase heat to high, and cook for 3–5 minutes to evaporate the tomato juice. Stir in the remaining ingredients and simmer the soup for 25 minutes, skimming off any foam that accumulates on top.

2. Remove the *bouquet garni* and puree the soup in a food mill or food processor. (NOTE: For this reason, it is important that the fish fillets be completely free of bones before you add them.) Return the soup to the heat and correct the seasoning. Serve *soupe de pêcheur* with croûtes rubbed with cut garlic.

POULTRY

LESSON 24

Chicken Breasts

◇

Techniques:

BONING AND POCKETING CHICKEN
  BREASTS

COOKING CHICKEN BREASTS

Master Recipe:

CHICKEN BREASTS STUFFED WITH BACON
  AND SMOKED CHEESE

Variations:

CHICKEN BREASTS WITH FIGS AND
  GORGONZOLA

—WITH ROQUEFORT, WALNUTS, AND
  PORT

—WITH APPLES, CHEDDAR, HAM, AND
  RAISINS

GRILLED CHICKEN FILLETS WITH LEMON
  GRASS AND HONEY

CHICKEN FILLETS WITH SILVER OAK
  MUSHROOMS AND AMARETTO

◇   ◇   ◇

The chicken breast is to the chef what a canvas is to an artist: a virgin space on which to paint one's imaginative colors. By itself, it is as bland a morsel as ever occupied a plate. It lends itself, however, to a wide variety of preparations, including poaching, baking, grilling, stuffing, and stir-frying. The chicken breast is low in fat and almost pure protein. It has the added advantage of coming in units suited to serving one person or many.

Chicken breasts are, of course, readily available boneless and skinless. But it is not difficult to bone your own. The easiest way is to remove the skin (simply peel it off) and lay the breast, bone side down, on a cutting board. Make an incision just to the right of the breastbone, running the length of the breast. Now, cut down, keeping the blade of the knife touching the ribs, and you will soon have a boneless half breast. Remove the left half breast the same way.

The breast itself comprises two muscles: a broad, flat one that forms the bulk of the breast, and a small, cylindrical muscle called the "fillet." When the breast is destined for stuffing, we remove the fillet. (It can be saved for making kebabs or sautés.) Usually, the fillet can be easily pulled away from the breast. It may be necessary to cut away the tail end with a knife.

Each fillet has a white tendon running its length which should be removed. Lay the fillet on a cutting board, tendon side down. Pinch the tendon between the knife and the board, and slide the blade along the tendon to remove it from the fillet. Some meat packers remove the fillets from the breasts before packaging.

To "pocket" a chicken breast, lay the breast flat on a cutting board, thick side at the edge. Press the breast flat with one hand, hold a sharp paring knife parallel to the cutting board in the other, and make a horizontal slice through the middle of the breast. Take care not to pierce the top or bottom. It helps to make small cuts at first, peeling back the top as you go. Obviously, the larger the breast, the easier it will be to pocket. A reasonable serving size is 1 large or 2 small half breasts.

As chicken breasts are inherently dry, the best way to cook them is with a gentle, moist heat. Brown the breast quickly on all sides to seal in the juices, then poach it gently in a little liquid (stock, wine, and/or cream) in a covered pan on the stove or in the oven.

Below are recipes for stuffing chicken breasts and using the fillets.

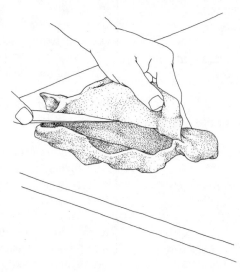

Chicken Breasts Stuffed with Bacon and Smoked Cheese

Quick to make, these stuffed chicken breasts contrast the smoky flavor of bacon and smoked cheese with the sweetness of Marsala wine (a fortified wine made in Sicily). The breasts are cooked by a method called "pan-braising": simmered in a little liquid in a sealed pan over low heat. Were this lesson to have a homework assignment, it would be to invent new stuffings, using the procedure below.

Serves 2 big eaters or 4 as a light main course

    2 large skinless, boneless chicken breasts (makes 4 halves)
    8 strips lean bacon or *pancetta*
    4 slices smoked mozzarella or other smoked cheese
      salt and fresh black pepper
    ½ cup flour
    6 tablespoons Marsala wine
    6 tablespoons heavy cream

1. Remove the fillets from the breasts, reserving them for another dish. (They can be frozen.) Cut the breasts in half, trim off any fat or sinew, and cut a pocket in each half, as described above.

2. Lightly brown the bacon over medium heat in a shallow, non-cast-iron sauté pan. Discard all but 1 tablespoon fat. Insert two strips bacon and a slice of smoked cheese in each breast half and pin the pockets closed with a toothpick. Season the breasts with salt and pepper and lightly dust with flour.

3. Lightly brown the stuffed chicken breasts on both sides in the bacon fat over high heat. Add the Marsala and cream and bring just to a boil. Reduce heat, cover the pan, and gently simmer the breasts for 10 minutes or until cooked. Transfer the breasts to a warm platter. Reduce the sauce by boiling until it is thick and well-flavored, adding salt and pepper as necessary. Pour the sauce over the chicken and serve at once. A Washington State merlot would go nicely.

CHICKEN BREASTS WITH FIGS AND GORGONZOLA

Gorgonzola is pungent blue cheese from Italy. Its salty tang is balanced by the sweetness of the figs. You can use either fresh figs or dried ones (the latter add a nice crunch).

Serves 2–4

    2 large, skinless, boneless chicken breasts
    4 slices pancetta or American bacon
    4 figs cut crosswise into ⅛-inch slices
    4 thin slices Gorgonzola cheese, plus 2 tablespoons,
        crumbled, for the sauce
      salt, fresh black pepper
    ½ cup flour
    6 tablespoons Madeira wine
    6 tablespoons cream

Stuff and cook the breasts as described in the master recipe above. Transfer to plates or a platter and keep warm. Boil the sauce to concentrate its flavor, whisking in the remaining Gorgonzola. Season to taste and pour the sauce over.

CHICKEN BREASTS WITH ROQUEFORT, WALNUTS, AND PORT: Prepare as in the basic recipe above, stuffing the chicken breasts with thinly sliced Roquefort cheese and chopped walnuts. Brown the breasts quickly in a little butter (in place of the bacon fat). Substitute port for the Marsala.

CHICKEN BREASTS WITH APPLES, CHEDDAR, HAM, AND RAISINS: Prepare as in the basic recipe above, stuffing the chicken breasts with slices of apple, cheddar, and smoked or Smithfield ham. Use port or hard cider in place of the Marsala and add to the sauce 3 tablespoons raisins plumped in hot water.

COOKING CHICKEN FILLETS

Boning and stuffing chicken breasts will leave you a large supply of chicken fillets, which can be frozen until you have enough to make a meal. Chicken fillets are delicious marinated and grilled, or thinly slivered and stir-fried. You can also use whole chicken breasts, cut into finger-sized lengths, for the recipes below.

GRILLED CHICKEN FILLETS WITH LEMON GRASS AND HONEY

Lemon grass is an aromatic, reedlike, lemon-flavored herb from Southeast Asia. It commonly comes dried, but occasionally you can find fresh. If unavailable, substitute lemon zest; that is, the oil-rich, outer peel of the fruit. (It is best removed in strips with a vegetable peeler.) Both lemon grass and sweet chili sauce can be readily found at Oriental grocery stores or gourmet shops.

Serves 8 as an appetizer, 2–4 as an entrée.

1 pound chicken fillets, tendons removed as described above

FOR THE MARINADE:

- 1 tablespoon soy sauce
- 1 tablespoon honey
- 1 tablespoon sesame oil
- 1 tablespoon sweet chili sauce
- 1 tablespoon lemon juice

1 tablespoon chopped lemon grass
1 tablespoon chopped scallion

bamboo skewers

1. Combine the ingredients for the marinade in a shallow glass bowl and marinate the chicken fillets, turning from time to time, for 6–12 hours.

2. Thread the fillets on skewers and grill them over charcoal or under a broiler for 2 minutes per side, or until firm and cooked.

VARIATION: To make Indonesian *saté*, add 2 tablespoons peanut butter to the marinade and prepare as described above.

CHICKEN FILLETS WITH SILVER OAK MUSHROOMS AND AMARETTO

This recipe is made with silver oak mushrooms, the name given to *shiitake* or Chinese black mushrooms grown fresh in the United States. Amaretto derives its nuttiness from apricot pits, not almonds. You could also use Grand Marnier.

Serves 4

1 pound chicken fillets, sinews removed
6 ounces fresh silver oak mushrooms, or 2 ounces dried
    shiitake mushrooms (see page 255)
2 tablespoons sesame oil
1 large clove garlic, peeled and minced
4 tablespoons fresh chopped parsley
1 tablespoon Amaretto
    juice of ½ lemon
    salt and fresh black pepper to taste

Cut the fillets into ½-inch chunks. Quickly wash the mushrooms, remove tough stems, and cut the large caps in half. Heat the oil in a wok or sloping-sided sauté pan. Add the chicken and mushrooms and stir-fry for 30 seconds. Add the garlic and parsley and cook for 15 seconds. Add the remaining ingredients and continue cooking for 1–2 minutes, or until the chicken is firm. Add more salt, pepper, Amaretto, or lemon juice to taste before serving.

LESSON 25

Chicken Sautés

◇

Techniques:

STOVE-TOP SAUTÉING

CARAMELIZING FRUIT

Master Recipe:

CHICKEN WITH CIDER AND APPLES

Variations:

BASQUE CHICKEN

CHICKEN WITH OLIVES

CHICKEN PAPRIKAS

◇   ◇   ◇

The first French dish I ever made was *coq au vin* (chicken with wine). It proved to be a good starting point, for it taught me not just a single recipe but a whole process of cooking. I learned the principle of stove-top sautéing: searing the chicken in hot fat to seal in the juices; the slow simmering in wine to produce a bird that was exceptionally moist and flavorful. I learned to cook the garnish separately—in this case, mushrooms, baby onions, bacon slivers—adding it at the end to preserve the individual flavors. Most important of all, I learned that by varying the cooking liquid—red wine, white wine, apple cider, cream, even clam broth—and by varying the garnish—wild mush-

rooms, caramelized apples, roasted red peppers, shrimp, or sauerkraut, one could make a myriad of different dishes.

For the following recipes, the chicken is cut the French way—into 8 pieces. This is similar to our way, except that each wing is removed with an inch or two of breast meat. (This makes for a more equitable division of the bird.)

◇　◇　◇

Chicken with Cider and Apples

This dish is perfect for the fall, when it can be made with fresh cider and crisp fall apples. Use a firm, tart apple, like a Spy, Baldwin, or Granny Smith.

Serves 4

    1 3-pound chicken, cut into 8 pieces
       salt and fresh black pepper
    4 tablespoons butter
    2 shallots, finely chopped (about ¼ cup)
    1 apple, peeled, seeded, finely chopped (about ¼ cup)
    2 tablespoons flour
    2 tablespoons calvados (French apple brandy) or applejack
    ½ cup dry white wine
    1 cup fresh apple cider
    ½ cup heavy cream
       bouquet garni

FOR THE GARNISH:

    4 firm, tart apples
    ½ lemon
    5 tablespoons butter
    5 tablespoons sugar
    4 tablespoons chopped fresh parsley

1. Season the chicken with salt and pepper. Melt 2 tablespoons butter in a large sauté pan (do not use aluminum or cast iron), and sear the chicken pieces on all sides, without crowding the pan. Start browning the chicken skin side down. (This helps melt out the subcutaneous fat.) When browned, transfer chicken to a platter, and discard all but 1 tablespoon fat.

2. Melt the remaining 2 tablespoons butter, add the shallots and apple, and sauté until soft. Stir in the flour, then return the chicken to the pan. Add the calvados and flambé. Add the wine and bring it to a full boil. Add the

cider and cream, bring to a boil again, scraping the bottom of the pan with a spoon to dissolve congealed meat juices. Add the *bouquet garni.* Reduce heat, and simmer the chicken for 20 minutes or until cooked, skimming off any fat that might rise to the surface. Correct the seasoning. To tell if the chicken is cooked, insert a skewer or paring knife into a thigh or drumstick: the meat should feel firm, and the juices should run clear.

3. Meanwhile, prepare the garnish. Peel the apples and rub with lemon to prevent discoloring. Cut the apples in half lengthwise and use a melon baller to remove the core. Cut each half in 3–4 wedges. Heat the butter to foaming in a heavy skillet. Dip the apples in sugar and fry them over high heat until golden brown and caramelized. You must use high heat, or the apples will fall apart: you want them to acquire a sugary crust. Add any pan juices to the chicken.

4. To serve, arrange the chicken on a platter. Taste the sauce one last time for seasoning, adding salt, pepper, calvados, even lemon juice as necessary. Strain the sauce over the chicken, and arrange the apples around the edge. Sprinkle with parsley.

A bone-dry hard cider, like English Bulmer's or Woodpecker, would be a perfect accompaniment.

Note: If you don't mind little pieces of apple and shallot in the sauce, you can simply add the caramelized apples to the chicken without straining the sauce.

BASQUE CHICKEN

The Basque country lies in the Pyrenees Mountains, straddling France and Spain. The Basques speak their own language and are fiercely independent. Their fondness for fiery chilis is more typical of Spanish cooking than of French. The seeds, by the way, are the hottest part of a chili. Discard them, unless you like your food *really* spicy. When you handle hot peppers, do not touch your face until you thoroughly wash your hands.

Serves 4

- 1 3-pound chicken, cut into 8 pieces
  salt and fresh black pepper
- 4 tablespoons olive oil
- 1 small onion, finely chopped
- 2 cloves garlic, minced
- 1 jalapeño chili (fresh or pickled), seeds removed, chopped
    (optional)
- 2 ounces diced prosciutto ham

1 tablespoon imported Hungarian paprika
3 ripe tomatoes, peeled, seeded, and chopped
2 tablespoons flour
1 cup chicken stock
  bouquet garni

FOR THE GARNISH:

2 green or yellow bell peppers
2 red bell peppers
3 tablespoons chopped fresh parsley

1. Season the chicken with salt and pepper. Heat 2 tablespoons olive oil in a large sauté pan and brown the chicken pieces on all sides, without crowding the pan. Transfer chicken to a platter, and discard all but 1 tablespoon fat.

2. Add the remaining 2 tablespoons olive oil, and sauté the onion, garlic, chili, ham, and paprika until the onions are soft. Add the tomatoes, increase heat to high, and cook for 3 minutes, or until most of the tomato liquid has evaporated. Return the chicken to the pan and stir in the flour. Add the stock and *bouquet garni,* and bring to a boil, scraping the bottom of the pan with a spoon to dissolve congealed meat juices. Reduce heat and simmer the chicken for 20 minutes or until cooked, skimming off any fat that might rise to the surface. Correct the seasoning.

3. Meanwhile, roast, peel, and core the peppers. Place them directly on a lit gas or electric burner and cook them, turning with tongs, until all sides are charred. Wrap the peppers in wet paper towels for 3 minutes. This steams off the skins. Peel the charred skin off under cold running water, using a brush or paring knife. Halve the peppers and remove the seeds. Cut each half into quarters. (For illustration and complete instructions see pages 261–62.)

4. About 10 minutes before the chicken is ready, add the peppers to the sauté. This is a peasant dish, so we won't bother to strain the sauce. (Do remember to remove the *bouquet garni,* however.) Correct the seasoning. Serve Basque chicken with a green salad, crusty French bread, and plenty of beer or cheap white wine to douse the fires.

◊   ◊   ◊

CHICKEN WITH OLIVES: Prepare as above, omitting the paprika and peppers, substituting ½ cup calamata olives and ½ cup green Sicilian olives. The olives should be blanched in boiling water for 2 minutes to remove some of the salt.

CHICKEN PAPRIKAS

Peppers, native to the New World, were introduced to Hungary in the sixteenth century, where they were adopted with gusto. (Other New World foods that became popular in Europe include potatoes, tomatoes, corn, chocolate, and turkey.) Hotter than our bell peppers, milder than cayenne, Hungary's pepper (*capsecum anuum*) yields the finest paprika in the world. Thus, it is important to use an imported brand. Note that flour is added to the sour cream, which prevents it from curdling when the sauce is boiled.

Serves 4

1 3-pound chicken, cut into 8 pieces
  salt and fresh black pepper
4 tablespoons lard or chicken fat
1 large onion, finely chopped (about ¾ cup)
1 clove garlic, minced
2 tablespoons imported Hungarian paprika
2 tomatoes, peeled, seeded, and chopped
  pinch of cayenne pepper
1 cup chicken stock
  bouquet garni
2 tablespoons flour
1 cup sour cream

1. Season the chicken with salt and pepper. Heat 1 tablespoon lard or chicken fat in a sauté pan and brown the chicken pieces on all sides over high heat.

2. Discard the fat and add the remaining lard to the pan. Cook the onion over medium heat for 3–4 minutes or until golden, adding the garlic and paprika halfway through. Add the tomatoes and cayenne, increase heat to high, and cook for 3 minutes or until the liquid from the tomatoes has evaporated. Return the chicken to the pan and add the stock and *bouquet garni*. Gently simmer the chicken for 20 minutes or until cooked. Arrange the chicken pieces on a platter and keep warm.

3. Skim off any fat and bring the sauce to a boil. Whisk the flour into the sour cream and whisk this into the sauce. Simmer for 3 minutes. Taste the sauce for seasoning—it should be quite spicy—and add more cayenne pepper if necessary. Return the chicken to the sauce to warm.

Serving: Chicken paprikas is delicious on a bed of spaetzle (see page 271) or noodles. Choose a Hungarian red wine, like Eger Bikavér, literally "blood of the bull."

LESSON 26

Roast Duck

————————◇————————

Techniques:
ROASTING DUCK
PREPARING ORANGE GARNISHES

Master Recipe:
STEAM-ROASTED DUCK

Variations:
ROAST DUCK WITH ORIENTAL MARINADE
DUCK WITH ORANGE SAUCE
DUCK WITH PORT SAUCE

◇   ◇   ◇

If duck were not so delectable, I would banish it from my kitchen. There is no other bird or beast that causes so much heartache. More than half of a Long Island duck is skin, bones, and fat. (The latter makes it *very* messy to cook.) A 5-pound chicken would feed 6–8 people; the same sized duck, only 2.

When the duck is good, however, it is very, very good. Especially when the skin is crackling crisp, and the meat so tender that it falls off the bone. Duck is a very fatty bird, so whatever the cooking method, it must concentrate on getting rid of the fat.

The French solve the fat problem by serving the bird in two courses. The duck is roasted in a blazing oven for 20 minutes. The breasts are removed and served rare, like steak. The thighs are returned to the oven or grilled until well done, and served as a subsequent course.

The Chinese adopt a different strategy in the preparation of Peking duck. They loosen the skin from the body, scrape out all the fat, and dry the skin in a special oven. The next day, the duck is roasted, and the skin, flesh, and carcass are served separately in the form of cracklings, meat, and soup.

Not long ago, my cooking class made a scientific effort to determine the best method for cooking duck. The winner was a method suggested by one of my students, Uta Retz. We pricked the skin with a fork (to release the fat). We then placed the duck on a rack over boiling water in a tightly covered pot and steamed it for 1 hour to melt out the fat. The bird was painted with honey and soy sauce and roasted in a hot oven to crisp the skin. The results were superior: the skin was fatless and crisp, the meat, tender and moist. Uta's method is the one you will find below.

◇   ◇   ◇

Steam-Roasted Duck

This duck recipe makes a fine dish in its own right, and it is the starting point for duckling with orange sauce or with currant sauce. Long Island ducks, by the way, are descended from Chinese ducks brought to Long Island in 1878.

Serves 2–3

- 1 4–5 pound Long Island duck
  salt and fresh black pepper
- 3 tablespoons soy sauce
- 2 tablespoons honey
- 2 tablespoons hot water

1. Ready the duck for roasting. Remove the giblets from the cavity. Remove the lumps of fat from the rear. Drain the duck, and sprinkle the inside with salt and pepper. Removing the wishbone is optional, but it will facilitate carving the bird. To remove it, turn the bird on its breast, reach in the neck cavity, and cut out the U-shaped bone you feel beneath the neck.

2. Truss the duck with a trussing needle and string. Have the duck on its back. Push the legs toward the front of the duck, so the drumsticks stand at a 45-degree angle. Insert the needle just below the bone in the right thigh, traverse the body, and push the needle out through the left thigh at the same spot. Now, invert the duck and insert the needle through the nearest wing. Pull the neck skin tightly over the back, pin it to the back with the string, and pierce the other wing in the same spot. Bring the two ends of string together, pull them as tight as possible, and knot. Cut off the excess neck skin and tuck the backside into the rear cavity. The bird should now stand proud and symmetrical, ready for roasting.

3. Prick the skin all over with a fork, toothpick, or skewer. This allows the fat to escape. Do not prick the actual meat, however, or you will lose valuable juices. Season with salt and pepper.

4. Steaming the duck: place 1 inch hot water in a wok, steamer, casserole, or other large pan. Place a rack an inch over the water and place the duck, breast side up, on top. Tightly cover the pan, using foil to make a tent if necessary: you want a hermetic seal. Place the pan over high heat and bring the water to a boil. Reduce heat to minimum and steam the duck for 1 hour, adding fresh water as necessary. When most of the fat in the skin has melted, remove the duck and gently pat dry. The duck can be prepared up to 4 hours ahead to this stage.

5. Roasting the duck: preheat the oven to 425°F. Prick the skin all over again. Combine the soy sauce, honey, and water, and brush the duck with this mixture. Roast the bird breast side up on a rack over a baking pan for

20 minutes, or until thoroughly browned. (Lining the roasting pan with foil will facilitate clean-up.) Baste the duck with soy sauce every 5 minutes. Remove duck from oven and let stand for 5 minutes before carving. Don't forget to remove the trussing string. To serve, cut the duck in 2 with poultry shears. Serve by itself or with one of the sauces below.

Duck goes well with many wines, including an Italian Barolo, French St. Julien, or California Cabernet Sauvignon.

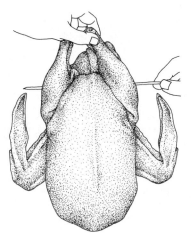

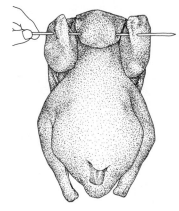

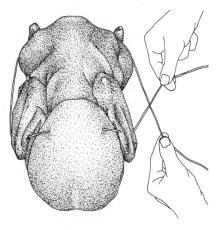

ROAST DUCK WITH ORIENTAL MARINADE

FOR THE MARINADE:

- 1 cup dark soy sauce
- ½ cup sherry
- 3 tablespoons honey
- 3 tablespoons sesame oil
- 1 inch ginger root, finely chopped
- 2 cloves garlic, peeled and minced
- ¼ cup chopped scallions

Combine the ingredients for the marinade. Prick the duck all over, and marinate it, turning from time to time, for 12–24 hours. Drain, reserving the marinade. Steam and roast the duck as described above, basting with reserved marinade.

DUCK WITH ORANGE SAUCE

The dark, rich meat of duck goes well with a sweet and sour fruit sauce. The sauce below is based on a *bigarade* (pronounced "bee-gahr-odd")—a mixture of caramelized sugar and vinegar.

FOR THE BIGARADE:

- 3 tablespoons sugar
- 2 tablespoons water
- 3 tablespoons red wine vinegar

TO FINISH THE SAUCE:

- 1½ cups well-flavored brown-bone chicken or veal stock
- 1 tablespoon orange marmalade
- ½ teaspoon grated zest and juice of 1 orange
- 2 teaspoons cornstarch
- 2 tablespoons Grand Marnier
- salt and fresh black pepper

1. Prepare the bigarade. Place the sugar and water in a heavy saucepan and place it over high heat. Cook, swirling the pan gently, until the sugar caramelizes; that is, turns golden brown. Remove the pan from heat, *stand back*, and add the vinegar. The pan will erupt with a Vesuvian hiss and the vinegar fumes will sting your eyes. Return this mixture to a low heat, and simmer it, whisking, till the sugar dissolves.

2. Add the stock, marmalade, and orange juice and boil the sauce until reduced by half. Dissolve the cornstarch in the Grand Marnier, and whisk

this mixture into the boiling sauce. Add salt and pepper to taste. Serve the orange sauce with the steam-roasted duck of the master recipe.

DUCK WITH PORT SAUCE

Patti Delia is a South Carolina cooking teacher and longtime friend of the Taste of the Mountains. Her port sauce for duck won first prize in a state-wide cooking contest some years back, and I am pleased to share the recipe here.

> 5 peppercorns
> 2 cloves
> 1 stick cinnamon
> 1 pinch cayenne pepper
>   zest (remove it in strips with a vegetable peeler) and juice
>   of 1 orange
> ¼ cup red currant jelly
> ¾ cup chicken stock
>   juice of ½ lemon
> ⅓ cup port wine
> 1 tablespoon orange marmalade
> 2 teaspoons cornstarch
>   salt
> 1 tablespoon butter

1. Combine the spices, orange zest, orange juice, currant jelly, and stock in a saucepan and simmer for 10 minutes or until the mixture is slightly reduced. Strain the sauce into another saucepan.

2. Add the lemon juice, all but 1 tablespoon port, and the marmalade, and simmer the sauce for 5 minutes. Dissolve the cornstarch in the remaining port and whisk it into the simmering sauce. Simmer for 30 seconds. Add salt to taste and stir in the butter. Serve the port sauce with the steam-roasted duck of the master recipe.

LESSON 27

Chicken Livers

◇

Techniques:
TRIMMING AND COOKING CHICKEN LIVERS

Master Recipe:
SILKY CHICKEN LIVER PÂTÉ

Variations:
CHICKEN LIVERS WITH BACON AND HOISIN
SAUCE
CHICKEN LIVERS WITH GREEN
PEPPERCORNS

◇ ◇ ◇

Chicken livers are like cats and Stravinsky. You either love them or hate them. I, myself, was a hater, having grown up on over-cooked livers. Then one day I tasted them properly prepared; that is, served pink in the center. On the spot I became a convert!

Chicken livers are inexpensive, nutritious, quick to prepare, and ideally suited to serving 1 or 2. If you have a quality butcher or poultry shop nearby, so much the better, for fresh livers taste better than frozen.

To prepare livers for cooking, spread them out on a paper towel and trim off any yellow fat or bitter green traces of gall bladder. Spread another paper towel on top and blot them dry. (This prevents the fat from spattering.) You are now ready for sautéing.

Chicken livers should be sautéed over high heat. We use clarified butter or a half-and-half mixture of butter and oil. (The two fats together can be heated to a higher temperature without burning.) The sauce is made directly in the pan in which you cooked the livers.

Below are recipes for the world's best chicken liver pâté, chicken livers with bacon and hoisin sauce, and chicken livers with green peppercorns.

◇ ◇ ◇

Silky Chicken Liver Pâté

This chicken liver pâté derives its silky smoothness from its base—pure creamed butter. If you are in a hurry, you don't have to strain the pureed chicken livers, but the pâté will not be as smooth. The butter can be added directly to the cooled liver puree in the processor, but the pâté won't be as light.

Serves 4–6 as an appetizer

- 8 ounces chicken livers
- 1 stick unsalted butter (at room temperature), plus 2 tablespoons for sautéing
- 2 tablespoons finely chopped shallots
- salt and fresh black pepper
- 1½ tablespoons port
- 1½ tablespoons cognac

1. Meticulously trim the chicken livers of all fat and sinews, and blot dry with paper towels. Heat 2 tablespoons butter to foaming in a small frying pan over high heat. Add the livers, shallots, and salt and pepper, and sauté over high heat, turning livers once or twice, for 2 minutes or until the livers are browned on the outside but very rare within. Add the spirits and flambé or boil until most of the liquid is evaporated.

2. Puree the chicken livers in a food processor. Force this mixture through a regular kitchen sieve, pressing with a spatula or the back of a spoon. Meanwhile, cream the butter; that is, beat it with a whisk in a large bowl until smooth, light, and fluffy. When the liver mixture is cool, gradually whisk it into the butter. Correct the seasoning, adding salt, pepper, or a few more drops port or cognac as necessary.

Serving: Mound the pâté in a bowl or ramekin, and working with a spatula moistened in cold water, make ridges on the top. Alternatively, pipe the liver pâté onto crackers, using a bag fitted with a ½-inch star tip (for full instructions on piping see page 278). Top each rosette with a black olive, as shown below.

Note: This pâté can be prepared up to 3 days ahead and refrigerated, but be sure to let it come to room temperature at least 2 hours before serving.

CHICKEN LIVERS WITH BACON AND HOISIN SAUCE

These broiled chicken liver kebabs make an unusual hors d'oeuvre. Hoisin sauce—a sweet-salty spicy Chinese condiment—is available at Oriental grocery stores or gourmet shops. This recipe was inspired by the vintage Wine Bar in Cambridge, Massachusetts.

Makes 12–14 pieces

1 pound chicken livers
1 cup hoisin sauce
6 strips bacon, cut into 3-inch lengths

toothpicks or bamboo skewers for broiling

Trim the chicken livers as described above, cutting any large ones in half. Marinate the livers in the hoisin sauce for at least 3 hours. Wrap each liver in a strip of bacon and thread it on a toothpick or skewer. Just before serving, cook the livers to taste on a grill or under the broiler, basting with hoisin sauce. This is a finger food, but be sure to provide napkins, because it is messy.

CHICKEN LIVERS WITH GREEN PEPPERCORNS

Green peppercorns are the fruit of the pepper tree, which, when dried, become black peppercorns. They have the flavor of pepper, without the fiery bite. Green peppercorns come packed in vinegar, in brine, or freeze-dried. The vinegar-packed have the most flavor.

Serves 2–3

1 pound chicken livers
  salt and pepper
3 tablespoons butter

FOR THE SAUCE:

2 tablespoons very finely chopped shallots
1 tablespoon drained green peppercorns (or to taste)
2 tablespoons cognac
3 tablespoons dry white wine
4 tablespoons brown stock
4 tablespoons heavy cream
2 tablespoons cold butter, cut into ½-inch cubes

1. Trim and dry the chicken livers. Sprinkle with salt and pepper. Melt the 3 tablespoons butter in a sauté pan (don't use cast iron or aluminum.)

When the butter foams, add the livers, and sauté over high heat, turning livers once or twice, for 2–3 minutes or until cooked to taste. Transfer the livers to a platter and keep warm.

2. Add the shallots and green peppercorns, and sauté until soft. Add the cognac and flambé. Add the wine, and boil until reduced by half. Add the stock and cream, and boil rapidly to reduce by half. Whisk in the butter, little by little, followed by salt and pepper to taste. NOTE: The butter should be whisked in over high heat, but once it is dissolved, do not let the sauce boil. (See lesson on reduction sauces on pages 140–41.) Pour the sauce over the livers and serve at once.

LESSON 28

Chicken Mousseline with Mosaic of Vegetables

———◇———

Techniques:
MAKING A CHICKEN MOUSSELINE
ASSEMBLING A VEGETABLE TERRINE
BAKING IN A WATER BATH
MAKING A "MOUSSE" SAUCE

Master Recipe:
MOSAIC OF VEGETABLES

Variations:
WATERCRESS SAUCE
PARSLEY SAUCE
SPINACH SAUCE

◇ ◇ ◇

A classic, a terrine is a sort of meatloaf baked in an earthenware mold. A pâté was baked in a pastry crust. Terrines were traditionally made with pork or game and garnished with tongue and ham. The mold was lined with strips of bacon or pork fat, which melted and basted the terrine as it baked.

Pork, ham, and bacon, however delicious, are not the stuff of healthy diets. In place of the traditional terrine, we propose this mosaic of vegetables. A light chicken mousseline replaces the pork mixture. Colorful chunks of carrots, green beans, and rutabagas are used for a garnish, while the mold is lined with grape leaves. This recipe may look difficult, but again it is just a series of simple steps.

Thanks to the food processor, the chicken mousseline can be prepared in a matter of minutes. There is one hitch: in the old days, the cream was laboriously beaten into the pureed chicken over ice. The whirling blade of the food processor tends to curdle the base mixture by overbeating the cream. To avoid this, we chill the pureed chicken, processor bowl and all, in the freezer for 20 minutes before adding the cream. (The mixture should be very cold but not frozen.) We add the cream, little by little, running the processor in bursts to prevent overbeating.

The mosaic tastes best baked a couple of days ahead, and as it is served cold, you don't have to worry about any last minute cooking.

◇ ◇ ◇

Mosaic of Vegetables

Vegetable mosaic is a guaranteed show-stopper, whether you serve it as an hors d'oeuvre, appetizer, or light entrée for lunch or brunch. This recipe makes 16 slices, enough to serve 8.

FOR THE CHICKEN MOUSSELINE:

    1 pound skinless, boneless chicken breasts
    3 egg whites
       juice of ½ lemon
   ½ teaspoon salt (or to taste)
       fresh black pepper, cayenne pepper, freshly grated nutmeg
1–1½ cups heavy cream

FOR THE VEGETABLE GARNISH:

    1 small rutabaga (yellow turnip), peeled, or parsnips, or white turnip
    3 carrots, peeled
  20 green beans, snapped
  12 mushroom caps, washed, stems removed
  12 grape leaves, rinsed and blotted dry (available in jars at Greek and Middle Eastern markets)
      Watercress Sauce (see recipe below)
      sprigs of fresh watercress or dill for garnish (optional)
      melted butter for buttering the mold

    1 5-cup terrine mold or narrow loaf pan

1. Prepare the chicken mousseline. Trim the chicken breasts of all fat and sinews. Cut them into 1-inch chunks and puree these to a smooth paste in the food processor. Add the egg whites and seasonings and puree until very smooth. Place the chicken mixture, processor bowl and all, in the freezer and chill for 20 minutes. The chicken should be very cold (but not frozen) before adding the cream.

2. Bring a small pan of water to a boil. Return the chilled chicken mixture to the processor and gradually add the cream, running the machine in short (20-second) bursts. The process should take 2 minutes. To test the mousseline for consistency and seasoning, poach a small ball of mixture (formed at the end of two wet spoons) in the boiling water for 1 minute. Taste it: it should be quite highly seasoned. Add salt, pepper, nutmeg, or lemon juice as necessary. If the mousseline seems rubbery, add a little more cream. Keep chilled until required to complete the terrine.

3. Meanwhile, prepare the vegetables. Cut the rutabaga lengthwise into ¼-inch slices. Cut these lengthwise into ¼-inch strips. Place the rutabaga

in 1 quart cold, salted water, and bring to a boil. Cook it for 3 minutes, or until it is quite soft (a little more than crispy-tender; this will make it easier to slice the mosaic). Remove with a slotted spoon, and refresh it under cold water. Drain. Cut the carrots lengthwise into ¼-inch strips. Cook these in the boiling rutabaga water until quite soft. Refresh and drain. Cook the green beans the same way. Pat the vegetables dry with paper towels. Double-butter the terrine mold; that is, brush it once with melted butter, freeze the pan, and brush it with butter a second time. (This is done to prevent any chance of sticking.) Line the bottom of the pan, then the sides with grape leaves. The leaves on the sides should hang an inch or so over the top.

4. Assemble the mosaic. Spoon enough mousseline mixture into the lined terrine mold to make a ¼-inch layer. Smooth it with the back of a wet spoon. Arrange symmetrical, alternating strips of rutabaga, carrot, and green beans running the *length* of the mold, pressing the vegetables lightly into the mousseline mixture. Add another ¼-inch mixture, smooth it down, and arrange more rutabaga strips, carrots, and green beans, varying the colors from the previous layer. Add more mousseline. Arrange the mushroom caps in a row down the center, slicing off the front and back of each cap so that the ends abut squarely. Flank the caps with green beans and strips of carrot. Add more mousseline.

5. Continue building the terrine in this manner, varying the pattern from the previous layer. You are aiming for a colorful mosaic effect when the terrine is sliced vertically. Top the last layer of vegetables with a last layer of mousseline mixture and smooth. Fold the ends of the grape leaves over the top. Add more grape leaves as necessary to completely cover the surface. Gently bang the terrine mold on the work surface 25 times to knock out air bubbles and compact the mousse. Cover it tightly with a piece of buttered foil. Bring 1 quart water to a boil.

6. Bake the vegetable mosaic. Place the terrine mold in a roasting pan just big enough to hold it. Add enough boiling water to come 1 inch up the side of the pan. (This is called a water bath and it ensures a moist, even heat.) Bake the mosaic in a preheated 350° oven for 40–50 minutes or until:

—the mousseline feels springy to the touch;

—it begins to shrink from the sides of the pan;

—an inserted toothpick or thin skewer comes out clean and *hot* to the touch.

Set the terrine on a cake rack to cool to room temperature. Refrigerate it at least 4 hours, preferably overnight, before serving. (Vegetable mosaic can be made up to 4 days ahead.)

7. Serving: invert the pan on a cutting board, and unmold the mosaic. (It may be necessary to warm the pan in hot water for a few seconds to melt the butter.) Using a slender, sharp knife, cut off one end, then cut the mosaic into ⅜-inch slices. Lay the slices flat on a metal spatula to move

them. Vegetable mosaic is equally spectacular served on a platter or on individual plates. For the former, arrange the slices around the outside of the platter, smaller ends facing out, inside corners touching. Spoon the watercress sauce inside. Place a sprig of watercress, fresh dill, or thyme in the center.

For individual plate presentations, spoon the sauce in the center of large, chilled salad plates. Rotate the plate to evenly coat the bottom with sauce. Arrange two slices of mosaic on top and garnish with a sprig of watercress. This spectacular dish calls for a festive beverage—champagne.

WATERCRESS SAUCE

This colorful sauce makes a beautiful foil for vegetable mosaic, not to mention for chicken breasts, fish, or a seafood mousse. Its intense green hue is obtained by quickly blanching the herb in rapidly boiling, salted water, then refreshing it under cold water. Use a blender to puree the watercress; a food processor blade does not turn fast enough. To save time, you could substitute ½ cup store-bought mayonnaise for the egg yolk, mustard, and oil in the recipe below.

Makes 1½ cups sauce

    1 bunch watercress, coarse stems discarded (about 2 cups)
      salt
    1 egg yolk
    1 scant teaspoon mustard
    ½ cup bland vegetable oil
    ⅓ cup chicken stock
      juice of ½ lemon (or to taste)

fresh black pepper, cayenne pepper
¼ cup heavy cream

1. Cook the watercress in 2 quarts rapidly boiling, heavily salted water for 30 seconds. Refresh it under cold water until completely cool, and wring dry.

2. Place the egg yolk, mustard, and ¼ teaspoon salt in the blender and blend at low speed. Add the oil in a *thin* stream; the mixture should thicken. Add the stock and watercress and puree until completely smooth. Add the lemon juice and seasonings—the mixture should be quite highly seasoned. Add the cream last of all, but do not run the blender for more than 5 seconds, or the sauce may curdle.

◇　◇　◇

PARSLEY SAUCE: Follow the recipe above, substituting a large bunch of flat-leaf parsley for the watercress.

SPINACH SAUCE: Follow the recipe above, substituting 5 ounces stemmed, washed fresh spinach for the watercress.

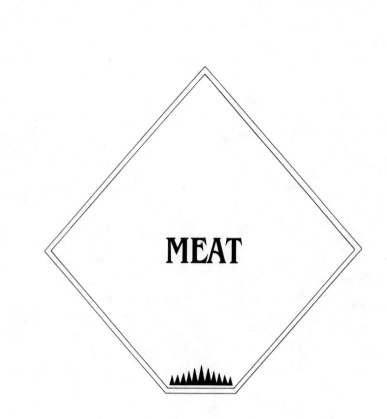

MEAT

LESSON 29

Rack of Lamb with Mustard Hollandaise

◇

Techniques:
FRENCHING LAMB
CRUMB-ROASTING
MAKING HOLLANDAISE

Master Recipe:
RACK OF LAMB WITH MUSTARD
   HOLLANDAISE

Variations:
RACK OF LAMB WITH GOAT CHEESE PESTO
LEG OF LAMB WITH MUSTARD
   HOLLANDAISE
HOLLANDAISE SAUCE
MUSTARD HOLLANDAISE
CURRY HOLLANDAISE
MALTAISE SAUCE

◇   ◇   ◇

Lamb is my favorite red meat, and the rack (rib roast) is my favorite cut of lamb. Rack of lamb is easy to prepare, speedy to cook (from start to finish it takes 25 minutes), and few sights are more spectacular than a neatly frenched rack, the ribs standing proudly, crowned with lacy cutlet frills.

The following recipe uses a technique I call "crumb-roasting": the lamb is painted with mustard (or honey or pesto) and dredged in herb-flavored bread crumbs. The crumb coating forms a crisp crust while keeping the meat moist and tender. Crumb-roasting can be used to cook poultry and seafood and the crumb mixture makes a delicious baked stuffed tomato.

◇   ◇   ◇

◇

TO FRENCH RACK OF LAMB

The French have become inextricably linked to all things fine and luxurious. Thus a French cuff has the added elegance of a cuff link; a French heel is the epitome of fashionable footwear; and a lover bestows not a peck on the cheek but a sensuous French kiss. In food, too, the French triumph: morning muffins pale in comparison to French toast, and the whole world has adopted the French fry. A frenched chop is one in which the rib has been meticulously scraped clean—a practice that flatters the eye, while keeping the fingers greaseless, should the diner wish to nibble the bone.

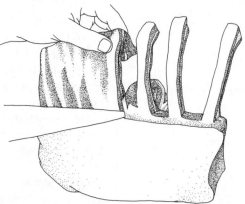

1. Using a sharp paring knife, cut around the shoulder blade (the cartilaginous wedge at the wider end of the rack) and remove it. Using the same knife, make a straight, deep cut perpendicular to the ribs, just above the "eye" (meaty part) of the rack where the meat meets the ribs.

2. Cut all the fat and meat off the ribs above the cut. Cut between the ribs to remove the fat as well. Now, scrape the ribs with the point of the knife until they are completely clean. (This is known as "frenching" the ribs.) Trim off the fell (papery skin) and most of the fat from the eye of the lamb, but leave a little fat for succulence.

◇ ◇ ◇

◇

To make toasted bread crumbs, grind fresh country-style white bread, or stale or lightly toasted French bread in the food processor. Spread the crumbs on a baking sheet and bake them for 5–10 minutes in a 400° oven.

Rack of Lamb with Mustard Hollandaise

Many butchers will be willing to "french" the rack for you, but if you wish to do it yourself, you will find detailed instructions above. Do ask your butcher to cut most of the way through the backbone to facilitate carving when the lamb is cooked. An eight-rib rack of lamb will serve 2–4 people, depending on their appetites and the size of the rest of the meal.

> 2 medium-sized racks of lamb, trimmed and frenched
> ½ cup grainy (Meaux-style) mustard
> salt and fresh black pepper
> oil for the roasting pan
> mustard hollandaise (see page 198)

FOR THE HERBED BREAD CRUMB MIXTURE:

> 1 cup lightly toasted fresh bread crumbs (see above)
> ¼ cup very finely chopped parsley, and/or other fresh herbs
> 2 cloves garlic, minced as finely as possible

1. Using a pastry brush, thickly paint the mustard on all sides of the racks but not on the ribs. Sprinkle on salt and pepper.

2. Combine the bread crumbs with the herbs and garlic. Dredge the racks in the crumb mixture, and place in an oiled roasting pan. The lamb can be prepared up to 1 hour ahead of time to this stage.

3. Roast the lamb in a preheated 425° oven for 20–25 minutes for medium rare, or until cooked to taste. To tell the degree of doneness, push the wider end of the rack with your finger: if it feels squishy, the lamb is very rare; if it feels slightly resilient, it is medium rare; if springy, the lamb is medium; if firm, it is well done. Alternatively, you can use a meat thermometer: medium rare lamb will register 120°F. (If you have never tasted lamb cooked medium-rare, you owe it to yourself to try it—it's delicious!)

4. Meanwhile, prepare the mustard hollandaise.

5. Serving racks of lamb: present the whole roast racks on a platter, then bring them back to the kitchen to stand for 5 minutes before carving. (This allows the blood to flow back to the edge of the roast.) Remove the chine (backbone), which the butcher loosened. Use a heavy chef's knife to carve the rack into ribs. For the actual serving, I prefer the plate presentation: the ribs of the chops crossed like raised sabres over a colorful array of vegetable purees (see Lesson 39). The mustard hollandaise can be spooned onto each plate or passed separately. The rich flavor of lamb requires a full-bodied red wine, like a Gruaud-Larose from St.-Julien, or an Alexander Valley Cabernet Sauvignon.

RACK OF LAMB WITH GOAT CHEESE PESTO: Prepare the recipe above, using the goat cheese pesto on page 83 in place of the mustard. The acrid piquancy of goat cheese makes a marvelous marriage with lamb.

LEG OF LAMB WITH MUSTARD HOLLANDAISE: Trim the fell and most of the fat off a 5-pound leg of lamb. Using a pointy paring knife, make small incisions all over the leg at 1-inch intervals, and in each insert a sliver of garlic, a blade of rosemary, and, optionally, a slice of anchovy. Coat and prepare the leg of lamb as described above, and roast it in a preheated 400° oven for 20 minutes for each pound of lamb. Test for doneness as described above. A 5-pound leg of lamb will serve 10 people.

◇　◇　◇

HOLLANDAISE SAUCE

Who was the first chef to combine egg yolks, butter, and lemon juice into that silky, rich, ethereal sauce known as hollandaise? History neglects to tell us. Its creator has no doubt been blessed by untold generations of epicures (mindful of eggs Benedict and asparagus with hollandaise), but this temperamental sauce has also been the bane of countless fledgling cooks.

Like mayonnaise, hollandaise is an emulsion, but here the egg yolks are cooked. The secret lies in gently poaching the yolks so that they thicken, but not so much so that they scramble (which happens at 165°F.). Most recipes call for cooking hollandaise sauce over a double boiler. The disadvantage of this method (aside from the fact that real men don't use double boilers!) is that it turns what should be a 5-minute sauce into a half-hour production. Work over a low flame, but have a bowl of cold water on hand: if the yolks start to overcook, you can cool the pan in the water.

Cook the yolks in a heavy, nonaluminum, slope-sided saucepan— heavy, so the heat will spread evenly; nonaluminum, because aluminum will turn the yolks green; slope-sided, so the whisk can easily reach into the corners of the pan.

BASIC HOLLANDAISE

Serves 6

    4 egg yolks
    1 tablespoon cold water
  1½ sticks unsalted butter, melted but tepid
       juice of ½ lemon (or to taste)
       salt, white pepper, cayenne pepper to taste

1. Place the yolks and water in a heavy nonaluminum saucepan and have a bowl of cold water nearby. Place the pan over a low flame and whisk the yolks as vigorously as you can. After 60 seconds or so, the mixture will become light and moussy; continue whisking until it thickens to the consistency of mayonnaise and you can see traces of the bottom of the pan with each stroke of the whisk. NOTE: Remove the pan from the heat as soon as the sauce begins to thicken, but continue whisking—the residual heat from the pan will continue cooking the yolks. If the yolks start to overcook (turn into scrambled eggs), immerse the pan in cold water. A trace of scrambling is normal and will not harm the final sauce.

2. Off the heat, add the butter in a very thin stream, whisking constantly. The sauce should thicken. It is better to add the butter too slowly, rather

than too quickly. Add the lemon juice by squeezing the lemon through your hand to catch the seeds in your fingers. Add the salt, white pepper, and cayenne, whisking all the while. Correct the seasoning, balancing the salt against the lemon juice: the sauce should be very highly seasoned.

RESCUING CURDLED HOLLANDAISE

No matter how careful you are, you will probably, once, curdle the hollandaise. To bring it back, first try whisking in a tablespoon of ice water. If this does not work, place another egg yolk at room temperature in a small bowl, and gradually whisk the curdled sauce into it.

There are recipes for hollandaise sauce made by pouring hot butter over cold egg yolks in the food processor or blender. Only by whisking the yolks over heat as described above will you achieve the fluffy richness of real hollandaise.

HOLDING AND SERVING ·

Hollandaise sauce cannot be reheated, nor should it be left on a burner, however low. To keep the sauce warm, place it on a grill or cake rack *over* a pan of hot, but *not* boiling, water. Hollandaise sauce is wonderful with steamed asparagus and broccoli, poached and grilled fish, poached eggs —almost anything.

◇　◇　◇

MUSTARD HOLLANDAISE: To the basic hollandaise add 1 tablespoon Meaux-style (grainy) mustard. Mustard hollandaise makes a perfect accompaniment to the crumb-roasted rack of lamb on page 195.

CURRY HOLLANDAISE: To the basic hollandaise add 1–2 teaspoons imported curry powder. This is excellent with fish and shellfish.

MALTAISE SAUCE (Orange-Flavored Hollandaise): Malta is famed for its sour oranges, and a mixture of orange juice and lemon juice achieves a similar effect. Prepare the basic hollandaise substituting fresh orange juice for the water at the beginning, adding a little more orange juice with the lemon juice at the end. Maltaise sauce is delicious on breaded, pan-fried fish, grilled lamb, and asparagus.

L E S S O N   3 0

Pan-Fried Veal

◇

Techniques:

CUTTING AND POUNDING SCALLOPINI

BREADING AND PAN-FRYING

CLARIFYING BUTTER

SEASONING A FRYING PAN

Master Recipe:

WIENER SCHNITZEL

Variations:

WEINER SCHNITZEL À LA HOLSTEIN

VEAL PICCATA

VEAL CORDON BLEU

◇   ◇   ◇

Wiener schnitzel literally means "Viennese slice." It was in this historic Austrian capital that pan-fried veal was elevated to what can only be called an art. That is not to say that the Viennese have a monopoly on this delicacy, for imagine Italian cuisine without *scallopini* or French without *escalope de veau*.

A *schnitzel* or *scallopini*, as it is commonly called in the United States, is a broad, thin slice of veal cut from the leg of a calf. The best comes from the *top round*, a broad, flat muscle on the outside of the leg. Scallopinis are also cut from the bottom round and eye of the round, but they are not nearly as tender. Thus, it's important to find a butcher who will cut it only from the top round. In his absence buy a whole top round and slice it yourself.

The second factor is equally important: the meat must be sliced *across* the grain. (Muscles, like wood, have a grain. When we saw a log in half, we are cutting it across the grain.) Cutting across the grain minimizes the length of each muscle fiber, thereby reducing toughness. Scallopini cut this way are also less likely to curl when cooked.

Restaurants obtain perfectly even slices by partially freezing the meat, and cutting it on a meat slicer. Most of us don't have meat slicers at home, but partial freezing will make it easier to slice the meat by hand. The proper thickness for slicing scallopini is ¼ inch. Pounding is optional, but the results will be more tender. Place the scallopini between two lightly moistened sheets of waxed paper or parchment paper. (The water acts as a lubricant, preventing the meat from tearing.) Gently hit the meat with a scallopini pounder or the side of a cleaver, sliding the pounder from the center to the edge. The idea here is to lightly flatten the veal, not pound it into a ragged pulp. The final thickness should be ³⁄₁₆ inch.

Because veal is a dry meat (it lacks the marbling of fat found in beef), it is best floured or breaded prior to cooking to seal in flavor and moistness. (A full discussion of breading will be found on page 63). For frying, use clarified butter or equal parts oil and butter, both of which have a higher burning point than regular butter. The best utensil for pan-frying is a cast-iron skillet, but any heavy pan will do.

◇　　◇　　◇

Wiener Schnitzel

The secret to great Wiener schnitzel is using fresh bread crumbs (page 194). Crumbs made from stale bread or the store-bought kind brown too much during frying.

Serves 4

> 1 pound veal scallopini, cut from the top round (each slice
>   will weigh approximately 2 ounces
>   salt and fresh black pepper
> ¾ cup flour
> 2 eggs, beaten with a pinch of salt
> 1 cup fresh bread crumbs (see page 194)
> 6 tablespoons clarified butter, or equal parts butter and oil
> 8 lemon wedges (see page 128)

1. Season the scallopini on both sides with salt and pepper. Place flour, egg, and bread crumbs in shallow bowls. Dip each piece of veal first in flour, shaking off excess, then in egg, finally in bread crumbs. Place the slices on a clean, dry plate until frying. The scallopini can be prepared up to 3 hours ahead to this stage but will taste better if breaded at the last minute.

2. Heat the butter or butter and oil in a large frying pan over a medium-high heat. The fat should be hot but not smoking: to test the temperature, dip in a piece of veal—if bubbles dance around it, it is ready. Fry the Wiener schnitzels on each side for 30 seconds. NOTE: Do not crowd the pan, or the veal will stew, rather than crisply fry. (Use two pans if necessary.) Serve the Wiener schnitzel as soon as it is cooked, with lemon wedges for squeezing. A dry white Austrian wine, like a Grünveltliner, goes well with the veal. Other accompaniments might include glazed carrots (see page 235), fiddle-head ferns (page 231), and spaetzle (page 271).

WIENER SCHNITZEL À LA HOLSTEIN

This is my favorite dish at the Bernerhof. Holstein is a German province on the Baltic Sea, where schnitzels come topped with fried eggs, capers, and anchovies. A no-stick pan is a great help for frying the eggs.

Serves 4

    1 batch of Wiener schnitzel
    4 eggs
    3 tablespoons butter for frying the eggs
   12 anchovy fillets
    4 tablespoons drained capers

Prepare the Wiener schnitzel as described above. Meanwhile, fry four eggs sunny-side-up. To serve, top each serving of Wiener schnitzel with a fried egg, and arrange three anchovies in a triangle around the yolk. Sprinkle capers on top.

TO CLARIFY BUTTER

Clarified butter is ideal for sautéing, because it can be heated to a higher temperature than stick butter without burning. (This is made possible by removing milk solids and other impurities.)

To clarify butter, melt it in a small saucepan. Using a spoon, skim off the white foam on the surface—these are the milk solids. The golden liquid underneath is clarified butter, ready to be spooned out with a small ladle. At the bottom is a thin layer of water. To remove it, chill the pan just until the butter resolidifies. Crack through it with a spoon and pour out the milky white liquid at the bottom.

Clarified butter will keep for several weeks.

VEAL PICCATA

This recipe calls for "medallions" of veal—small, medallionlike steaks that measure ¼–½ inch thick and 2–3 inches across. Medallions are best cut from the ribs, loin, or tenderloin, but you can also use top round. Instead of breading the veal, we use a cheese-flavored batter. The best Italian grating cheese is parmigiano-reggiano; unless these words are stamped into the rind, you have not bought the real McCoy.

Serves 4

8 veal medallions, each weighing 2–3 ounces
1 lemon

FOR THE BATTER:

3 eggs
½ cup freshly grated Parmesan cheese
2–3 tablespoons flour

TO FINISH THE VEAL PICCATA:

salt and fresh black pepper
1 cup flour
6 tablespoons clarified butter, or half-and-half oil and butter
1 heaping tablespoon drained capers

1. Trim any fat or sinews off the veal. Carefully cut the rind off the lemon to expose the flesh. (The French call this "skinning alive.") Cut the lemon widthwise into paper-thin slices and carefully remove the seeds.

2. Whisk together the ingredients for the batter, adding more flour if necessary: the batter should be slightly thicker than heavy cream. The recipe can be prepared ahead to this stage.

3. Just before cooking, salt and pepper the veal. Dredge each piece in flour and shake off the excess. Heat the butter in a skillet over a medium-high flame. Dip each veal medallion in batter, drain for a moment, and fry for 1 minute per side, or until the veal is cooked to taste. To serve, top each medallion with a slice of lemon and a few capers. A dry Italian white, like a Gavi or Orvieto, would go well with veal piccata.

VEAL CORDON BLEU

In French a *cordon bleu* ("blue ribbon") is both a champion cook and the badge she receives for excellence. The dish must surely be one of the most sadly abused. The original veal *cordon bleu* was a splendid combination of scallopini, prosciutto, and pungent Gruyère cheese. These days you are more apt to be served veal burgers filled with boiled ham and Velveeta. The Bernerhof serves a particularly fine *cordon bleu*, which we are proudly restoring to gastronomic grace.

The veal is best cut on a meat slicer: each slice should be ³⁄₁₆-inch thick and at least 4 inches across. Use Westphalian ham, which is a heavily smoked, dry-cured ham, or prosciutto.

Serves 4

8 broad, very thin slices veal
4 very thin slices Westphalian ham or prosciutto

4 very thin slices imported Gruyère cheese (or enough to
cover the ham)
salt, fresh black pepper
¾ cup flour
2 eggs beaten with a pinch of salt
1 cup fresh bread crumbs
6 tablespoons clarified butter, or half-and-half oil and butter

1. Lay a slice of veal on a sheet of lightly moistened waxed paper or
parchment paper. Lay a slice of ham on top, followed by a slice of Gruyère
and another slice of veal. Place a second sheet of lightly moistened waxed
paper on top, and *gently* flatten the cordon bleu with the side of a cleaver.
Repeat, using the remaining veal, ham, and cheese. The recipe can be
prepared up to 6 hours ahead to this stage.

2. Dip each *cordon bleu* first in flour, then in egg, finally in bread
crumbs. Heat the butter in one or two large skillets over a medium-high
heat, and brown the veal quickly on both sides. Finish cooking the *cordons
bleu* right in the frying pan in a preheated 400° oven for 4–6 minutes. A
spicy Gewürztraminer from Alsace would be a perfect wine.

L E S S O N   3 1

Stews

◇

Let "gourmets" have their filets mignons: when it comes to honest eating, I raise my fork for stew. Give me a tough, flavorful cut of meat, slow-simmered with aromatic vegetables till it can literally be cut with a fork. I tell you that there is no gastronomic glory greater than the humble stew.

Our term "stew" (which has variously meant a "pond," a " pheasant pen," and a "house of prostitution") comes from the French word *etuver*, "to bathe," literally, and by extension, to cook in lots of liquid. Stewing is similar to braising (see Lesson 18) in that both are moist cooking methods. A single large chunk of meat can be braised, while in stews the meat is cut into small pieces.

Stewing is well suited to tough, inexpensive cuts of meat, like chuck, round, and brisket. Such cuts owe their toughness—and flavor—to large amounts of connective tissue. Connective tissue is made of a protein called collagen (from the Greek *kolla,* meaning "glue"), which melts in the presence of prolonged moist heat. Prolonged heat has a tendency to toughen muscle fibers, however, so it is important to cook stews at a low temperature: a bare simmer on the stove or at 300°F. in the oven.

Season stews only partially at the beginning, as the juices will reduce while cooking. Correct the seasoning before serving.

Below are recipes for spring lamb stew, mock wild boar stew, and classic beef *bourguignonne.*

◇   ◇   ◇

Spring Lamb Stew

This dish is traditionally made in springtime, using spring lamb and the first of the season's vegetables. The vegetables are cooked separately and added to the stew at the end to preserve their individual flavors.

Serves 6–8

- 3 pounds boneless leg or shoulder of lamb
  salt and fresh black pepper
- 2 tablespoons oil
- 2 tablespoons butter
- 1 medium onion, finely chopped
- 1 large carrot, finely chopped
- 2 stalks celery, finely chopped
- 3–4 *ripe* tomatoes, or 1 pound imported canned tomatoes, drained, peeled, seeded, and chopped
- 2 cloves garlic, peeled
- 2 tablespoons flour
- 2–3 cups brown stock or chicken stock
- 2 tablespoons tomato paste
  bouquet garni

FOR THE GARNISH:

- ½ pound new carrots
- ½ pound new turnips
- ½ pound new potatoes
- ½ pound green beans, ends snapped
- 1 pound fresh peas, shucked
- 2 tablespoons chopped fresh herbs, such as basil, tarragon, or rosemary
- 4 tablespoons chopped fresh parsley

1. Cut the lamb into 1½-inch cubes, trimming off any large pieces of fat. Season with salt and pepper. Heat the oil and butter in a large (3-quart) casserole. Brown the lamb pieces, on all sides, in several batches, over high heat. Avoid overcrowding the pan, or the meat will stew rather than sear. Use fresh butter and oil as needed. Transfer the cooked pieces to a platter. Discard all but 3 tablespoons fat.

2. Add the chopped onion, carrot, and celery to the pan and cook over medium heat for 3 minutes or until the vegetables are soft. Add the tomatoes and garlic, increase heat to high, and cook for 2 minutes to evaporate some of the liquid from the tomatoes. Return the lamb to the casserole and thoroughly stir in the flour. Stir in stock to cover, the tomato paste, and the *bouquet garni*. Bring the stew to a boil, reduce heat, and gently simmer the

lamb, covered, for 1 hour, or until the meat is tender. It may be necessary to add more stock as the stew simmers. You should end up with approximately half the liquid you started with.

3. Meanwhile, prepare the garnish. Peel each of the root vegetables. Unless they are very tiny, cut each in 1-inch pieces, or turn them (see page 234 for instruction and illustration). Cook the carrots, turnips, and potatoes separately, placing each in cold, salted water, which you gradually bring to a boil. Cook each root vegetable for 3–4 minutes or until crispy-tender, and refresh under cold water. Cook the green beans and peas in rapidly boiling, salted water for 2–3 minutes or until crispy-tender, and refresh under cold water.

4. To serve the stew, remove the *bouquet garni* and discard. Gently stir in the vegetables and herbs. Correct the seasoning and cook the stew until the vegetables are thoroughly heated. Sprinkle with parsley. Most stews can be served the next day; indeed, they improve with age.

Spring lamb stew would be wonderful on a bed of fresh-cooked pasta. A Pomerol, Côtes-de-Nuits, or Franciscan Vineyards Merlot would make an excellent beverage.

MOCK WILD BOAR STEW

This recipe comes from chef Fernand Chambrette, instructor at La Varenne cooking school and former owner of the Boule d'Or restaurant in Paris. It is called mock wild boar stew, because it is made with very tame pork roast that you would find at any supermarket. The overnight marinade gives the pork its gamy flavor. Real wild boar would be cooked the same way. Juniper berries are the primary flavoring of gin.

Serves 6–8

  1 five-pound pork roast

FOR THE WILD GAME MARINADE:

    1 bottle dry red wine
  ¼ cup red wine vinegar
    1 large onion, chopped (about ¾ cup)
    2 carrots, chopped
    2 stalks celery, chopped
    3 shallots, chopped
    3 cloves garlic, minced
  20 peppercorns
    5 cloves
  10 juniper berries or ¼ cup gin
    1 sprig parsley
    5 bay leaves

1½ teaspoons thyme
2 tablespoons olive oil

TO FINISH THE STEW:

   salt and fresh black pepper
3 tablespoons butter
3 tablespoons oil
2 tablespoons flour
   bouquet garni
1 cup brown stock
2 tablespoons red currant jelly (or to taste)
½ cup heavy cream
   sprigs of fresh coriander leaf for garnish

1. Trim the fat and bones off the pork and discard. Cut the meat into 2-inch cubes. Combine the ingredients for the marinade, and marinate the pork overnight. If you have less time, you can bring the marinade to a boil, let it cool, then marinate the pork for only 5–6 hours.

2. Strain the pork, reserving the marinade. Separate the meat from the vegetables, blot both dry with paper towels, and reserve. Season the meat with salt and pepper. Heat the butter and oil in a large casserole over high heat, and brown the pork on all sides in several batches. Use fresh butter and oil as necessary. Transfer the pork to a platter, discard all but 3 tablespoons fat from the pan, and cook the reserved vegetables until soft. Return the pork to the pan and stir in the flour. Add the reserved marinade, *bouquet garni,* and stock. Bring the stew to a boil, reduce heat and, stirring from time to time, simmer for 1½ hours or until the pork is tender. Remove the meat with a carving fork and transfer it to a warm serving dish. Whisk in the red currant jelly and cream into the sauce and simmer for 3 minutes. Add salt and pepper to taste. The sauce should be a little sweet, so add more jelly if necessary. Remove the *bouquet garni.* Strain the sauce over the meat and garnish with fresh coriander leaves.

Mock wild boar stew would be delicious over spaetzle (see page 271) or with toast points (see page 215). It calls for a robust, spicy wine: a California zinfandel perhaps or Croze-Hermitage from the Rhône.

VARIATIONS: This game marinade can be used to turn any meat into its wild counterpart: steak into venison, lamb into mountain goat; chicken into pheasant (for the latter, use white wine and white wine vinegar instead of red).

BEEF BURGUNDY

This robust beef stew exemplifies country French cooking. You needn't use a Romanée-Conti (the region's most expensive wine) for cooking, but you should use a decent Burgundian table wine, like a *bourgogne rouge* or *passe-tout-grains*. In a pinch, a Californian pinot noir (made from the classic Burgundian grape) will do. Avoid domestic jug wines marked "Burgundy," however; they have nothing to do with the real thing. For extra flavor, you can marinate the beef with the wine, chopped vegetables, and spices overnight, as described in the preceding recipe.

Serves 6–8

2½–3 pounds stew beef (chuck or round)
  ¼ pound slab bacon
    salt, fresh black pepper
  1 onion, finely chopped
  2 carrots, finely chopped
  2 ribs celery, finely chopped
  2 cloves garlic, minced
  2 tablespoons flour
  ¼ cup brandy
    approximately 1 bottle dry red wine (preferably from Burgundy)
    bouquet garni

FOR THE GARNISH:

  12 ounces fresh mushrooms
  ½ pound small silverskin onions
    salt, pepper, freshly grated nutmeg
    a little fresh lemon juice
  2 tablespoons butter
  2 tablespoons sugar
  12 ½-inch slices French bread (for toast points—optional)
  3 tablespoons melted butter for the toast points
  4 tablespoons finely chopped fresh parsley

1. Cut the beef into 2-inch cubes, discarding excess fat or gristle. Cut the bacon into ¼-x¼-x1-inch slivers. Fry the bacon in a large (4-quart) casserole over medium heat to render the fat and *lightly* brown the bacon. Transfer the bacon with a slotted spoon to a paper towel to drain.

2. Season the beef cubes and brown them on all sides in several batches. Discard all but 3 tablespoons fat, and cook the chopped vegetables in it until soft. Return the beef to the pan, stir in the flour until absorbed, and stir in the brandy and most of the wine. Add the *bouquet garni*. Bring the stew to a boil, reduce heat, and very gently simmer for 2–3 hours or

until the beef is tender. It may be necessary to add more wine as the stew cooks. In any case, be sure to save ¼ cup to refresh the sauce at the end.

3. Meanwhile, prepare the garnish. Wash the mushrooms (see page 253), cutting large ones in quarters, medium-sized ones in half. Peel the onions. Cook the mushrooms in ¼-inch water with salt, pepper, nutmeg, and lemon juice in a covered saucepan over a medium heat for 3 minutes. Drain and add the mushroom liquid to the stew. Place the onions in cold, salted water, bring to a boil, and simmer for 5 minutes or until tender. Drain. Melt the 2 tablespoons butter in a small skillet and sauté the onions with the sugar over high heat until golden brown and glazed. Brush the bread slices lightly with melted butter. Bake them in a preheated 400° oven for 10 minutes or until golden brown, turning once. Cool on a cake rack.

4. Serving beef Burgundy. The French would transfer the beef to a platter, strain the sauce, and return it to the casserole with the beef, mushrooms, onions, and reserved bacon slivers. If you don't mind having tiny pieces of onion, carrot, and celery in your stew, simply stir in the garnishes and simmer till thoroughly heated. Remove the *bouquet garni.* Correct the seasoning with salt and pepper and add a little red wine to "refresh" the sauce. Serve the stew on the toast points, sprinkled with fresh parsley.

This stew, too, would go well with pasta or spaetzle (see page 271). Almost any red burgundy, from a Chambertin to a Santenay, would be appropriate.

LESSON 32

Marinades and Grilling

◇

Techniques:
MARINATING
SKEWERING
GRILLING

Master Recipe:
BEEF TERIYAKI

Variations:
SATÉ
TANDOORI

◇   ◇   ◇

Our story begins on the steppes of Asia Minor, where Mongol nomads paused from their marauding and pillaging to roast horse meat impaled on their sabres over campfires. The Turks called such fare *sis kebabi,* literally "sword meat"—the origin of the modern shish kebab. Skewer cookery remains popular the world over, from the Indonesian *saté* to the Indian *tandoori* to Russian *shashlik* to Greco-American shish kebab.

There are three components to any shish kebab: the meat, the marinade, and the skewer. The meat should be cut into uniform pieces to insure even cooking. Don't stint on fat; it absorbs the smoky flavor from the coals and tenderizes the meat as it melts. You can use a water pistol to control any flareups caused by dripping fat.

Marinades are essential for any kebab, not only as a flavoring but also as a tenderizer. Thus marinades always contain an acid—wine, vinegar, citrus juice, yogurt—which helps break down tough muscle fibers. Acids tend to dry meats out, however, so a fat—oil or melted butter—is added to the marinade to keep the food moist during grilling. The kebab should be basted with marinade during cooking to keep it from drying out.

The skewer is the backbone of any kebab—if you use metal ones, choose the flat or square kind; these prevent the chunks from slipping when you turn them. I like the disposable bamboo skewers sold in Oriental markets—soak them in water beforehand to keep them from catching fire during grilling. (If the ends start to burn, they can be protected with pieces of foil.)

Nothing can rival kebabs grilled over fresh coals or gas-heated lava stones. The coals or stones should be thoroughly heated before you actually start grilling, so that they quickly sear in moisturizing meat juices. The darling of barbecue chefs these days is mesquite, the wood from a scrubby tree native to Texas that lends a unique smoky perfume to food grilled over it. But let us not forget alder, cherry, and hickory, which have long been standbys at the American smokehouse. Spendthrifts can grill directly over mesquite or hardwood coals, but an excellent smoke flavor can be obtained by throwing wood chips (soak them in cold water for 1 hour beforehand to make them smolder) on preheated charcoals or lava stones. The kebabs can also be cooked in your oven, under the broiler.

◇　◇　◇

Beef Teriyaki

Energy resources have shaped the world's cuisines as dramatically as the availability of individual ingredients. Thus, Northern Europe, with its vast forests and coal fields, traditionally favored such prolonged cooking methods as roasting, braising, and baking. In Japan, where fuel has always been scarce, chefs evolved quick cooking methods, like steaming, stir-frying, and grilling over a tiny hibachi. The marinade below is based on a sweet-salty sauce called teriyaki. It is equally good with meat, poultry, and seafood.

Serves 4

FOR THE MARINADE:

- 4 tablespoons *mirin* (or white wine sweetened with a little sugar)
- 4 tablespoons soy sauce
- 3 tablespoons sesame oil
- juice of ½ lemon
- 1 clove garlic, minced
- 1 ½-inch slice fresh ginger, finely chopped
- 2 scallions, finely chopped
- 2 tablespoons maple syrup

- 1½ pounds beef sirloin or shell steak cut into ¼-inch strips
- 3 tablespoons sesame seeds

Combine the ingredients for the marinade. Add the beef and marinate for 2–4 hours, turning 2 or 3 times. Thread the meat onto skewers and grill over hot coals for 1 minute per side, or until cooked to taste, basting the kebabs with leftover marinade. Sprinkle the kebabs with sesame seeds 30 seconds before removing from grill.

PORK SATÉ

Satés (pronounced "sah-tay") are served throughout Southeast Asia, where they are marinated with fiery chili pastes and grilled over portable charcoal braziers. The quantity of chili paste called for below will be tolerable to most palates. Feel free to add more or less.

Serves 4

FOR THE MARINADE:

> 4 tablespoons dark soy sauce
> 2 tablespoons sugar
> juice and grated zest of 1 lemon
> 1 teaspoon ground cumin
> 1 teaspoon coriander seeds
> ½ teaspoon chili paste, or a splash of hot chili oil
> 1 clove garlic, minced
> 4 tablespoons peanut butter
> 2 tablespoons sesame oil

> 1½ pounds pork tenderloin, cut into ¾-inch cubes

1. Combine the ingredients for the marinade. Marinate the meat for at least 6 hours.
2. Thread the meat onto skewers and grill over hot coals for 2 minutes per side or until cooked to taste, basting the kebabs with leftover marinade.

TANDOORI

A *tandoor* is a clay oven heated with charcoals, in which spice- and yogurt-marinated meats are grilled on vertical skewers. In most Indian restaurants this dish takes its Mercurochrome orange color from an edible vegetable dye. The marinade quantities below are sufficient for 2 cut-up game hens or 1½ pounds lamb.

Serves 4

FOR THE MARINADE:

> 1 cup plain yogurt
> ¼ cup fresh lemon juice
> ½ inch fresh ginger root, finely chopped
> 3 cloves garlic, finely chopped
> 1 hot chili, minced, or ½ teaspoon crushed dried red peppers
> 2 bay leaves, crumbled
> 2 tablespoons Hungarian paprika

1 teaspoon ground cumin
1 teaspoon ground coriander
1 teaspoon ground cinnamon
1 teaspoon turmeric
½ teaspoon fresh ground black pepper
¼ teaspoon ground cardamom
   pinch of ground cloves
½ teaspoon salt (or to taste)

1½ pounds lamb, cut into 1-inch cubes

1. Combine ingredients of marinade and marinate the lamb for at least 8 hours, preferably overnight.

2. Thread the meat onto skewers and grill over hot coals, basting with the marinade, for 2 minutes per side, or until cooked to taste.

Note: When making chicken or game hen tandoori, deeply score the meat to enable the marinade to penetrate to the bone.

LESSON 33

Beef in the Raw

————————◇————————

Technique:
SERVING RAW BEEF

Master Recipe:
THE WORLD'S BEST STEAK TARTARE

Variations:
YUK HWE (KOREAN UNCOOKED,
   MARINATED BEEF)
CARPACCIO (ITALIAN UNCOOKED BEEF
   PLATTER)
BEEF TENDERLOIN WITH GOAT CHEESE

◇   ◇   ◇

The sagest chefs and most cagey kitchen truants share one point of wisdom. They know when *not* to cook. Just as a hardy stew warms the cockles of the heart in winter, few dishes are more refreshing than steak tartare amid summer's heat. Uncooked beef dishes have long been popular in Europe, and they're beginning to enjoy a heyday in the United States.

Serving raw beef isn't particularly dangerous, but there are some points to keep in mind.

Foremost among them is to serve the best meat money can buy. Unless you have absolute trust in your butcher, buy large cuts of meat and chop them yourself at home. This assures you that the beef has not come in contact with equipment used for grinding pork, which is dangerous, of course, because it may contain trichinae.

I prefer to chop beef by hand, as the food processor tends to mash, not cut, the meat. To slice meat paper-thin either by hand or in the food processor, it helps to *partially* freeze the meat first. Handle the ingredients as little as possible. The heat and salt from your fingertips actually "cook" the meat. In general, raw beef dishes are best assembled at the last minute. Below is an international assortment of uncooked beef dishes.

◇   ◇   ◇

The World's Best Steak Tartare

Steak tartare is the world's most famous raw beef dish. The recipe below comes from the Locke-Ober Cafe, a venerable Boston restaurant where wry sexagenarian waiters prepare it at tableside amid the clubby elegance of a nineteenth-century men's bar. It is perfectly polite, and even a mark of distinction, to ask to prepare your own tartare in a restaurant. Steak tartare is a wonderful party dish.

Serves 6–8 as an appetizer, 3 as a main course

- 1 pound beef tenderloin
- 1 tablespoon A-1 steak sauce
- 1 teaspoon Worcestershire sauce
  juice of 1 lemon
- 2 tablespoons extra-virgin olive oil
- 1 tablespoon brandy
- 1 tablespoon Dijon-style mustard
- 1 raw egg yolk
  salt and plenty of fresh black pepper
- 6 anchovy fillets, finely chopped, plus several fillets, cut in half
  lengthwise, for garnish
- 1 onion, very finely chopped (about 6 tablespoons)
- 3 tablespoons capers, drained
  sprigs of parsley for garnish
  toast points (see below)

1. Trim all fat and sinews off the meat and discard. Chop the beef as finely as possible by hand, in a meat grinder, or food processor. (The processor is the least preferred method, but acceptable results can be obtained by chopping the beef a little at a time, and running the machine in bursts.)

2. Meanwhile, prepare the toast points as described below.

3. Combine the liquid ingredients in a wooden salad bowl and stir them to a smooth paste. Add the meat and remaining ingredients and thoroughly mix with salad forks. Mixing should be done at the last minute and as lightly as possible.

4. To serve, mound the tartare on the toast points to make open-face sandwiches and decorate each with a strip of anchovy and a sprig of parsley. Alternatively, mound the tartare on lettuce leaves on a platter and arrange the toasts around it. (A nice garnish for the latter is a ring of raw onion with a raw egg yolk in the center.) Ale or stout makes a better beverage than wine.

BUTTER-BAKED TOAST POINTS

The simplest dishes are often the hardest to make. Consider, for example, that culinary accessory, the toast point. The toast points served at most restaurants are anemic white bread wilted to a soggy disgrace under a warming lamp. The French are famed for their *croûtes*—crisp, usually deep-fried, bread rounds, as delectable as they are bad for the arteries.

The best toast points I ever tasted, however, were those made by a French pastry chef named Albert Jorant, who brushed them lightly with butter, then baked them crisp in a hot oven. Butter-baking serves equally well for French bread and country-style white.

Makes 24 croûtes

6 thin slices country-style white bread, crusts removed,
　　diagonally cut in quarters, or
1 loaf of French bread, cut diagonally into ⅓-inch slices
4 tablespoons melted butter

Lightly brush the bread slices on both sides with melted butter. Bake them on a hot baking sheet (leave it in the oven) in a preheated oven, turning once, for 15 minutes, or until golden-brown on both sides. (Watch the toasts carefully—they are very quick to burn.) Transfer the toasts to a cake rack to cool (this prevents them from becoming soggy).

VARIATIONS: If destined for bouillabaisse, the croûtes could be brushed with olive oil and rubbed with a cut clove of garlic after baking. To make croutons, simply cut the bread into 1-inch pieces and toss them with melted butter. The crispness of these toast points makes them ideal for floating on soups.

YUK HWE

KOREAN UNCOOKED MARINATED BEEF

Most nations have a version of steak tartare, proving the universal appeal of raw beef. The Korean rendition, called *yuk hwe* (pronounced "you-kway"), is flavored with sesame oil and hot chili oil, both available at Oriental grocery stores.

Serves 4–6

1 pound beef tenderloin

FOR THE MARINADE:

2 tablespoons sugar
4 tablespoons dark soy sauce
4 tablespoons finely chopped scallions
1–2 cloves garlic, minced
2 teaspoons freshly grated ginger root (or to taste)
2 tablespoons sesame oil
1 teaspoon hot chili oil

FOR SERVING:

    1 raw egg yolk
    3 tablespoons toasted sesame seeds
  12 lettuce leaves (washed and dried), or butter-baked toast
         points (see recipe on page 215)

1. Trim all fat and sinew from the beef and discard. Cut the beef into julienne (matchstick-like slivers). To do so, cut the beef across the grain into ⅛-inch slices. Stack these slices flat on the cutting board, and cut them again into ⅛-inch slivers.

2. Combine the ingredients for the marinade. Stir in the meat and marinate it in the refrigerator for 20 minutes.

3. To serve, mound the *yuk hwe* on a lettuce leaf in the center of a platter. Make a depression in the center and in it place the raw egg yolk. Sprinkle on the sesame seeds. Arrange the remaining lettuce leaves around the beef. Let each guest roll up the beef in a lettuce leaf and pop it into his mouth.

Note: To toast sesame seeds, see page 132.

CARPACCIO
ITALIAN UNCOOKED BEEF PLATTER

Carpaccio is an Italian version of steak tartare, supposedly invented at Harry's Bar in Venice for a customer who could not eat cooked beef. The secret lies in slicing the meat as thinly as possible; this is facilitated by partially freezing it.

Serves 4

  1 pound beef tenderloin
  5 tablespoons extra-virgin olive oil
     juice of 1 large lemon, plus lemon wedges for garnish
     plenty of salt and fresh black pepper
  2 tablespoons very finely chopped shallots
  2 tablespoons very finely chopped parsley
  2 tablespoons very finely chopped scallions
  2 tablespoons very finely chopped fresh tarragon, basil, or
     other fresh herb
  2 tablespoon capers
  2 tablespoons green peppercorns, lightly crushed with the
     side of a knife

1. Trim all fat and sinew from the beef and discard. Slice the meat as thinly as possible and spread it out on four chilled dinner plates. Sprinkle

each plate with the remaining ingredients. Wait 5 minutes before serving (keep the plates in the refrigerator) to let the flavors mellow. Garnish with lemon wedges. (See page 128 for instructions on how to cut proper wedges.)

BEEF TENDERLOIN WITH GOAT CHEESE

Chèvre, French goat cheese, has become the Brie cheese of the eighties. This unusual appetizer is best made with soft, tangy goat cheese, like lingot, pyramide, or montrachet. This recipe was inspired by Odette Bery, owner of Another Season restaurant on Boston's Beacon Hill.

Makes 20 pieces

¾ pound beef tenderloin
½ pound French goat cheese
4 tablespoons extra-virgin olive oil
juice of 1 lemon (or to taste)
salt and fresh black pepper

Cut the beef into paper-thin slices and the cheese into finger-sized cork shapes. Wrap each piece of cheese in a slice of raw beef, and secure it with a toothpick. Just before serving, sprinkle the beef with *plenty* of olive oil, lemon juice, salt, and pepper.

L E S S O N 3 4

Sweetbreads

◇

Techniques:
DISGORGING SWEETBREADS
BLANCHING SWEETBREADS
COOKING SWEETBREADS

Master Recipe:
BRAISED SWEETBREADS WITH BACON,
  WILD MUSHROOMS, AND OLIVES

Variations:
GRILLED SWEETBREADS WITH MALTAISE
  SAUCE
PAN-FRIED SWEETBREADS WITH LEMON
  AND CAPERS

◇ ◇ ◇

M ost people regard sweetbreads with suspicion, if not outright hostility. This is a shame, because few foods are more delectable or unique. Sweetbreads have a fine, delicate flavor, and firm yet creamy consistency. They have been erroneously identified as brains, pancreas, or even testicles. They are in fact the thymus (a growth gland), which explains why they are found in calves and lambs but not in full-grown steer or sheep. A whole sweetbread consists of two lobes, one smooth and round, the other narrow and veined. The former, called the "nut" or "kernel," is the more desirable. (Sweetbreads are hard to find in many communities. You might try ordering fresh ones from a reputable butcher at least one week ahead.)

Sweetbreads can be braised, sautéed, or grilled, but they must be conscientiously washed, blanched, and trimmed beforehand. The first step is called "disgorging." The sweetbreads are rinsed, then soaked in several changes of cold water for 2 hours. The best way to disgorge sweetbreads is to place them in a bowl in the sink under the faucet, and let a thin stream

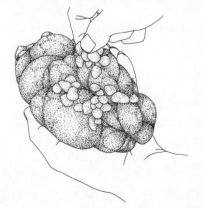

of cold water trickle continuously into the bowl. (Make certain that nothing blocks the drain!) Alternatively, change the soaking water every 20–30 minutes. Disgorging is important, because it helps remove the blood from the organ.

The next step is blanching. Place the sweetbreads in cold water to cover and bring them gradually to a boil. Reduce heat, simmer for 5 minutes, and drain. Blanching partially cooks the sweetbreads and removes surface impurities. Place the sweetbreads between two plates, the top one weighted with a small saucepan, and let them cool. Weighting gives the sweetbreads a nice oval shape.

The last step is to trim the sweetbreads. Using your fingers or a small paring knife, carefully remove any gristly ducts, lumps of fat, blood vessels, or dark spots. Separate any large sweetbreads into individual lobes. Do *not* peel off the fine membrane covering the individual lobes: it is needed to hold the sweetbreads together during cooking. You are now ready to try one of the recipes below.

◇   ◇   ◇

Braised Sweetbreads with Bacon, Wild Mushrooms, and Olives

This dish is actually an adaptation of an eighteenth-century dish served with a belly-bludgeoning garnish of truffles, tiny veal dumplings, and even cocks' combs. Use whatever fresh wild mushrooms are in season; if these are unavailable, use white mushrooms.

Serves 4

1½ pounds veal sweetbreads
    salt and fresh black pepper
    flour for dredging
3 tablespoons butter

FOR THE BRAISING MIXTURE:

2 ounces prosciutto or smoked ham, diced
1 onion, diced
1 carrot, diced
1 rib celery, diced
1 clove garlic, minced
2 cups brown stock, or to cover
    bouquet garni

FOR THE GARNISH:

> ¼ pound lean slab bacon, or Smithfield or smoked ham
> 2 tablespoons butter
> 6 ounces fresh chanterelle, shiitake, or other wild
>   mushrooms, or white mushrooms
> 1 cup pitted black olives
> 8 toast points (optional—see recipe on 215)
> 4 tablespoons chopped parsley

TO FINISH THE SAUCE:

> ¼ cup heavy cream
> 2 teaspoons cornstarch
> 3 tablespoons Madeira

1. Disgorge, blanch, trim, and press the sweetbreads as described above.

2. Season the sweetbreads with salt and pepper and dust them with flour, shaking off the excess. Heat the butter in a nonaluminum, non–cast-iron frying pan over a medium-high heat and brown the sweetbreads on all sides. Transfer them to a platter.

3. Add the ham and vegetables to the pan and sauté until lightly browned. Return the sweetbreads to the pan, add the stock and *bouquet garni,* and bring the liquid to a boil. Cover the pan and braise in a preheated 350° oven or over a low flame for 30–40 minutes, or until tender. The recipe can be prepared ahead to this stage.

4. Meanwhile, prepare the garnish: cut the bacon into 1-inch-by-¼-inch-by-¼-inch slivers. Melt the butter and fry the bacon until golden brown but not too crisp. Drain on paper towels. (If using ham, cook it the same way.) Discard all but 2 tablespoons of the fat from the pan.

5. Gently wash the mushrooms, discarding dirty stems, cutting the larger mushrooms into quarters or halves. Sauté the mushrooms over high heat in the reserved bacon fat until soft, about 1 minute. Drain the mushrooms, pouring any juices into the sweetbreads.

6. Place the olives in a saucepan with cold water to cover, boil for 2 minutes, and drain. Prepare the toast points. The garnishes can be prepared ahead to this stage.

7. Prepare the sauce: transfer the sweetbreads to a platter or cutting board and keep warm. Strain the cooking liquid from the sweetbreads into a saucepan, pressing hard to extract the juices from the vegetables. Add the cream and bring the sauce to a boil. Dissolve the cornstarch in the Madeira, and whisk it into the boiling sauce. Correct the seasoning with salt and pepper.

8. To serve, cut the sweetbreads diagonally into ¼-inch slices. Add the garnishes to the sauce and simmer just long enough to heat them. Arrange

the sweetbreads with the toast points on warmed dinner plates or a platter and spoon the sauce and the garnish on top. Sprinkle with parsley.

Serving: This dish deserves your best wine: a Richebourg, Romanée-Conti, Echézeaux, or Heitz "Martha's Vineyard" Cabernet Sauvignon.

Note: Chicken or veal chops are excellent braised as described above.

GRILLED SWEETBREADS WITH
MALTAISE SAUCE

I first tasted grilled sweetbreads at a bistro in Paris called Nicholas. The crumbs should be fresh, as dried ones will brown too much during grilling. (For a full discussion of breading, see pages 63–64.)

Serves 4

1½ pounds sweetbreads
   salt and fresh black pepper
 1 cup flour
 2 eggs, beaten
 1 cup fresh bread crumbs
 ¼ cup melted butter
   Maltaise Sauce (see recipe on page 198)

 8 bamboo or metal skewers

1. Disgorge, blanch, trim, and press the sweetbreads as described above.

2. Cut the sweetbreads into 1-inch cubes, and season with salt and pepper. Dip each cube in flour, shaking off excess, then in egg, and finally in bread crumbs. Thread the cubes on skewers. It is best not to bread the sweetbreads more than 10 minutes ahead.

3. Grill the sweetbreads over coals or under the broiler, for 3–4 minutes per side, or until nicely browned, basting with melted butter. Set the grill rather far away from the coals so that the sweetbreads cook without burning the crumbs. Alternatively, lightly brown the sweetbreads on all sides in butter and bake them in a preheated 350° oven for 10–15 minutes. Serve the grilled sweetbreads on a bed of rice pilaf (see recipe on page 267), with the Maltaise sauce on the side.

PAN-FRIED SWEETBREADS WITH
LEMON AND CAPERS

Capers are the buds of a small, trailing shrub that are pickled in brine. The small ones have a better flavor than the large ones.

Serves 4

1½ pounds sweetbreads
 1 cup seasoned flour (see page 128)
 5 tablespoons clarified butter, or a half-and-half mixture of
     butter and oil
   juice of 1 lemon
 4 tablespoons capers
   salt and fresh black pepper
   lemon wedges (see page 128) and sprigs of parsley for
     garnish

1. Disgorge, blanch, trim, and press the sweetbreads as described above.

2. Cut the sweetbreads on the diagonal into ¼-inch slices. Just before cooking, dip each slice in seasoned flour and shake off the excess. Heat the butter or butter and oil in a large frying pan. Sauté the sweetbread slices over medium heat for 5–6 minutes per side or until golden brown. Transfer the slices to a warm platter or plates. Add the lemon juice and capers to the hot pan, bring just to a boil, and pour this mixture over the sweetbreads. Sprinkle lightly with salt and pepper and garnish with lemon wedges and parsley. Serve immediately.

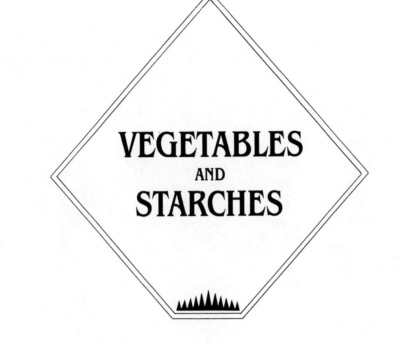

VEGETABLES
AND
STARCHES

Human history can be charted by the broad swings of revolution and counterrevolution. The same is true of the evolution of cooking. Consider the vegetable. For countless decades, vegetables were regarded with the utmost distrust, deemed unsafe to eat until they'd been boiled to olive-drab mush. Then in the early seventies, these garden denizens were vindicated by the vegetarian movement on college campuses in the United States and by *la nouvelle cuisine* in France.

For almost the first time in history, chefs took pains to preserve the pristine crunch of green beans, the moist crispness of the zucchini. Root vegetables were reduced to matchstick slivers before you could say *julienne.* (The advent of the food processor helped.) But like the "Terror" of the French Revolution, the vegetable movement had its frenzied extremists. Within no time, both hands were required to cut into a string bean, and carrots and broccoli were not being served merely *al dente* but actually raw.

We at the Taste of the Mountains urge moderation in all things, including cooking. Vegetables *are* important, and they should be cooked with restraint and sensitivity to preserve their freshness. At the same time, if human beings had been intended to eat vegetables raw, they would have been furnished with four-chambered stomachs like cows. This section covers the various methods of cooking vegetables—boiling, steaming, stir-frying, and braising, as well as how to handle some of the lesser-known vegetables, like Jerusalem artichokes and fiddlehead ferns.

◇　◇　◇

Green Vegetables

◇

Techniques:

BOILING GREEN BEANS

COOKING FIDDLEHEAD FERNS

STEAMING KALE

Master Recipe:

GREEN BEANS WITH SHALLOTS AND
COUNTRY HAM

Variations:

GREEN BEANS WITH SUN-DRIED
TOMATOES

FIDDLEHEAD FERNS WITH LEMON AND
BUTTER

STIR-FRIED FIDDLEHEADS WITH
CORIANDER AND HONEY

KALE STEAMED WITH ORIENTAL
FLAVORINGS

◇   ◇   ◇

Boiling and steaming are the easiest ways to cook green vegetables, and a preliminary step for glazing or braising root vegetables. Being French-trained, I favor the former, which consists of cooking the vegetable in plenty of rapidly boiling, heavily salted water until crispy-tender. There are many key words in this seemingly simple definition.

By plenty I mean at least 3 quarts of water for 1 pound of vegetables. Like pasta, vegetables require lots of water, or they become mushy and lose their bright color. Green vegetables (and vegetables that grow above the ground in general) go directly into rapidly boiling water. Root vegetables go into cold water and are brought to a boil gradually.

Boiling water "fixes" the color and texture of green vegetables. Starting with cold water allows the starches naturally found in root vegetables to expand gradually, preventing a mealy consistency at the end.

Salt is important because it not only preserves but intensifies the color of green vegetables and carrots. By "heavily salted" I mean 2 teaspoons per quart of water (don't worry, by the time the vegetable is refreshed under cold water, it won't taste salty at all). Crispy-tender describes the degree of doneness of a vegetable the way *al dente* describes pasta. It is not a question of cooking a string bean for exactly two minutes or three minutes— rather, it is a question of continually tasting the vegetable (run it under cold water so you don't burn your tongue) until you have reached the proper texture. By crispy-tender we mean completely cooked yet ever-so-slightly crisp or resilient when bitten.

The vegetable can be served as soon as it is crispy-tender. (Toss it with a little butter or extra-virgin olive oil, lemon juice, fresh black pepper, and fresh chopped parsley or other herbs.) But in most cases it is easier to "refresh" the vegetable and reheat it prior to serving. To refresh a vegetable, we drain it thoroughly in a colander and run it under cold water until *completely* cool. Refreshing prevents overcooking; once refreshed, a vegetable can be held up to 24 hours before serving. To reheat the vegetable we sauté it in butter or oil, steam it, or return it quickly to boiling water.

Steaming is similar to boiling, except that we use very little water and the vegetables are cooked on a rack. Steaming has the virtue of removing fewer vitamins than boiling and is ideal for leafy vegetables like spinach or kale.

Green Beans with Shallots and Country Ham

This dish is inspired by a specialty of the *Landes,* a flat, wooded plain south of Bordeaux. It is equally delicious made with an uncooked ham like prosciutto or Smithfield, or a smoked cooked ham, like Harrington ham, which is made in Vermont. When buying green beans, select the smallest, firmest beans you can find.

Serves 6

1½ pounds green beans
    salt
3–4 tablespoons olive oil or butter
  3 ounces uncooked or smoked country-style ham of the best
      quality, diced as finely as possible
  4 tablespoons minced shallots
  1 clove garlic, minced (or to taste)
  4 tablespoons finely chopped fresh parsley
    fresh black pepper
    salt to taste

1. Snap the stems off the beans, pulling out any strings. Cook the beans in 3 quarts rapidly boiling, heavily salted water for 2–3 minutes, or until crispy-tender. Refresh under cold running water till cool. The beans can be prepared up to 6 hours ahead to this stage.

2. Just before serving, heat the oil in a large frying pan. Sauté the ham for 30 seconds. Add the shallots and garlic and sauté another 30 seconds. Add the beans, parsley, pepper, and, perhaps, a little salt (the ham is quite salty), and cook the beans over medium heat for 1–2 minutes, or until completely warmed and coated with garnish. Green beans prepared this way are an excellent accompaniment to lamb.

VARIATIONS: Any green vegetable—asparagus, broccoli, fiddlehead ferns— can be prepared this way. Instead of using ham, you could use bacon, pancetta, smoked beef, or pepperoni. Olive oil will give you a Mediterranean flavor; butter, a Northern European one.

GREEN BEANS WITH SUN-DRIED TOMATOES: Carol Powers has been a close friend and tireless assistant in my classes since 1981. She makes the above recipe using sun-dried tomatoes (see page 140) in place of the ham, adding a few drops of lemon juice at the end.

◇   ◇   ◇

FIDDLEHEAD FERNS

The backwoods of New Hampshire hold a special surprise for students of the spring session of Taste of the Mountains. Each May, thousands of ostrich ferns begin to unfurl their leafy crowns, producing a delicacy—fiddlehead ferns. The ferns resemble a bishop's crozier or the scrolled head of a violin (whence the name), and their taste suggests spinach, asparagus, and okra. The season lasts a mere three weeks, for the ferns must be tightly curled when eaten.

Fiddlehead ferns have more than their unusual flavor to recommend them: they contain twice as much vitamin A as string beans, more iron than beet greens, and substantial amounts of vitamin C, niacin, and potassium. Thanks to air freight, fiddlehead ferns are available in specialty markets in most major cities.

FIDDLEHEAD FERNS WITH LEMON AND BUTTER

The first time you try fiddlehead ferns, cook them this simple way, to appreciate their unique flavor. If fiddleheads are unavailable, substitute asparagus or green beans, and adjust the cooking times accordingly.

Serves 4

1 pound fresh fiddlehead ferns
salt
2–3 tablespoons butter
fresh black pepper
a few drops fresh lemon juice

1. Wash in several bowls of cold water and pick through the fiddleheads, discarding any brown husks. Cut off any discolored ends. Cook the fiddleheads in 3 quarts rapidly boiling, heavily salted water for 2–3 minutes or until crispy-tender. If serving at once, toss the ferns with butter, pepper, and a *little* lemon juice.

If you wish to prepare the fiddleheads ahead of time, cook as described above, refresh under cold water, and drain. Just before serving, sauté the ferns in butter until thoroughly heated.

FIDDLEHEADS WITH HOLLANDAISE SAUCE: Cook the fiddleheads in rapidly boiling, salted water till crispy-tender. Serve them with the Hollandaise Sauce on page 197.

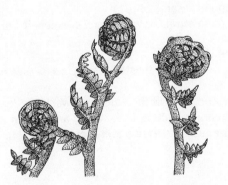

STIR-FRIED FIDDLEHEADS
WITH CORIANDER AND HONEY

Coriander is a pungent spice used in making pickles and curry. It takes its name from the Greek *koris,* meaning "bedbug"—a reference to the odd "buggy" odor of the leaves of the coriander plant.

Serves 4

1 pound fiddlehead ferns
1 tablespoon vegetable oil
1 tablespoon sesame oil
½ teaspoon ground coriander
1 tablespoon honey, dissolved in 2 tablespoons boiling water
   salt and fresh black pepper

1. Clean and trim the fiddleheads as described above. Heat the oils in a wok. Stir-fry the fiddleheads with the coriander over high heat for 1 minute. Add the honey water and cook the ferns for 1–2 minutes more, or until tender. Season with salt and pepper and serve at once.

KALE STEAMED WITH ORIENTAL FLAVORINGS

Kale is a perfect food for the health-conscious eighties. Its broad, crimped leaves are low in calories and rich in vitamins A and C. It is popular in Portugal, where it is used to make "green soup"—and in our own Deep South, where it is simmered with vinegar and bacon. The best way to cook kale (and other leafy vegetables) is by steaming. The smaller the leaves, the more tender.

Serves 4

1 pound kale
2 tablespoons dark soy sauce
1 tablespoon sesame oil
1 tablespoon *mirin* (or white wine sweetened with a little
   sugar)
   juice of ½ lemon
4 tablespoons lightly toasted sesame seeds (see page 132)

Cut the stems and ribs off the kale, and wash the leaves in cold water. Place kale in a steamer with ½ inch water, and steam for 4–5 minutes or until the leaves are tender. Do not overcook. Just before serving, stir in the seasonings.

LESSON 36

Glazed Root Vegetables

◇

Techniques:
GLAZING VEGETABLES
TURNING VEGETABLES
MAKING CARROT FLOWERS

Master Recipe:
GLAZED CARROTS

Variations:
CARROTS GLAZED IN GRAND MARNIER
GLAZED SCALLIONS
TURNIPS GLAZED IN CIDER

◇   ◇   ◇

Colorful mounds of glazed vegetables—all trimmed into neat ovals and shining with butter and sugar—make a bright accompaniment to a roast. Glazing is well suited to most root vegetables, especially carrots and turnips. The principle is simple enough: the vegetable is parboiled in water or fruit juice and then cooked over high heat with butter and sugar. The sugar caramelizes with the vegetable juices, forming a syrupy glaze. Take care to keep the vegetables crisp and not to burn the sugar.

Traditionally, vegetables to be glazed are "turned;" that is, whittled into neat, seven-sided ovals, which enables them to roll easily in the syrup. Turning vegetables is one of the many ways French chefs have tortured their apprentices, making them reduce seemingly endless quantities of root vegetables into mountains of tiny footballs. The process is not as wasteful as it seems, because you can save the scraps for stocks or soups. Alternatively, carrots and similarly shaped vegetables can be cut into "flowers," as explained below.

Turning Carrots:

1. Peel the carrot and cut it into 1-inch slices. Cut any thick slices lengthwise into 2 or 3 pieces. (Turnips and other round vegetables must be cut into 1-by-¾-inch boxes for turning.)

2. If you are right-handed, hold each piece in your left hand, pinched between your thumb and forefinger. Hold a sharp paring knife by the base of the blade in your right hand. Starting at the top end, pulling the blade toward your thumb, cut an arc-shaped slice off the side of the carrot. The cut part of the carrot should look rounded like the side of a barrel. Rotate the carrot slightly and cut off another arc-shaped piece. Continue rotating and cutting until you are back where you started. You should wind up with an olive-shaped piece with flat top and bottom. (Turned vegetables traditionally have seven sides.) The trick lies in keeping the top and bottom flat, so that the carrot can be tightly grasped as it pivots. Once you get the hang of it, turning vegetables goes more quickly. This method is used for a variety of root vegetables.

Cutting Carrot "Flowers":

Peel the carrot. Using a fluting knife, cut parallel grooves the length of the carrot, spaced ¼ inch apart. Now, cut the carrot widthwise into ¼-inch slices. Each slice should look like a petaled flower.

Glazed Carrots

This recipe can be used for glazing any root vegetable. Turning is optional, but the pieces should be of uniform size to ensure even cooking.

Serves 4

> 1 pound carrots, peeled, turned, cut into flowers (see
> instructions, page 234), or simply cut into uniform pieces
> salt and fresh black pepper
> 2–3 tablespoons granulated sugar or brown sugar
> 2–3 tablespoons butter
> 1 tablespoon chopped fresh herbs, such as parsley, chives,
> tarragon, and/or chervil

1. Place the carrots in a heavy saucepan in cold water to cover with salt, pepper and 1 tablespoon sugar. Cook carrots over high heat for 5 minutes, or until they are crispy-tender but more on the crisp side. (Carrot flowers will cook more quickly than turned carrots.) Refresh the carrots under cold water and drain. Blot the carrots dry. This step can be done up to 24 hours ahead.

2. Melt the butter with the remaining sugar in the saucepan. Add the carrots, and cook over high heat, stirring with a wooden spoon, for 1–2 minutes or until the butter and sugar caramelize, coating the carrots with syrupy glaze. Carrots can also be cooked ahead to this stage and rewarmed, but be extra careful not to overcook them. Toss with chopped herbs before serving.

Note: Baby onions, rutabagas (yellow turnips), parsnips, and chestnuts are glazed the same way. If you are serving more than one vegetable (and you should), glaze them separately, as the cooking time differs for each.

◇　◇　◇

CARROTS GLAZED IN GRAND MARNIER: Follow the previous recipe to step 2, cooking the carrots a minute less. Combine the butter, sugar, and 2 tablespoons Grand Marnier in the saucepan and glaze the carrots in this mixture. Chopped fresh tarragon makes a nice garnish. You could also use an *eau-de-vie* such as calvados (French apple brandy) in place of Grand Marnier.

GLAZED SCALLIONS

Serves 4–6

4 bunches scallions
salt
2 tablespoons butter
2 teaspoons sugar
fresh black pepper

1. Discard the top 3 inches of the scallions and the root end. Peel off any dried outside leaves, and cut the scallions into 2-inch lengths. Tie these into small bundles with string, to prevent the scallions from falling apart.

2. Cook the scallions in rapidly boiling, salted water for 1 minute. Discard the strings, refresh under cold water, and drain. Just before serving, melt the butter in a large skillet with the sugar and pepper. Cook the scallions over high heat for 2–3 minutes or until glazed and hot.

Glazed scallions go well with chicken.

TURNIPS GLAZED IN CIDER

In this recipe we cook the turnips in apple cider instead of water. Because we are using a limited amount of liquid, there is no need to drain and refresh the vegetables before glazing.

Serves 4

1 pound baby turnips, peeled, or large turnips cut into 1-inch
    ovals
approximately ¾ cup apple cider (enough just barely to
    cover the turnips)
salt and freshly ground black pepper
2 tablespoons butter
2 tablespoons sugar

Combine all the ingredients in a saucepan and cook over high heat for 6–8 minutes or until the cider has evaporated. The turnips should be soft and coated with syrupy glaze. If the turnips are still too firm, it may be necessary to add more cider.

LESSON 37

Braised Vegetables

◇

◇ ◇ ◇

As we saw in Lesson 18, braising is a moist cooking method well suited to cooking fibrous foods. Thus, braising is ideal for such stringy vegetables as celery, Belgian endive, and leeks, not to mention strong-flavored vegetables, like cabbage. The procedure is much the same as for braising meats, except that instead of browning the vegetable first, we blanch it in boiling water. The braising liquid can be served as sauce: boil it down to coating consistency and strain. Braised vegetables make a delicious accompaniment to roasts.

◇ ◇ ◇

Braised Belgian Endive

Endive is a compact, white, cylindrical vegetable with an intriguing bitter flavor. Most of the world's crop comes from Belgium—whence the name. Use a glass or earthenware dish to minimize discoloration.

Serves 4–6

1½ pounds Belgian endive
salt
juice of ½ lemon
3 tablespoons butter
1 small onion, finely chopped
1 carrot, finely chopped
1 branch celery, finely chopped
1 clove garlic, minced
2 ounces cooked ham, preferably prosciutto, finely chopped
freshly ground black pepper
¾ cup brown stock (see recipe on page 25)
bouquet garni
3 tablespoons chopped fresh parsley (for garnish—optional)

1. Discard any brown or wilted leaves from the endive and trim away any brown or tough spots. Cut a small X through the base—this fosters even cooking. Blanch the endive in rapidly boiling, heavily salted water with the lemon juice for 1 minute and drain.

2. Melt the butter in a small frying pan over medium heat. Add the chopped vegetables, the garlic and ham and sauté for 3–5 minutes, or until the vegetables are soft and just beginning to brown. Spread the vegetables in a baking dish just large enough to hold the endive. Arrange the endive on top. Add a little salt, the pepper, stock, and *bouquet garni*—the stock should come halfway up the sides of the endive. Press a piece of buttered foil or parchment on top of the endive and cover the pan with a lid. This recipe can be prepared up to 12 hours ahead to this stage.

3. Bake the endive in a preheated 400° oven for 30 minutes or until tender. If too much stock evaporates, add more. To serve, transfer the endive to a warm platter. Boil the braising liquid in a small saucepan until 5–6 tablespoons liquid remain. Adjust the seasoning and strain this liquid over the endive. Garnish with chopped parsley.

◇　◇　◇

BRAISED LEEKS: Prepare as described above, using 2 to 2½ pounds leeks. Figure on 2 leeks, each ½ to ¾ inch in diameter, per person. Cut off the dark green tops and the roots and wash as described on page 29. Before blanching, tie the leeks with string to prevent them from falling apart. Braise for 20 minutes, or until the leeks are tender.

BRAISED CELERY: Prepare as described above, using 2 pounds of celery. Cut off the leafy tops and the base. Peel the celery with a vegetable peeler to remove the strings, and cut the stalks into 3-inch lengths. Bake for 25 minutes, or until the stalks are tender. Serves 6–8.

BRAISED CABBAGE

Most varieties of cabbage can be braised. I am especially partial to Savoy cabbage, which is distinguished by its light-green, ruffled leaves. Juniper berries have the clean, pungent flavor one associates with gin, of which they are the primary flavoring. (Indeed, our term "gin" comes from the French *genévrier,* for juniper.) This dish could be turned into a main course by adding whole smoked sausages, such as knockwurst or kielbasa.

Serves 6

1 medium head Savoy or other green cabbage
¼ pound heavily smoked bacon or kielbasa, diced
1 onion, finely chopped
1 branch celery, finely chopped
1 clove garlic, minced
¼ cup dry white wine
½ cup brown stock
6 juniper berries or ¼ cup gin
bouquet garni containing 3 cloves
salt and fresh black pepper

1. Slice the cabbage in half through the stem. Make a V-shaped cut on either side of the stem to remove the core. Cut the cabbage crosswise into ½-inch strips.

2. Render the bacon in a large casserole over medium heat, but do not let it brown. Discard all but 3 tablespoons fat. Add the onions and celery, and cook for 2–3 minutes or until the onion softens. Stir in the garlic and cook for 30 seconds. Add the cabbage and stir over medium heat until all the pieces are coated with fat. Add the wine and bring it to a boil. Stir in the remaining ingredients and cover the casserole. The recipe can be prepared ahead to this stage.

3. Bake the cabbage in a preheated 400° oven for 40 minutes or until the cabbage is soft. If the cabbage dries out, add more stock. If it is too moist, leave the pan uncovered for the last 10 minutes to evaporate the excess liquid. Remove the *bouquet garni* before serving.

LESSON 38

Vegetable Gratins

◇

Techniques:

MAKING GRATINS

MAKING WHITE SAUCE AND MORNAY
 SAUCE

Master Recipe:

GRATIN DAUPHINOIS

Variations:

GRATIN OF BROCCOLI AND CAULIFLOWER

FENNEL GRATIN

◇   ◇   ◇

Like most people, I'm a sucker for any dish made with butter, cream, and potatoes. Nothing is surer to bring a smile to my lips than *gratin dauphinois* (bubbling *gratin* potatoes). I have a great recipe (given below) that I often prepare; and once, when I was out of potatoes, I tried it with yams. "The discovery of a new dish does more for human happiness than the discovery of a new star," observed the French epicure Brillat-Savarin, and in this case I had discovered not only a new dish but a whole new way of cooking vegetables.

Gratins represent a process ideally suited to a wide range of root vegetables. The vegetable is parboiled and then layered with salt, pepper, nutmeg, and cheese in an ovenproof baking dish. Heavy cream is poured over the whole to keep the ingredients moist. As a gratin bakes in the oven, the cheese melts, forming a thick, golden-brown crust on top. This crust is the best part, and it must be patiently scraped from the corners of the pan. This is how gratins got their name, for the French word for "to scratch" or "scrape" is *gratter.*

◇   ◇   ◇

Gratin Dauphinois
GRATIN POTATOES

The Dauphinois is a hilly region in France that borders Switzerland and is famous for its baking cheeses, like Gruyère and Comté. There are as many recipes for gratin potatoes as there are cookbooks: this one comes from chef Fernand Chambrette, former owner of the Boule d'Or restaurant in Paris. The potatoes are boiled in milk to make them sweeter.

Serves 6

    6 large baking potatoes
    2 cups milk
    1 clove garlic, cut
    4 tablespoons butter, melted
      salt and freshly ground black pepper
      freshly grated nutmeg
1–1½ cups grated Gruyère cheese
1–1½ cups heavy cream

    1 10-inch gratin dish (traditionally of earthenware, but glass or heavy metal will do)

1. Peel the potatoes and cut them into ⅛-inch slices. Place them in a heavy saucepan with the milk and enough water to cover. Gradually bring the potatoes to a boil, reduce heat, and simmer for 5–6 minutes, or until the potato slices are partially, but not completely, cooked. Stir the potatoes from time to time, lest the ones on the bottom stick and burn. Pour into a colander and drain.

2. Meanwhile, rub the gratin dish thoroughly with garlic and brush it with melted butter. Arrange a layer of potato slices in the bottom of the dish and sprinkle with salt, pepper, nutmeg (used very sparingly), grated cheese, and some melted butter. Continue layering the potatoes with the seasonings, cheese, and butter, reserving ¼ cup cheese and 2 tablespoons butter for the top. Pour the cream over the top, and sprinkle with the remaining cheese and butter. The gratin can be prepared to this stage up to 24 hours ahead. Just be sure to remove it from the refrigerator and bring it to room temperature before baking, lest the sudden heat shatter the glass.

3. Bake the gratin in a preheated 400° oven for 30 minutes or until the potatoes are soft, the cream is bubbling, and the cheese on top is golden brown. (If necessary, run the gratin under the broiler to thoroughly brown the top.) Allow it to set for 5 minutes before serving.

GRATIN OF BROCCOLI AND CAULIFLOWER

The rich cheese sauce in this recipe goes well with the musky flavor of broccoli and cauliflower. For a dramatic visual effect, alternate rows of jade-green broccoli with rows of pearly cauliflower. Notes on making flour-thickened sauces are found on page 157.

Serves 8

1 head broccoli
1 head cauliflower
  salt
3 tablespoons melted butter for the gratin dish and for the
    broccoli

FOR THE MORNAY SAUCE:

  3 tablespoons butter
  3 tablespoons flour
1¾ cups milk
  1 teaspoon Dijon-style mustard
  1 cup grated Gruyère or cheddar cheese
    salt, white pepper, cayenne pepper
    freshly grated nutmeg

1. Cut the broccoli and cauliflower into florets. (Cut the stem off quite close to the flowering part; the floret must be able to stand upright.) Cook each vegetable separately in rapidly boiling, salted water until crispy-tender. Refresh under cold water and drain. Use 1 tablespoon of the butter to coat an ovenproof gratin dish or baking platter.

2. Prepare the sauce. Melt the butter in a saucepan over high heat. Stir in the flour and cook for 3 minutes to make a roux. Add the milk off the heat, and, whisking constantly, bring it to a boil. Simmer the sauce for 3 minutes. Remove the pan from the heat and whisk in the mustard and cheese followed by the seasonings—the sauce should be quite spicy. NOTE: Do not boil the sauce once the cheese has been added, or it will become stringy.

3. Spread half the sauce on the platter. Arrange the vegetables in rows by color. Spoon the remaining sauce on top of the cauliflower; do not spoon any of the sauce on the broccoli or you will spoil the striped effect. Brush the broccoli with melted butter. The gratin can be prepared ahead to this stage.

4. Just before serving, bake the gratin in a preheated 400° oven for 10 minutes or until the vegetables are hot and the sauce bubbly.

FENNEL GRATIN

Fennel is a bulbous root in the celery family, and it tastes like licorice. Popular with Italians (ask for *finocchio* in an Italian market), fennel is in season in late April. The leaves look like dill sprigs and can be hung upside down and dried. (Toss them on hot coals when grilling fish.)

Serves 6–8

> 3 large bulbs fennel, green stalks removed
> salt
> 2 ounces *pancetta* (Italian bacon), or regular bacon, cut into
> ¼-inch slivers
> 1 clove garlic, cut
> salt and fresh black pepper
> freshly grated nutmeg
> 1 cup grated Gruyère cheese
> 1 cup heavy cream

1. Cut the fennel widthwise into ¼-inch slices and cook in rapidly boiling, heavily salted water for 3 minutes or until crispy-tender. Drain and refresh under cold running water until cool. Blot dry.

2. Render the bacon fat in a large skillet, and remove the lightly browned bacon pieces with a slotted spoon and reserve them. Discard all but 3 tablespoons fat. Increase heat to high, and lightly brown the fennel slices on both sides in two or three batches.

3. Rub a 10-inch gratin dish with cut garlic, and arrange a layer of fennel on the bottom. Sprinkle with salt, pepper, freshly grated nutmeg, some of the cheese, and some of the bacon. Arrange another layer of fennel on top, and add more flavorings. Repeat until all the ingredients are used up, except for a handful of cheese. Pour the cream over the fennel. Sprinkle the remaining cheese on top. The gratin can be prepared to this stage up to 24 hours ahead of time.

4. Just before serving, bake the gratin in a preheated 400° oven for 20 minutes or until the fennel is well-heated and the cheese on top is bubbly and browned.

LESSON 39

Vegetable Purees

◇

Technique:
PUREEING VEGETABLES

Master Recipe:
BROCCOLI PUREE

Variations:
SWEET POTATO PUREE
CELERY ROOT PUREE
RED CABBAGE PUREE

◇   ◇   ◇

Vegetable purees can be as simple as cafeteria mashed potatoes . . . or as exotic as a celery root puree. To the cynic they may seem like glorified baby food. To me they are the apotheosis, the Platonic Ideal of the commonplace garden vegetable.

Vegetable purees are made by boiling vegetables in salted water, stock, or milk and pureeing them through a sieve or in a food processor. The sieve produces a finer result, because it eliminates coarse vegetable fibers. The food processor is infinitely quicker and easier to clean, and unless you are extremely fussy, it will produce a very acceptable puree. Purees made from stringy vegetables, like leeks or celery, should be forced through a sieve. Watery vegetables, like mushrooms and green beans, are often cooked and pureed with potatoes to give them extra body. Fruits make an interesting addition to many vegetable purees, like apples with cabbage or pears with spinach.

I like to serve several different-colored vegetable purees at once, creating the effect of a painter's palate. Use a wet soupspoon for mounding the various purees, as pictured here.

GUIDELINES FOR MAKING VEGETABLE PUREES

1. Chop the vegetables as finely as possible. (Because this reduces their surface area, they cook quickly and evenly without overcooking.) Cook white vegetables in a half-and-half mixture of milk and water to preserve their whiteness. Use plenty of salt for all other vegetables to preserve their

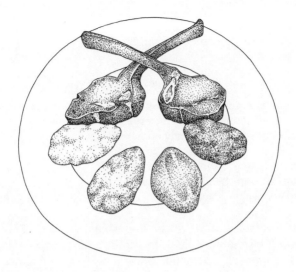

bright color. The vegetables are cooked when they are easily squished between thumb and forefinger.

2. Pour the vegetables into a strainer and rinse under cold water to prevent them from overcooking. Drain very thoroughly and puree. If the puree is too wet, cook it in a wide pan over a high heat to evaporate the excess liquid.

3. Beat in enough softened butter and cream to obtain the consistency of soft ice cream. The butter can be added directly in the food processor. Be careful adding cream in the processor: a continuously whirling blade will cause it to curdle. The basic seasonings are salt, pepper, cayenne pepper, and perhaps a little lemon juice, but let your imagination be your guide.

4. To keep several different purees warm, place them in small sauce-pans or bowls in a roasting pan with 1 inch of simmering water. Dot each puree with butter to prevent a crust from forming. Purees can be prepared up to 8 hours in advance.

◇   ◇   ◇

Broccoli Puree

You may wish to save a few whole broccoli florets to garnish the puree. Purees of cauliflower, green beans, and artichokes would be prepared the same way.

Serves 4–6

> 1 bunch broccoli (about 1½ pounds), coarse stems discarded,
>   small stems and florets very finely chopped
> 1 potato, peeled and finely chopped
>   salt
> 2 tablespoons butter (or to taste)
> 2–4 tablespoons heavy cream (or to taste)
>   black pepper, cayenne pepper, a few drops of lemon juice

Cook the vegetables in rapidly boiling, salted water for 5–6 minutes or until quite soft. Rinse under cold water, drain, and puree, working in butter, cream, and flavorings. Keep the puree warm as described above.

SWEET POTATO PUREE

The starchy flesh of sweet potatoes makes them excellent for pureeing. For a Thanksgiving feel, we use such autumnal flavorings as maple syrup, ginger, cinnamon, and nutmeg. Purees of chestnuts and yams would be prepared the same way.

Serves 4–6

> 1½ pounds sweet potatoes, peeled and diced
>   salt
> 2 tablespoons maple syrup (or to taste)
> 2 tablespoons brown sugar
> ½ teaspoon cinnamon
> ¼ teaspoon each nutmeg and powdered ginger
> ⅛ teaspoon each ground cardamom and ground cloves
> 2 tablespoons butter (or to taste)
> 2–4 tablespoons heavy cream (or to taste)

Cook the sweet potatoes in rapidly boiling, salted water for 6–8 minutes, or until quite soft. Rinse under cold water, drain, and puree, working in the flavorings, butter, and cream. Keep the puree warm as described above.

CELERY ROOT PUREE

Celeriac, or celery root, is a knobby root vegetable with a subtle celery flavor. The stalks of the celeriac can be used sparingly in stocks but are much too bitter to eat. Purees of carrot and parsnip (the latter excellent with pears) would be prepared this way.

Serves 4–6

> 1½ pounds celeriac, peeled with a paring knife and rubbed with
>   cut lemon to prevent it from discoloring
> 1 cup milk
>   salt
> 2 tablespoons butter (or to taste)
> 2–4 tablespoons heavy cream (or to taste)
>   pepper, cayenne pepper, lemon juice

Prepare the puree as described above, cooking the celeriac in a half-and-half mixture of milk and water. (The milk helps preserve its white color.)

RED CABBAGE PUREE

When pureeing red cabbage (and other watery vegetables), it is necessary to cook them over high heat to evaporate the excess liquid. The vinegar gives the cabbage a distinctive purple color. Purees of spinach, leek, and watercress would be prepared this way, omitting the apple and vinegar.

Serves 4–6

> 1 pound cored, chopped red cabbage (for instructions on
>   coring cabbage, see page 239)
> 1 apple, peeled, cored, and chopped
> 1 potato, peeled and chopped
> 2 teaspoons red wine vinegar
>   salt
> 2 tablespoons butter
>   fresh black pepper, cayenne pepper

Cook the cabbage, apple, and potato with the vinegar in rapidly boiling, salted water. Rinse under cold water, drain and puree. Place the puree in a wide saucepan and cook it over a high heat, stirring with a wooden spoon, to evaporate the excess liquid. Stir in the butter and seasonings.

LESSON 40

All About Eggplants

◇

Techniques:
DISGORGING EGGPLANTS
ROASTING EGGPLANTS

Master Recipe:
EGGPLANTS NIMOISE

Variations:
POOR MAN'S CAVIAR
BABA GHANNOOJ

◇   ◇   ◇

The eggplant achieved the rank of "cult vegetable" during the vegetarian revolution of the seventies. Now, that's what I call progress! In the Middle Ages, this bulbous vegetable was considered a cause of insanity—whence its Italian name *melanzàna,* from the Latin *mala insanum,* literally "mad apple." This is not as crazy as it sounds, for the eggplant belongs to the nightshade family, many of whose members are poisonous.

Eggplants contain bitter juices, which must be purged before the cooking. The French called this process *dégorgement,* "disgorging." The eggplant is sliced and sprinkled with kosher salt (2–3 tablespoons for a medium-sized eggplant), which draws out the bitter juices. Unlike most vegetables, eggplant tastes best not *al dente* but well done.

There are numerous species of eggplants: the slender Japanese, the miniature Italian, the rare albino eggplant (for which the plant is named in English). The recipes below call for the regular, large purple eggplant—the heavy, unbruised specimens of which are the best.

◇

TO DISGORGE EGGPLANT

For dishes calling for sliced eggplant, cut the eggplant widthwise into even slices. Arrange these on a tray or baking sheet and sprinkle with 2–3 tablespoons kosher salt. Turn and sprinkle the other sides. Let stand for 20 minutes, during which time a brownish juice will be drawn to the surface. Rinse the slices under cold water and blot dry. They are now ready to be floured and fried.

For dishes calling for whole eggplant, cut the eggplant in half lengthwise. Score each cut side deeply; that is, make a series of crisscrossing slashes through the flesh, almost to the skin. Sprinkle each half with kosher salt. Let stand for 20 minutes. Squeeze each half over the sink to wring out bitter juices. Rinse thoroughly in cold water and blot dry. The eggplant is now ready for grilling or baking on an oiled baking sheet, cut side down.

◇   ◇   ◇

Eggplants Nimoise

Nîmes is a town in the south of France, famed for a soft-blue cloth called denim (from the French words *de Nîmes* ("from Nîmes"). The town is also known for its eggplants and vine-ripened tomatoes. Choose long, slender eggplants if possible for this dish.

Serves 6–8

- 2 eggplants (about 1½ pounds)
- 2–3 tablespoons kosher salt
  flour for dusting (about 1 cup)
  oil for frying (1–2 cups)
- 4 ripe tomatoes
- 2–3 cloves garlic, minced
- 3–4 tablespoons dried or fresh chopped herbs, including parsley, oregano, and basil
- 3 tablespoons extra-virgin olive oil
  fresh black pepper and perhaps a little salt

1. Cut the eggplants into ⅜-inch slices and disgorge, rinse, and dry as described above.

2. Dredge the slices in flour, and then shake off the excess. Meanwhile, heat ¼ inch of oil in a large frying pan over medium-high heat. Fry the eggplant slices 30 seconds per side, or until lightly browned, turning with tongs. Transfer the slices to paper towels and blot dry.

3. Cut the tomatoes into as many slices as you have eggplant slices. Arrange these alternating with and overlapping the eggplant slices on an ovenproof platter. The result should be striped like a zebra. Sprinkle the platter with the garlic, herbs, olive oil, pepper, and perhaps a little salt.

(Remember that the eggplant has been salted already.) The dish can be prepared up to 4 hours ahead to this stage.

4. Bake the eggplants Nimoise in a preheated 350° oven for 15–20 minutes, or until the tomatoes and eggplants are soft. This dish is delicious with lamb. In fact, you could bake the ingredients in a circle around the edge of a large ovenproof platter and set a roast leg of lamb in the center.

Note: Frying eggplant is a case where more is less. The more oil you use (provided it is sufficiently hot), the less the eggplant will absorb. Try to keep at least ¼ inch in the pan. To tell when the oil is the right temperature, immerse the edge of a slice of eggplant: tiny bubbles should appear at once. Never let the oil get so hot it smokes.

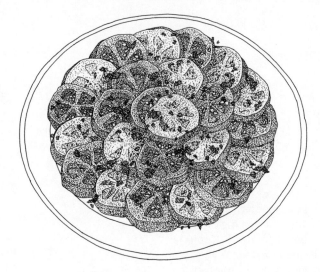

POOR MAN'S CAVIAR

Poor man's caviar is a Russian dish, so named because it has the consistency of caviar but costs only a fraction of the price. This recipe comes from a fine cook and dear friend named Bob Ginn.

Serves 6 as an appetizer

> 2 medium eggplants (about 1½ pounds)
> 2–3 tablespoons kosher salt
> ¼ cup extra-virgin olive oil (or to taste)
> 2 pounds *ripe* tomatoes, or 1 2-pound can Italian plum
>   tomatoes, peeled, seeded, and chopped (see page 66)
> 2 whole carrots, peeled
> 2 whole Italian or cubanelle peppers, cored and seeded
> 1 small chili pepper, cored and seeded

2 cloves garlic, minced
¼ teaspoon ground sage
freshly ground black pepper and perhaps a little salt
juice of 1 large lemon (or to taste)
wedges of toasted pita bread for dipping

1. Peel the eggplants and cut them into ½-inch cubes. Toss these cubes with the kosher salt and let stand in a colander over a bowl for 20 minutes. Squeeze the eggplant between your fingers to wring out the bitter juices, then rinse and drain the cubes. Chop the remaining ingredients.

2. Lightly oil a roasting pan or baking sheet with sides. Mix the vegetables and seasonings, spread them on the baking sheet, and bake in a preheated 250° oven for 2 hours. Turn off the heat and leave the eggplant mixture in the oven overnight.

3. The next day, finely chop the vegetables by hand or in a food processor. Do not reduce the mixture to a puree, however—it should have the grainy consistency of caviar. Season to taste, adding additional salt, pepper, and lemon juice or olive oil as necessary. Poor man's caviar can be served chilled as an appetizer or warm as a vegetable. You could also spoon the mixture into hollowed plum tomatoes, mushroom caps, or zucchini and bake until the vegetables are soft.

BABA GHANNOOJ

EGGPLANT DIP

Baba ghannooj (pronounced "ga-noosh") is a Middle East eggplant dip flavored with garlic, lemon juice, and *tahini* (sesame seed paste). But what distinguishes an ordinary dip from superlative *baba ghannooj* is the way the eggplant is cooked: it should be roasted over an open fire. Roasting is best accomplished on a barbecue grill, but it can also be done over a gas flame or even under the broiler. The skin should be completely charred, for this is what imparts the distinctive smoke flavor. Sour cream is an unconventional substitute for *tahini,* but the result is delicious.

Serves 6

2 small or 1 large eggplant (about 1 pound)
1–2 cloves garlic, minced
1 very small onion, minced (about 2 tablespoons)
2–3 tablespoons extra-virgin olive oil
4 tablespoons *tahini* or sour cream
juice of 1 lemon (or to taste)
4 tablespoons very finely chopped fresh parsley
salt, freshly ground black pepper, cayenne pepper to taste

1. Roast the eggplant on all sides on a barbecue grill (or under the broiler, or over a gas flame with the eggplant impaled on a carving fork) for 15–20 minutes or until completely charred on all sides. The flesh inside should be very soft. Let it cool. Cut the eggplant in half lengthwise, and scrape out the flesh with a spoon.

2. In a large bowl mash the eggplant flesh to a smooth puree with a fork. Beat in the remaining ingredients. Alternatively, puree the remaining ingredients in a food processor. Use the lemon juice, salt, and pepper as necessary—the mixture should be very spicy.

Serving: Serve *baba ghannooj* with warm pita bread for dipping. If you prefer, cut the pita bread in wedges and toast it on a baking sheet (or standing up in a muffin tin) in a preheated 400° oven for 10 minutes or until crisp.

LESSON 41

Of Mushrooms White and Wild

◇

Techniques:

WASHING MUSHROOMS

SLICING AND CHOPPING MUSHROOMS

IDENTIFYING WILD MUSHROOMS

MAKING DUXELLES

Master Recipe:

MUSHROOMS SAUTÉED WITH GARLIC-
PARSLEY BUTTER

Variations:

SHIITAKE MUSHROOMS WITH SNOW PEAS
AND WALNUT OIL

SCRAMBLED EGGS AND TRUFFLES

MUSHROOM DUXELLES

DUXELLES-STUFFED MUSHROOM CAPS

◇ ◇ ◇

Few foods have made as much progress in the last twenty years as *agaricus bosporus,* the common mushroom. When I was growing up, mushrooms invariably meant "sink stoppers"—the rubbery canned variety. Today, fresh mushrooms are as commonplace as onions, and a host of wild mushrooms are available at specialty shops and even large supermarkets. In this lesson we take up the various species of mushrooms—how to clean them and how to cook them.

TO CLEAN MUSHROOMS: Mushrooms are like sponges. They must be washed quickly to prevent them from becoming waterlogged. Fill a large bowl with cold water. Add the mushrooms, sandy stems and all, in small batches, and agitate them with your fingers. Fish them out at 10 seconds and transfer to a colander. Pour off the dirty water (not onto the clean mushrooms!), replenish the bowl with clean water, and wash the mushrooms again. Repeat the process as necessary. (Usually, it will take 2–3 times.) At no point should the mushrooms be in water for more than 10 seconds.

After the mushrooms are washed, cut off and discard the sandy stems. The stems are removed after washing to prevent the caps from becoming waterlogged. (For the same reason, we wash strawberries before we remove the hulls.) Blot the caps dry with paper towels.

SLICING MUSHROOMS: To slice mushrooms, cut the stems off flush with the base (stems can be added to stock or *duxelles*—see below). Lay each mushroom flat and, using the tip of a sharp paring knife, cut it into thin slices.

CHOPPING MUSHROOMS: Mushrooms are best chopped in a food processor, but care must be taken not to reduce them to soggy mush. Chop no more than 1 cup of washed mushrooms at a time. Run the processor a few seconds at a time, not continuously, until the mushrooms have been reduced to ⅛-inch pieces. *Stop.* Transfer the chopped mushrooms to a bowl and sprinkle with lemon juice to prevent them from discoloring. Chop the remaining mushrooms the same way. To chop mushrooms by hand, use a large chef's knife. First slice them as described above, and then chop them finely.

COOKING WITH WILD MUSHROOMS: Fresh wild mushrooms are washed and cooked the way common ones are. If they are not too dirty, you may want to wipe them off with a damp paper towel. When possible, leave them whole, so that you can appreciate their unusual shapes.

Dried wild mushrooms must be reconstituted; pour boiling water over them to cover and let them stand for 30 minutes. The soaking liquid will be loaded with flavor—and sand, so be sure to strain it through cheesecloth or a coffee filter before using. European dried mushrooms tend to be very gritty; you may need to wash them in two or three changes of water. (The second and third can be discarded, as they will lack the flavor of the first soaking.) Three ounces of dried mushrooms are the equivalent of 1 pound of fresh ones. Wild mushrooms are very expensive. You can stretch them by blending wild with white.

A GUIDE TO WILD MUSHROOMS

Of the 40,000-odd mushroom species, 2,000 are regularly eaten by man. A dozen, popular in Europe and Asia, are available in this country.

OYSTER MUSHROOMS: Named *pleurottes* ("weepers") in French, these elongated, gray mushrooms look like freshly shucked oysters, and there is something oystery about their soft, moist texture. Minimize sautéing time, as they are easily overcooked.

STRAW MUSHROOMS: Because of their perishability, these cone-shaped mushrooms are usually sold canned. Their flavor is not unlike that of common mushrooms—perhaps a little more intense. They are popular throughout the Orient.

SHIITAKE MUSHROOMS: The workhorse of the Orient, shiitakes have a dark-brown cap, tan gills, and a pungent, woodsy flavor familiar to anyone who has eaten hot-and-sour soup or *moo shi* pork. The mushroom takes its name from the *shii* tree, on logs of which it is grown; it is also called Chinese mushroom or black mushroom. *Silver oak mushrooms* are shiitakes grown in this country. They dry well, but whether you use dried or fresh ones, be sure to discard the tough stem.

ENOKI MUSHROOMS: Popular in Japan, these cream-colored mushrooms have tiny caps and a long, slender stem, looking not unlike an overgrown straight pin. Enoki are delightful in salads; they are too delicate to cook.

CHANTERELLES: Chanterelles look like miniature orange trumpets. The flavor has been alternately described as meaty, winelike, and peppery. These mushrooms don't dry well, but fortunately they are widely available fresh.

TRUMPET OF DEATH MUSHROOMS: Hardly a reassuring name for a member of a plant family renowned for its toxic species. Nonetheless, these black, horn-shaped mushrooms are not only edible, but delicious, boasting a delicate, earthy flavor.

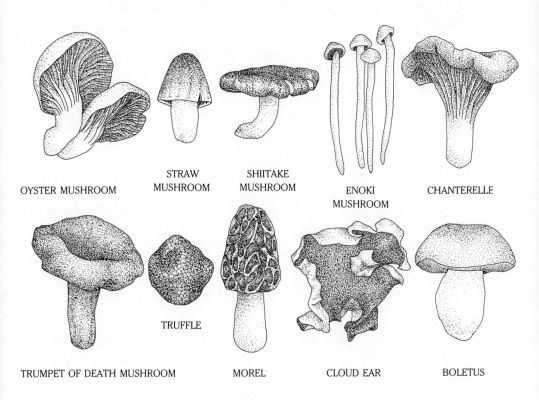

OYSTER MUSHROOM STRAW MUSHROOM SHIITAKE MUSHROOM ENOKI MUSHROOM CHANTERELLE

TRUMPET OF DEATH MUSHROOM TRUFFLE MOREL CLOUD EAR BOLETUS

TRUFFLES: The truffle looks like a knobby, black golfball. The smell, particularly of the white ones, reminds me of wool socks that have moldered too long in a gym locker. Nonetheless, these pungent fungi, which grow underground and are hunted by specially trained pigs, command over $300 a pound!

There are two species: the *black* found in Perigord in France, and the *white* (actually a dusty tan) from Piedmont in Italy. The black ones are generally consumed cooked; the white ones, raw, thinly sliced on top of risotto or pasta. Black truffles are widely available canned—be sure to use the juice. Fresh black truffles can be stored in brandy; white ones do best buried in dried rice in the refrigerator. One of the best ways to enjoy black truffles is in scrambled eggs (see recipe below).

MORELS: Morels are my favorite wild mushrooms, distinguished by their dusty brown hue, their honeycombed cone shape, their penetrating, almost smoky fragrance. Dried morels are good, but they tend to be sandy.

CLOUD EARS: This wafer-thin fungus is not esteemed for its flavor—it has none—but rather for its texture, which is pliable, chewy, and crisp. The Chinese name is *mu er,* which poetically translates as "cloud ears." They are always sold dried; the smaller ones are more highly prized than the larger.

BOLETUSES: These stout-stemmed, broad, spongy-capped mushrooms have a woodsy aroma and a rich, meaty tang. The French call them *cèpes;* the Germans, *Herrenpilz* ("lord mushrooms"); the Italians, *porcini* ("pig mushrooms," an allusion to their popularity with pigs). Boletuses are seldom seen fresh in this country; the dried ones look like tiny wood chips and tend to be very sandy.

◇   ◇   ◇

Mushrooms Sautéed with Garlic-Parsley Butter

This is my favorite way to prepare mushrooms. You can use either escargot butter or the garlic-parsley butter below. Flat-leaf parsley has more flavor than the curly leaf.

Serves 4

    1 pound fresh white mushrooms, chanterelles, shiitakes,
        oyster mushrooms, boletuses, and/or trumpets of death
    4 tablespoons butter, olive oil, or walnut oil
  1–2 cloves garlic, minced
    4 tablespoons chopped fresh flat-leaf parsley
      salt and freshly ground black pepper

Wash and dry the mushrooms as described above. Cut the large ones in quarters, the medium-sized ones in half, and leave the small ones whole. Melt the butter in a large frying pan over high heat. Add the mushrooms and cook for 1 minute. Add the garlic, parsley, salt, and pepper and continue sautéing for 1 or 2 minutes or until the mushrooms are soft. Serve at once.

◇   ◇   ◇

MUSHROOMS IN CREAM SAUCE: Follow the recipe above, adding ¼ cup cream 1 minute after you add the garlic and parsley. Cook the mushrooms in the cream for 2–3 minutes. This cream sauce goes particularly well with morels. For a nice, meaty flavor, add 3 tablespoons finely chopped prosciutto with the garlic.

SHIITAKE MUSHROOMS WITH
SNOW PEAS AND WALNUT OIL

This recipe was inspired by a dish at the Four Columns Inn in Newfane, Vermont. Naturally it tastes better with fresh mushrooms, but it can also be made with dried ones. Walnut oil is available in most gourmet shops; once opened, it should be refrigerated. The nutty taste of the Amaretto goes perfectly with the earthy flavor of the mushrooms.

Serves 4 as an appetizer or vegetable

    ½ pound fresh shiitake mushrooms, or 2 ounces dried
    6 ounces fresh snow peas, snapped
    3 tablespoons walnut oil
      salt and pepper
      juice of ½ lemon
    2 teaspoons Amaretto

  1. Clean and dry the mushrooms as described above. Cook the snow peas in rapidly boiling, heavily salted water for 15 seconds, refresh under cold water, and drain. Blot the mushrooms and snow peas dry.

2.   Heat the walnut oil in a frying pan over high heat. Add the mushrooms and sauté for 2 minutes. Add the snow peas and cook for 1 minute. Add the salt, pepper, lemon juice, and Amaretto and bring the mixture just to a boil. Serve at once.

SCRAMBLED EGGS AND TRUFFLES

This may be the ultimate way to enjoy truffles. The French make their scrambled eggs in a double boiler. The result is closer to hollandaise sauce than what we call scrambled eggs. Instead of whole truffles, you can use canned truffle pieces, which are considerably less expensive.

Serves 4

8 eggs
1 small (½ ounce) fresh black truffle or canned truffle or
    truffle pieces with juice
4 tablespoons heavy cream
4 tablespoons butter, cut into small pieces
    salt and fresh white pepper
8 toast points (optional; see page 215)

1. Crack the eggs in the top of a double boiler or saucepan (non-aluminum) and beat for 2 minutes. If using a fresh truffle, brush it lightly under cold running water. Chop fresh or canned truffle finely. Add the truffles, cream, butter, salt, and pepper to the eggs and beat for 2 more minutes.
2. Place the pan over gently simmering water in the bottom of a double boiler or in a shallow pot. Cook the eggs at the barest simmer, stirring constantly with a wooden spoon, for 3–4 minutes, or until the eggs have thickened to the consistency of mayonnaise. Do not overcook (the French like their scrambled eggs very loose). Correct the seasoning and serve with toast points.

MUSHROOM DUXELLES

This rich mushroom stuffing is named for the Marquis d'Uxelles, employer of the father of modern French cuisine, François Pierre de La Varenne.
  Duxelles (pronounced "duke-cell") is made by cooking mushrooms, parsley, and shallots over high heat until *all* the liquid has evaporated. The

absence of moisture has two advantages: it intensifies the mushroom flavor, and it enables this watery vegetable to be used as a stuffing without making the surrounding food soggy.

Makes ¾ cup duxelles

12 ounces fresh white mushrooms
   juice of ½ lemon
3 tablespoons butter
3–4 shallots, minced (approximately 3 tablespoons)
3 tablespoons finely chopped fresh parsley
   salt and freshly ground black pepper
   cayenne pepper
   freshly grated nutmeg

Wash and finely chop the mushrooms as described above. Sprinkle them with lemon juice to prevent discoloring. Melt the butter in a large frying pan over high heat, and cook the shallots for 30 seconds. Add the mushrooms and parsley. Cook the mixture over high heat, stirring with a spatula, for 4–5 minutes, or until all the mushroom liquid has evaporated and the volume is reduced by half. Add the seasonings and spices: the mixture should be quite highly seasoned.

Storing

Mushroom duxelles will keep in the refrigerator for 2–3 days. It can be frozen almost indefinitely. Should you ever have more fresh mushrooms than you can use, turn them into duxelles and freeze it.

Uses

The uses of mushroom duxelles are almost limitless. Use it to stuff mushroom caps (see below), hollowed-out zucchini, chicken breasts, pork chops or veal chops (cut a horizontal pocket in the chop), tarts (see recipe on page 109), filo dough triangles, crêpes, papillotes, etc. Add duxelles to white sauce to make a mushroom sauce; add it to the basic cheese soufflé on page 76 to make a mushroom soufflé. Mix it with a little sour cream and broil on toast points to make an easy hors d'oeuvre.

VARIATIONS: Duxelles can also be made from fresh or dried wild mushrooms.

DUXELLES-STUFFED MUSHROOM CAPS

Stuffed mushroom caps can be served as an appetizer or a vegetable. For an unusual touch, make the duxelles with wild mushrooms.

Makes 15–20 caps

15–20 large mushroom caps
Mushroom Duxelles from preceding recipe
½ cup heavy cream
oil for the baking dish
½ cup sour cream (for garnish—optional)
sprigs of fresh dill or paprika (for garnish)

1. Wash the mushrooms. Remove the stems and hollow out the caps with a melon baller or a teaspoon. The stems can be chopped and added to the duxelles.

2. Prepare the duxelles as described above. Add the heavy cream and simmer 5 minutes. Spoon this mixture into the mushroom caps. The recipe can be prepared up to 12 hours ahead to this stage.

3. Bake the caps in a lightly oiled baking dish for 15 minutes or until soft. Just before serving, pipe a rosette of sour cream on the center of each mushroom cap, and top with a sprig of dill or a sprinkle of paprika.

LESSON 42

Picking Peppers

◇————◇

Technique:
ROASTING PEPPERS

Master Recipe:
ROASTED BELL PEPPER SALAD

Variations:
SICILIAN SALAD
"RUST" SAUCE FOR FISH
RED PEPPER BUTTER SAUCE

◇   ◇   ◇

Peter Piper picked a peck of pickled peppers. He's not the only one. Peppers have become some of the "hottest" ingredients of the eighties, and I don't mean just spicy. Winners of the pepper popularity contest include plump red, yellow, and even brown peppers from Holland, not to mention Mexico's insidiously hot chilies.

Like the tomato and potato, the pepper was native to the Americas. When Columbus first encountered it in the Caribbean, he mistook it for *piper nigrum,* the black peppercorn. (Black pepper was so popular and expensive in Europe that Columbus's explorations were largely motivated by the hope of finding a cheap source.) Actually, Columbus had bitten into one of the spicier varieties of *capsicum,* the chili pepper. The *capsicum* family (from the Greek *capto,* "I bite") embraces the mild bell pepper and paprika, as well as the fiery jalapeño. According to food historian Waverley Root, it is the most widely cultivated spice in the world.

Peppers range in color from green to yellow to red, depending on the degree of ripeness. When handling chili peppers, be sure not to touch your face or eyes. The hottest part of any pepper is the seeds. Bell peppers taste best when roasted and peeled.

HOW TO ROAST AND PEEL A PEPPER

As a rule, cooks try to avoid burning food, but to peel a pepper it is essential to burn it first. The pepper is roasted *directly* on the burner until it is completely charred. Roasting loosens the skin from the flesh, and it has the happy side effect of imparting a delectable smoke flavor. If you have a gas stove, roast the pepper directly on the burner. If you have an electric stove, you can either roast the pepper on the burner or under the broiler. Best of all is to roast the pepper on a grill.

1. Place the whole pepper(s) directly on a high burner, and cook, turning frequently with tongs, until the skin is charred and black on all sides. Wrap the peppers in paper towels moistened with cold water and let stand for 10 minutes. (The moisture will steam off the skin.) Scrape the pepper with a brush or paring knife under cold running water to remove all bits of black. Blot dry. Chilies as well as bell peppers are roasted in this fashion.

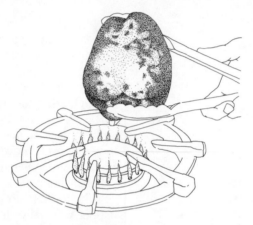

2. To core and seed the pepper, cut around the stem and discard it. Split the pepper, and scrape out the seeds with a knife. Thus roasted and seeded, peppers can be stored in oil for several weeks.

◇   ◇   ◇

Roasted Bell Pepper Salad

This roasted bell pepper salad is one of my all-time favorites, especially when made with the meaty red, yellow, and brown bell peppers imported from Holland. If possible, use a colorful combination of red, yellow, and green or brown peppers. If only one species is available, red or yellow is preferable.

Serves 4–6

6 large roasted bell peppers (2 red, 2 yellow, and 2 brown or
green, if possible), cored and seeded

FOR THE MARINADE:

> 6–8 tablespoons extra-virgin olive oil
> 1½ tablespoons red wine vinegar
> juice of ½ lemon (or to taste)
> salt and freshly ground black pepper
> 2 tablespoons slivered fresh basil or oregano
> 2 cloves garlic, peeled and lightly bruised but left whole

1. Cut each pepper in quarters or strips and layer them in a shallow dish. Combine and stir the marinade ingredients and sprinkle each layer of peppers with the marinade.

The salad can be eaten immediately, but the flavor will improve if the peppers are allowed to marinate for 4–6 hours.

◇   ◇   ◇

PEPPER SALAD WITH ANCHOVIES AND CAPERS: Prepare the salad as described above, adding 6 drained, coarsely chopped anchovy fillets and 4 table-spoons rinsed, drained capers.

SICILIAN SALAD

This is actually more of a dip than a salad, and variations are served all around the Mediterranean. This particular version comes from Tony Trio, Boston's premier purveyor of pasta. Note that the tomatoes are peeled by roasting instead of boiling.

Serves 4–6

> 3 large red peppers, roasted, peeled, and cored
> 3 large *ripe* tomatoes
> 6 tablespoons extra-virgin olive oil
> 1½ tablespoons red wine vinegar
> salt and freshly ground black pepper
> a loaf of French or Italian bread, cut into chunks and lightly
>   toasted, for dipping

Cut the peppers into thin slivers. Roast the tomatoes at the end of a carving fork over a high flame until the skins blister and peel. Peel the tomatoes, cut them in half widthwise, and wring out the seeds by squeezing with the palms of your hands. Chop finely. In a bowl, combine the peppers and tomatoes with the oil, vinegar, and the seasonings. Sicilian salad is eaten on dunked chunks of bread.

"RUST" SAUCE FOR FISH

"Rust" sauce is traditionally served on fried bread slices with fish soup or *bouillabaisse.* The sauce takes its rust color from the saffron and freshly roasted red peppers. The sauce is traditionally made with a mortar and pestle, but the food processor works well, too.

Makes 1½ cups

2 slices dense white bread, crusts removed
2 large red peppers, roasted, peeled, and cored
2 cloves garlic, peeled (or to taste)
    generous pinch saffron
1 egg yolk
5 tablespoons extra-virgin olive oil
    salt and freshly ground black pepper
    generous pinch cayenne pepper

Moisten the bread slices in warm water and wring dry between your fingers. Puree the peppers, bread, garlic, saffron, and egg yolk to a very smooth paste in a food processor or blender or with a mortar and pestle. Gradually blend in the olive oil and seasonings. The sauce should be very spicy.

Serve rust sauce with the fish soup and *bouillabaisse* on pages 160–63 or with grilled fish, chicken, or steak.

Note: If fresh red peppers are unavailable, use bottled pimientos plus a pinch of sugar.

RED PEPPER BUTTER SAUCE

This red pepper butter sauce is more delicate than the preceding recipe. Serve it with poached fish or shellfish. For a full discussion on making butter sauces, see pages 140–42.

Makes 1 cup sauce

¾ cup dry white wine
¼ cup white wine vinegar
3 tablespoons very finely chopped shallots
¼ cup heavy cream
12 tablespoons (1½ sticks) cold, unsalted butter, cut into
    ½-inch pieces
    salt, fresh white pepper, cayenne pepper
1 large or 2 small roasted red peppers, cored and seeded

1. Bring the wine, vinegar, and shallots to a boil in a heavy, nonaluminum or cast-iron saucepan. Rapidly boil the mixture until only ⅓ cup of liquid remains. Add the cream and continue boiling until only 5–6 tablespoons liquid remain.

2. Add the butter, piece by piece, whisking vigorously. The first piece of butter should be almost melted before you add the next. When all the butter has been added, let the sauce come just to a boil. Remove the pan from the heat. Add salt, pepper, and cayenne pepper—the sauce should be highly seasoned. Puree the sauce with the roasted red pepper in a blender. Correct the seasoning and serve.

LESSON 43

Rice

◇

Technique:
MAKING RICE PILAF

Master Recipe:
RICE PILAF "TASTE OF THE MOUNTAINS"

Variations:
INDIAN-STYLE RICE
TURKISH PILAF (WITH NUTS AND FRUIT)
WILD RICE

◇ ◇ ◇

"**A** meal without rice is like a beautiful girl with only one eye" goes a Chinese saying. This tiny white grain is a staple for an estimated six out of ten people in the world. Asians lead in world rice consumption with an average of 265 pounds per person per year (compared to 6 pounds in the United States). But that has not prevented rice from playing an important role in American history: rice was called "Carolinian gold" during the Revolutionary War, and to improve our seed stock, Thomas Jefferson smuggled purloined grains from Italy. Today, the United States grows an impressive 10 billion pounds a year, most of it for export.

But which rice? Confucius urged his followers to eat white rice. When I was in college, I was fed near-lethal doses of brown rice. The Japanese have a glutinous rice which is used for making special desserts and sushi. From the marshlands of Minnesota comes wild rice, which technically isn't rice but a kind of grass seed.

Most of the rice sold in the United States comes in three lengths: long grain, medium grain, and short grain. The first (4–5 times as long as it is wide) cooks the most quickly, producing firm, fluffy, individual grains. The latter (respectively, twice as long as wide and virtually round) cook into a softer, stickier mass popular in the Orient, where their stickiness makes them easy to eat with chopsticks. All rice starts as brown rice—the individual grain with husk removed but the fiber-rich bran left intact. The crown prince of the rice kingdom is costly *basmati*, a grain grown in India and renowned for its distinctive nutty flavor. All recipes in this lesson call for long-grain rice or *basmati*.

Rice is usually cooked by one of three methods: boiling (in the Caribbean), steaming (used throughout the Orient), and pilaf-style, which originated in Turkey. To make a pilaf, the rice is sautéed with onion and garlic till translucent, then simmered or baked with relatively little liquid. I prefer the pilaf-style for three reasons: it is the least temperamental of the three, it can be simmered or baked depending on the availability of burners or oven, and the finished rice has more flavor and a firmer texture.

BASIC FORMULA FOR RICE PILAF

For each cup of rice:

> 3 tablespoons fat (butter, olive oil, etc.), plus 2–3 tablespoons
>   butter at the end for "fluffing" the rice
> ½–1 cup vegetable or fruit garnish (chopped onions, garlic,
>   celery, peppers, figs, prunes, etc.)
> 1½ cups liquid (water, chicken stock, fish broth, etc.)

Serving information:
One cup dried rice makes 3 cups cooked. One-half to two-thirds cup cooked rice makes a normal side-dish serving.

◇　◇　◇

Rice Pilaf "Taste of the Mountains"

Our term "pilaf" comes from the Persian *pilaou* ("cooked rice"). Depending on the frying fat (butter, olive oil, or goose fat) and the cooking liquid (water, chicken stock, clam broth), you can infinitely vary the results. For an Indian accent, the rice would be sautéed with onions, garlic, coriander, and cumin; for a Mexican accent, with tomatoes and peppers. That glorious national dish of Spain—*paella*—is nothing more than rice pilaf cooked with saffron, seafood, and chicken.

Serves 4–6

> 3 tablespoons butter (or fat of your choice), plus 2
>   tablespoons butter for serving (optional)
> 1 medium-sized onion, finely chopped
> 1 branch celery, finely chopped
> 1 clove garlic, minced
> 1 red pepper, cored, seeded, finely chopped (optional)
> 1 cup long-grained rice
> 1½ cups water or chicken stock
>   *bouquet garni*
>   salt and fresh black pepper

1. Melt the butter in a heavy 10-inch frying pan (one with an ovenproof handle) and sauté the vegetables over medium heat for 3 minutes or until soft. Add the rice and sauté it for one minute or until translucent and shiny. Add the remaining ingredients, increase heat to high, and bring the liquid to a boil. NOTE: Do not stir the rice once the liquid has been added, or it will become starchy.

2. Tightly cover the pan with a lid. Bake the pilaf in a preheated 400° oven for 18–20 minutes (or until the rice grains are soft). The rice should be cooked but firm—you should be able to taste and chew each individual grain. Alternatively, you can cook the pilaf on the stove: turn the heat as low as possible and cook the rice for 20 minutes or until all the liquid has been absorbed.

3. To serve, "fluff" (gently mix) the rice with a fork, adding the remaining butter. Correct the seasoning. Rice pilaf can be cooked up to one hour ahead of time and kept warm in the pan on the stove, but fluff it just before serving. Pilaf can be served in the pan in which it was cooked. For a fanciful presentation, spoon the rice into a buttered 5-cup ring mold, gently press to compact it, and invert it onto a round platter.

INDIAN-STYLE RICE

Basmati is the world's most luxurious rice, costing up to $3–4 a pound. Its fine nutty flavor makes it every bit worth the price. Coconut cream is made from the pulp of a coconut. Both the rice and the cream can be purchased at an Indian or Near East specialty shop.

Serves 4–6

3 tablespoons butter
1 onion, diced
1 clove garlic, minced
½ teaspoon each ground cumin and coriander
⅛ teaspoon each saffron, ground cardamom, cloves
1 cup *basmati* rice
1 cup coconut cream (optional) and 1 cup water, or 2 cups
   chicken stock or 2 cups water
salt and fresh black pepper

Melt the butter and sauté the vegetables with the spices as described above. Continue following the master recipe, but cook the rice for 10–15 minutes longer.

TURKISH PILAF

(WITH NUTS AND FRUIT)

This pilaf—loaded with nuts and dried fruits—is almost a meal in itself. It goes well with lamb; indeed, it would make a delicious stuffing for a boned breast or butterflied leg of lamb.

Serves 4–6

¼ cup coarsely chopped dried figs
¼ cup coarsely chopped dried apricots
¼ cup coarsely chopped pitted prunes
4 tablespoons butter
¼ cup chopped or coarsely slivered almonds
¼ cup pine nuts
1 onion, finely chopped (about ½ cup)
1 cup long-grain rice
2 sticks cinnamon
  bouquet garni containing 4 cloves
  pinch saffron (optional)
  salt and fresh black pepper
1½ cups hot chicken stock or water

1. Pour boiling water over the dried fruits and let stand for 20 minutes. Drain and blot dry.

2. Melt the butter in a large cast-iron or enamelware skillet. Sauté the nuts until lightly browned. Add the onion and sauté until soft. Add the rice and sauté until the grains are shiny. Stir in the fruit, flavorings, and stock, and bring to a rapid boil. (NOTE: Do not stir the rice after the stock has boiled.) Press a piece of buttered foil or parchment paper on top of the rice and tightly cover the pan.

3. The pilaf can be baked in a preheated 400° oven for 20 minutes, or cooked on the stove over the lowest possible heat. Uncover the rice and fluff with a fork just before serving.

WILD RICE

Wild rice is no rice at all, but the seeds of a marsh grass that grows wild in Minnesota. It is traditionally harvested by canoe: the Indians paddle through the marshes, beating the plants with sticks. The grains that land in the boat are packaged and sold. Ninety percent of the rice falls in the water, though, which accounts for the expense of this luxury item. Wild rice takes much longer to cook than regular.

Serves 6

1 cup wild rice
4 strips bacon, cut into ¼-inch slivers
1 onion, diced (about ½ cup)
2 stalks celery, diced (about ½ cup)
1 clove garlic, minced
4 cups chicken stock (see recipe on page 24) or water
  bouquet garni
  salt and fresh black pepper

1. Rinse the rice under cold water and drain. Render the bacon in a large saucepan. The pieces should be lightly browned. Transfer them with a slotted spoon to a paper towel to drain. Pour off all but 3 tablespoons bacon fat.

2. Sauté the onion, celery, and garlic over medium heat for 2–3 minutes or until soft. Add the rice and sauté until all the grains are shiny. Gently stir in the remaining ingredients, minus the bacon, and bring the rice to a boil.

3. Gently simmer the rice, covered, for 40–50 minutes or until tender, stirring from time to time to keep the grains on the bottom from burning. (Because the rice is simmered, not baked, and because it is cooked for so much longer than pilaf, it must be stirred from time to time.) Add more stock or water if the mixture dries out; if it is too wet, cook uncovered for the last 10–15 minutes to evaporate the excess liquid. Return the rendered bacon to the rice for the last 5 minutes. Correct the seasoning. Wild rice is excellent with poultry of any sort, especially game birds.

L E S S O N 4 4

''Comfort Foods''

DUMPLINGS, BISCUITS, AND POTATO PANCAKES

---◇---

Technique:
FORMING AND COOKING SPAETZLE

Master Recipes:
SPAETZLE
MAMA SPACH'S DROP BISCUITS
STEVE'S POTATO PANCAKE

Variations:
CHEESE SPAETZLE
HERB SPAETZLE

◇   ◇   ◇

This last lesson on vegetables brings us to what I call "comfort foods," those hardy starch dishes that leave us feeling not only well fed but well nurtured. The first is *spaetzle*, tiny egg dumplings from Central Europe. The second is drop biscuits, made according to an old family recipe from North Carolina. The third is a potato pancake, which the author prepares at least once a week. All three have the added advantage of being quick and easy to make.

◇   ◇   ◇

Spaetzle

TINY EGG DUMPLINGS

Spaetzle (pronounced "shpehtz-le") means "little sparrow," an apt description for these tiny egg dumplings, each no bigger than a pea. Spaeztle originated in Germany, where they are nicknamed "Wurtemberg potatoes"; variations are found throughout Eastern Europe. Their small size makes them ideal for soaking up gravies.

Spaeztle are made from a loose dough of eggs, milk, and flour. Traditionally, the dough is cut into boiling water using a special cutter, which looks like a perforated metal rectangle surmounted by a movable, open-topped box. As the box slides back and forth, tiny droplets of dough fall through the holes in the bottom. A spaetzle cutter can be improvised using a round cookie cutter and a slotted spatula. You can even force the dough through the holes in a colander (one with very wide holes). All this may sound more complicated than it really is, for spaetzle can be made from start to finish in under 15 minutes. These tiny dumplings go well with almost any dish with gravy.

Serves 6–8

2½ cups flour
scant teaspoon salt, fresh white pepper, freshly grated nutmeg
3 eggs
1 scant cup milk
1 tablepoon oil (for cooking)
1 teaspoon salt

FOR SERVING SPAETZLE:

4 tablespoons butter
salt and fresh pepper
4 tablespoons fresh chopped parsley

1. Sift the flour and seasonings into a large bowl, and make a "well," or depression, in the center. Beat the eggs with most of the milk until smooth. Quickly whisk this mixture into the flour to form a soft, sticky dough. (It should be the consistency of apple sauce—add more flour or milk as necessary.) Let stand for five minutes, but use within an hour of making the batter.

2. Bring at least 2 quarts water to a rolling boil with the oil and 1 teaspoon salt. (As it does with pasta, the oil will help prevent the dumplings from sticking together.) Place the spaetzle cutter over the pan, load it with dough, and cut tiny droplets into the water. Cook for 1 minute or until the

water returns to a boil and the spaetzle rise to the surface. When they are cooked, fish the spaetzle out with a slotted spoon, and cook the remaining batter in this fashion. The dumplings can be served as they are or with melted butter or a little sour cream.

Note: It is easier, sometimes, to cook spaetzle ahead of time and reheat at the last minute. To do this transfer the cooked dumplings with a slotted spoon to a bowl of cold water (this prevents them from overcooking). When all the spaetzle are cooked, drain off the cold water, and toss them with a little oil to prevent the individual dumplings from sticking. Covered and refrigerated, they will keep up to 48 hours.

To reheat the spaetzle, melt the butter in a large pan over high heat, and sauté the dumplings till hot. (Many people, including myself, like to cook them till golden brown and crusty.) Sprinkle with salt and pepper as necessary, and fresh parsley.

◇ ◇ ◇

CHEESE SPAETZLE: To the recipe above add ½ cup grated Parmesan cheese. Cook as described above.

HERB SPAETZLE: To the recipe above add ¼ cup finely chopped fresh basil, parsley, oregano, and/or other fresh herbs, or ¼ teaspoon saffron.

Mama Spach's Drop Biscuits

"Mama" Spach is actually Ted Spach, a strapping, 180-pound cabinetmaker and longtime friend of the Taste of the Mountains. He learned how to make biscuits growing up in North Carolina. The secret to light biscuits lies in mixing the dough as *little* as possible.

Makes 10 biscuits

> 2 cups all-purpose flour (or ½ cup whole wheat flour and 1½
>   cups white flour)
> 1 scant tablespoon baking powder
> 1 scant teaspoon salt
>   approximately ¼ cup oil
> 2 eggs
> ⅓ cup heavy cream
>
>   lightly greased baking sheet

1. Preheat the oven to 400°F. Combine the dry ingredients in a large bowl. Combine the wet ingredients in a large measuring cup and beat until

thoroughly mixed. You should have 1 cup liquid: add oil or cream as necessary.

2. Combine the wet ingredients with the dry ones and beat with a wooden spoon just to mix. Using 2 soupspoons, drop 3-inch mounds of dough on the baking sheet, leaving 2 inches between each. Bake in the preheated oven for 15–20 minutes, or until puffed and golden brown.

Serve Mama Spach's biscuits with butter, honey, and freshly brewed coffee.

◇　◇　◇

Steve's Potato Pancake

This crisp potato pancake would be called a *galette* (flat-cake) in French. The secret is to use a nonstick frying pan and to keep the pancake thin. The potatoes can be grated, skins and all, by hand or on the grating disk of a food processor. The pancake should be started on the stove, but once both sides are browned, it can be finished in the oven.

Serves 2–4

2 medium baking potatoes
5 tablespoons butter
 salt and freshly ground black pepper

1 10-inch, nonstick frying pan

1. Grate the potatoes into matchstick-sized slivers. Melt 3 tablespoons butter in the frying pan over medium heat. Add the grated potatoes and press them into a flat cake. Sprinkle with salt and pepper. Fry the potato pancake for 5–10 minutes or until the bottom is crisp and browned, but not burned—you may have to reduce the heat.

2. Flip the pancake: shake the pan to loosen the pancake, then flick your wrist to flip it. (I usually flip it over the sink, just in case.) If flipping pancakes makes you nervous, place a large round platter over the frying pan and invert the pancake onto it. Then slide the pancake back into the pan. Cut the remaining butter into 3 or 4 pieces and add these to the pan at the edge of the pancake. Sprinkle with more salt and pepper.

3. Cook the bottom side of the pancake for 5–10 minutes, or until browned and very crisp. If you prefer, bake it in a preheated 400° oven. To serve, slice the potato pancake into wedges, like a pie.

DESSERTS

LESSON 45

Dessert Preliminaries

◇

Techniques:
WHIPPING CREAM
LOADING AND USING A PIPING BAG

Master Recipe:
WHIPPED CREAM

◇　◇　◇

Few kitchen procedures are as magical as the process by which ordinary cream is transformed into snowy clouds of whipped cream. In this lesson we take up two techniques essential to many desserts: whipping cream and using a piping bag.

Cream comes in many grades. The best for whipping is nonpasteurized heavy cream (its minimum butterfat content is 36 percent). Whipping cream (minimum butterfat content of 30 percent) is, in fact, inferior to heavy cream. Medium cream and light cream are too light to whip.

The temperature has a lot to do with how cream whips: the rule is the colder the better. The cream should be refrigerated before you start. Chill the bowl and beaters in the freezer. When whipped cold, not only is cream less likely to separate, but it also whips higher.

◇　◇　◇

Whipped Cream

1 cup heavy cream
¼ cup confectioner's sugar
½ teaspoon vanilla
1 tablespoon Grand Marnier, rum, whiskey, or spirit of your
　　choice

Place the cream in a chilled bowl and beat by hand or by machine with chilled beaters.

Start beating slowly, picking up speed after 30 seconds. Beat the cream until soft peaks form. Sift in the confectioner's sugar. Add the flavorings at this point—earlier they would have interfered with the thickening process. When pouring liqueurs, hold your thumb over the bottle to control the flow. Continue beating until the cream is stiff. What is happening on the microscopic level is that each stroke of the whisk beats in minuscule air bubbles. The butterfat in the cream supports the walls of these bubbles. If you beat the cream too much, these walls will congeal into butter.

When preparing whipped cream ahead of time, whip it almost to stiff peaks. There is always time to "tighten it up" just before using. The same is true of machine beating: I always like to finish machine-beaten cream by hand.

Note: It is best to whip cream within 2 hours of when you plan to use it.

◇   ◇   ◇

TO FILL AND USE A PIPING BAG

The piping bag, along with knives and saucepans, is one of the most important tools in the kitchen. Not only is it essential for decorating cakes and piping fanciful swirls of whipped cream on cakes and mousses: it speeds up many a recipe by enabling you to quickly "squirt" a filling into mushroom caps, hard-cooked egg halves, even terrine molds. Many people are intimidated by piping bags, but their operation is simple. The results delight the eye as well as the palate.

First, the bag. You'll want at least three (one for savory fillings, two for desserts); 12 inches is a good length. Piping bags come in a variety of materials. I prefer nylon, which is the easiest to clean. Avoid canvas bags: they tend to leech water out of whipped cream. Some bags are very stiff when new: simply boil them for 10–15 minutes to soften them. To clean a pastry bag, scrub it both inside and out. I put mine through the washing machine.

The companion to the piping bag is the conical metal tip at the end. Tips come in an almost infinite range of shapes and sizes. For the recipes in this book, you'll need a ⅛-inch, ¼-inch, and ½-inch round tip, and a ¼-inch and ½-inch star tip. The round tips are used for piping fillings and cream puffs; the star tips for piping decorative rosettes. Be sure to buy tips that are big enough for your bag. (You may have to trim off the end of the bag to fit the tip.) Cake decorators use special bags fitted with a plastic nut at the end so that the tips can be unscrewed and changed while the bag is full. These are not recommended for general kitchen use, because the tips are too small.

LOADING THE BAG

Filling a piping bag has tripped up more than one otherwise able cook. When done properly, both the outside of the bag and your hands should be clean. Follow these simple steps and you'll never have trouble with piping bags.

1. Insert the tip in the bag. If using a star tip, take care not to pierce the side of the bag with one of the sharp points.

2. Twist the bottom of the bag into the tip to prevent the filling from leaking out.

3. Fold the top of the bag over to form a 2-inch cuff. If you are right-handed, hold your left hand in a U-shape. Drape the cuff over your thumb and fingers.

4. Use a spatula to transfer the filling to the bag. Scrape the spatula clean against your thumb and forefinger. Remember to keep your hand in a U-shape. Repeat as often as necessary to fill the bag.

5. Now unfold the cuff. Your holding hand should be perfectly clean. Bring the top of the bag together in pleats. Now twist it down until the filling appears at the tip. If the filling is runny, like choux pastry, you'll want to have the tip slightly raised when you twist.

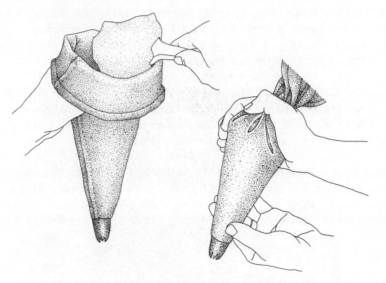

PIPING

Now comes the actual piping. Try to keep three things in mind as you pipe. First, keep the top of the bag pinched closed between the base of your thumb and forefinger. Second, as the bag empties, keep twisting the top, and lowering the spot you pinch. Third, hold your fingers together: apply pressure by gently closing your hand. It should *not* feel as though you're wringing the neck of a chicken.

Hold the bag almost perpendicular to the baking sheet or the object to be filled or decorated. To make a round shape, squeeze the bag gently, the point about ⅓ inch above the baking sheet. When you reach the desired shape, stop squeezing *completely*. Bring the tip of the bag in a close circle around the shape, then lift it. If you lift the tip while you are still piping, you will wind up with a Hershey's kiss or a tadpole.

DECORATING WITH A STAR TIP

Star tips are used for desserts with icing and whipped cream. When using a star tip, there are four basic shapes: stars, rosettes, ridged stripes, and ruffled boarders.

STARS: These are the easiest shapes. To make a star, hold the bag vertically, ⅓ inch away from what you are decorating. Squeeze gently, stop, and lift. You will have produced a perfect five- or six-pointed star. Stars of whipped cream are used to decorate the tops of cakes, pies, and mousses.

ROSETTES: Rosettes are just like stars except that you rotate the tip of the bag in a tiny circle as you are squeezing. Remember to stop piping before you lift the bag. Rosettes are perfect for decorating deviled eggs and individual servings of mousse, pies, and cakes.

RIDGED STRIPES: Ridged stripes are made just like stars except that you move the bag in a straight line as you pipe, holding the bag at a slight angle. Pipe parallel rows of ribbed stripes in one direction, then in another at a 60-degree angle to make a decorative lattice for cakes.

RUFFLED BORDERS: Ruffled borders are made just like rosettes, except that you move the bag in a straight or curved line as you pipe, holding the bag at a slight angle. Ruffled borders are often used to decorate the perimeter of a pie or cake.

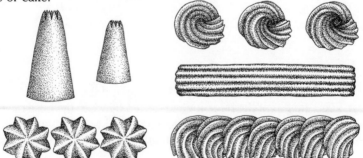

LESSON 46

Fruit Desserts

◇

Technique:
POACHING PEARS AND OTHER FRUIT

Master Recipe:
PEARS POACHED IN WINE AND CRÈME DE
    CASSIS

Variations:
PEARS BELLE HÉLÈNE
STRAWBERRY SOUP
STRAWBERRIES "BLUE STRAWBERY"

◇ ◇ ◇

In many parts of the world, dessert begins and ends with fresh fruit. Fruit desserts have the dual advantage of being light and refreshing and quick and easy to make. Below are four of my favorites: pears poached in red wine with *crème de cassis,* pears *belle Hélène* (with ice cream and chocolate sauce), strawberry soup, and strawberries "Blue Strawbery."

Two of the recipes call for poached fruit. Fruit should be gently simmered in a syrup made with wine or water, flavored with sugar and spices to taste. Test doneness by inserting a skewer in the thickest part of the fruit. When it meets just a little resistance, the fruit is cooked. Remember that the fruit will continue cooking as it cools.

◇ ◇ ◇

Pears Poached in Wine and
Crème de Cassis

The best pear for this simple dessert is the comice, distinguished by its reddish skin and intense pear perfume. (It is available at specialty greengrocers.) *Crème de cassis* is a black currant liqueur from Burgundy. It is well known as an ingredient in *kir*—an aperitif made by mixing 4 or 5 parts dry white wine to 1 part black currant liqueur. The pears can be poached up to 48 hours ahead of time; the plates are assembled at the last minute. This dish was inspired by Ann Sterling, a fine cook who worked aboard the luxury barge *Etoile de Champagne.*

Serves 6

2 cups dry red wine
1 cup *crème de cassis*
½ cup sugar (or to taste)
2 cinnamon sticks
5 whole cloves
5 cardamom pods
½ inch fresh ginger root, peeled and thinly sliced
3 large ripe comice pears (or Anjou or bosc pears; the ripeness is the important thing here)
2 strips lemon peel (remove them with a vegetable peeler), plus the cut lemon

FOR THE GARNISH:

½ cup cream beaten to stiff peaks
12 fresh mint or watercress leaves
1 maraschino cherry, cut into 6 slivers (optional)

6 chilled dessert plates

1. Combine the wine, *crème de cassis,* sugar, spices, and lemon peel in a wide saucepan, and bring to a boil. Meanwhile peel the pears: use the tip of the vegetable peeler to cut out the ends, then remove the peel in clean, longitudinal strips. Cut the pears in half and remove the cores with a melon baller. Rub the pear halves with the cut lemon to prevent them from discoloring.

2. Place the pears in the wine, round side down, and gently simmer for 5–10 minutes, or until each pear is very easily pierced with a skewer. (Test from the core side, to keep the round side unblemished.) Remove the pears with a slotted spoon and transfer them to a cake rack set on a tray (to catch drips) to cool. Continue to boil the poaching liquid until only 1½ cups

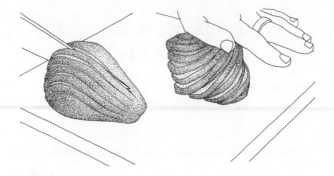

liquid remain. Strain this sauce and chill. The pears and poaching liquid should be kept in the refrigerator until serving.

3. Fan out the pears. Place each pear half, cut side down, on a cutting board. Using a paring knife and starting at the wide end of the pear, make a series of parallel vertical cuts almost to the stem end. Do not cut all the way through, however; the slices must be attached at one end. Gently flatten the pear toward one side with the palm of your hand to fan out the slices. Slice and fan out all the pear halves this way.

4. To serve, spoon ¼ cup sauce on each plate and set the fanned-out pear in the center. Pipe a rosette of whipped cream (for complete instructions on using the piping bag see page 278) on the narrow end of each pear and in it set a cherry sliver. Set two mint leaves in each rosette of whipped cream.

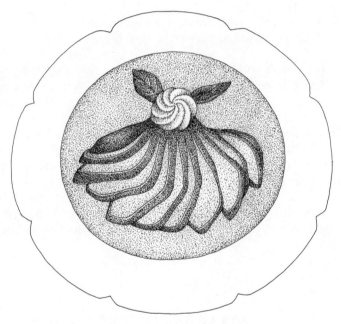

PEARS BELLE HÉLÈNE

PEARS WITH ICE CREAM AND HOT CHOCOLATE SAUCE

Pears "lovely Helen" is the French equivalent of a banana split. As you eat it, imagine you are sitting at a sidewalk table at La Coupole, a fashionable café in Montparnasse famed equally for its people-watching and its desserts.

Serves 6

3 large ripe pears poached in simple syrup as described below
1 pint vanilla ice cream
    chocolate sauce (see below)
¼ cup lightly toasted almonds

FOR THE SIMPLE SYRUP:

½ lemon
½ cup sugar
2 cups water
2 strips lemon zest

FOR THE CHOCOLATE SAUCE:

½ cup heavy cream
8 ounces semisweet chocolate, finely chopped
2 tablespoons Grand Marnier, or spirit of your choice

1. Peel the pears and rub with cut lemon to prevent discoloring. Core the pears with a melon baller. Bring the water, sugar, and zest to a boil and poach the pears in this mixture for 5 minutes, or until the pears can easily be pierced with a skewer. Drain and cool on a cake rack.

2. Prepare the chocolate sauce: bring the cream to a boil. Stir in the chocolate off the heat (if necessary, return the pan to a low heat—the chocolate should be completely melted). Stir in the Grand Marnier. The sauce is now ready but can be kept warm in a double boiler.

3. To assemble the pears *belle Hélène,* place a scoop of ice cream in each of 6 saucer-shaped champagne glasses or goblets. Top each with a poached pear. Spoon the hot chocolate sauce on top, and sprinkle with the toasted almonds.

STRAWBERRY SOUP

This unusual dessert is another creation of Breton chef Louis LeRoy. It is served in a brandy snifter, which funnels the enticing scents of fresh berries and mint to the nose. *Fraise* is a fruit brandy made with strawberries; substitute *framboise* (raspberry brandy) or Cointreau.

Serves 6

2 pints fresh, ripe strawberries
3–4 tablespoons sugar (or to taste)
    juice of 1 lemon (or to taste)
6 splashes *fraise* or spirit of your choice

3 tablespoons finely slivered fresh mint leaves

6 brandy snifters

1. Wash and hull the berries, reserving and halving 9 perfect berries. Puree the rest in a blender or food processor, with sugar and lemon juice to taste.

2. Divide the strawberry puree neatly and evenly among the brandy snifters, adding three strawberry halves and a splash of *fraise* to each. Sprinkle fresh mint on top, and serve with long-handled spoons.

STRAWBERRIES "BLUE STRAWBERY"

The success of any recipe lies in the whole being greater than the sum of the parts. One of the best examples I know is a dessert of startling simplicity, served at the Blue Strawbery (no double "r") restaurant in Portsmouth, New Hampshire. The combination of sour cream and brown sugar also goes well with pineapple.

Serves 4

1 pint ripe, unblemished strawberries
1 cup sour cream
1 cup brown sugar

Wash and blot dry the strawberries, leaving the stems on, and place them in a bowl. Place the sour cream and brown sugar in separate bowls. Let each guest dip his strawberries first in sour cream, then in brown sugar, and finally in his mouth. The flavor combination is as delicious as it is unexpected.

LESSON 47

Crème Anglaise and Zabaglione

CUSTARD SAUCE AND ITS DERIVATIVES

◇

Techniques:
COOKING CRÈME ANGLAISE
COOKING ZABAGLIONE

Master Recipe:
BASIC CRÈME ANGLAISE
ZABAGLIONE

Variations:
CHILLED ZABAGLIONE FOR FRUIT

◇   ◇   ◇

Crème *anglaise* (pronounced "krem ang-lez"), literally "English cream," is a dizzyingly rich custard sauce made from milk, sugar, and egg yolks. *Zabaglione* (pronounced "za-by-own-e") is an Italian dessert consisting of whole eggs and wine whisked with sugar to a cloudlike foam. The secret to both lies in cooking the yolks enough to thicken them but not so much that they scramble. *Crème anglaise* is discussed directly below; *zabaglione,* on page 288.

By itself, *crème anglaise* makes a delicious sauce for poached fruit and fresh berries. It is also the base for numerous desserts. Bavarian cream is a *crème anglaise* set with gelatin and enriched with whipped cream. A cold soufflé or chiffon pie filling is a Bavarian cream lightened with stiffly beaten egg whites. *Crème anglaise* is also the base of French ice cream—the best in the world.

◇   ◇   ◇

Basic Crème Anglaise

Basic *crème anglaise* makes an excellent sauce for fresh blueberries or raspberries. The vanilla bean is optional, but it adds depth to the flavor. Add any alcohol-based flavorings after the sauce has cooled (otherwise, the heat evaporates the alcohol, and you will have to use twice as much).

Makes 2 cups, 8 servings

- 1 vanilla bean (optional)
- 2 cups milk
- 6 egg yolks
- 6–8 tablespoons sugar (depending on the sweetness of the flavoring)
- 2–3 teaspoons flavoring of your choice (Grand Marnier, Poire Williams, Drambuie, Kahlua, etc.)

1. If using a vanilla bean, split it lengthwise and infuse it in the milk in a large, heavy, nonaluminum saucepan over the lowest possible heat for 15 minutes.

2. Bring the milk to a full boil. Meanwhile, whisk the egg yolks with the sugar. (Whisk these ingredients just to mix—overwhisking will make too much foam.) Have ready a fine-meshed strainer.

3. Whisk the hot milk in a *thin* stream into the yolk mixture. Return this mixture to the saucepan and place it over a medium-high heat. Cook the *crème anglaise* for 2–3 minutes, stirring constantly with a wooden spoon (whisking here would also make too much foam). As the sauce reaches the correct consistency, there will be three telltale signs:
—the foam on top will begin to subside;
—the yolks will lose their raw egg smell;
—the mixture will thicken to the consistency of heavy cream.
The classic test for doneness is to draw your finger across the back of the coated wooden spoon: if the mixture is sufficiently thick so that your

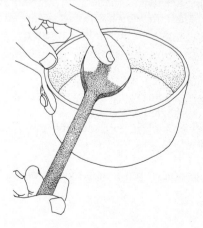

finger leaves a clean line, the custard is cooked. Do not let the mixture boil or the yolks will scramble. (If it curdles, you must throw it out and start again.)

4. Immediately pour the sauce through the strainer back into the bowl. Add the flavoring when the sauce is cool. (Grand Marnier-flavored sauce goes well with raspberries; Poire Williams sauce with poached pears.) If using the *crème anglaise* for a Bavarian cream, add the gelatin while the sauce is still hot.

◇   ◇   ◇

Zabaglione

Few dishes have a more curious history than the frothy, Italian egg dessert zabaglione. The Marechal Baglione defended Florence against the Castracani in the fourteenth century. Reduced to eggs and brandy (the enemy having captured the provision wagon), the marshal's chef invented a sweet dessert, which he called *zuppa baglioni*—"Baglioni's soup." In time the term was shortened to *zabaglione.*

Zabaglione owes its lightness to the high proportion of liquid to eggs. As the mixture is very fragile, we work over a pan of gently boiling water, not on direct heat. Successful zabaglione requires a vigorous beating, so use a springy whisk or an electric beater. We beat the mixture to ribbon stage; that is, until it is sufficiently thick to fall from a raised whisk in a thick, silky ribbon. If overcooked, however, the zabaglione will collapse.

Zabaglione is delicious by itself; it is equally lovely served hot over fresh raspberries or blueberries. It can also be mixed with whipped cream or set with gelatin and served chilled as a mousse.

Traditionally, this dessert is made with Marsala, a sweet wine from Sicily. I prefer to use Madeira, which is not as sugary and is more interesting as a wine. Zabaglione can also be made with sherry, port, and French and German dessert wines. Adjust the sugar to suit the sweetness of the wine.

Serves 4

 4 egg yolks
4–6 tablespoons sugar (or to taste)
 ½ cup Madeira, Marsala, port, sauterne, or a French or German
     dessert wine

Combine the ingredients in a nonaluminum bowl. Place the bowl over

a pan of gently boiling water and whisk vigorously for 3 minutes, or until the mixture is:
—light and frothy;
—tripled in volume;
—and falls in a thick ribbon when the whisk is raised.
Spoon the zabaglione into martini glasses and serve at once.

CHILLED ZABAGLIONE FOR FRUIT

The advantage of this chilled zabaglione is that it can be prepared several hours ahead of time. Spoon it over the fresh fruit of your choice.

Serves 6

  5 egg yolks
  ½ cup Marsala wine
  ¼ cup dry white wine
  3 tablespoons sugar
  ¾ cup heavy whipping cream
  1 pint strawberries, blueberries, or raspberries, picked over
      and washed

Cook the first four ingredients over boiling water as described in the master recipe. Let cool slightly. Meanwhile, beat the cream to stiff peaks. Working over a bowl of ice, fold the whipped cream into the yolk mixture. The recipe can be prepared up to 6 hours ahead to this stage.

To serve, spoon the zabaglione mixture into wine glasses and garnish with fresh berries.

LESSON 48

Bavarian Creams and Dessert Mousses

———◇———

Techniques:
WORKING WITH GELATIN
MAKING PRALINE

Master Recipe:
LEMON MOUSSE

Variations:
CAFÉ AU LAIT MOUSSE
PRALINE MOUSSE
FRENCH VANILLA ICE CREAM

◇   ◇   ◇

A Bavarian cream is a *crème anglaise* thickened with gelatin and enriched with whipped cream. To make a dessert mousse, add stiffly beaten egg whites to a Bavarian cream. When *crème anglaise* is combined with whipped cream and frozen, it becomes French ice cream. This lesson takes up all three.

Gelatin is a protein extracted from animal bones and skins (and also from Irish moss). It owes its thickening properties to its ability to absorb up to 10 times its own volume in water. Until this century, cooks used natural gelatin in the cumbersome form of sturgeons' bladders and calves' feet. In the 1890s a salesman from Johnston, New York, Charles B. Knox, had the idea to sell powdered gelatin in easy-to-use packages. The most widely used unflavored gelatin still bears his name.

To use powdered gelatin, we soften it first over *cold* water or other liquid, using 4 tablespoons liquid for every envelope gelatin. (Hot water tends to make gelatin lumpy.) After a few minutes, the mixture will look soft and spongy. It can now be whisked into hot *crème anglaise,* but as further precaution against lumps, I prefer to melt the sponged gelatin in a shallow pan of boiling water before adding it to the base mixture.

Gelatin sets when cool. To speed up the process, we can place the mixture over a bowl of ice, stirring frequently with a rubber spatula. If lumps form, try whisking them out. If this fails, set the pan over simmering water, melt the mixture, and try chilling again. The whipped cream and/or stiffly beaten egg whites are added when the base mixture is on the verge of setting—it should wiggle like Jell-O but not be completely firm. Bavarian cream and dessert mousses should be made at least 2 hours before serving; the night before is even better.

Gelatin-based desserts should be firm but not rubbery. As a rule of thumb, 1 envelope gelatin will properly thicken 2 cups of liquid. (If you can bounce a fork off the finished product, you know you've added too much.) Fresh pineapple, by the way, contains an enzyme that prevents gelatin from thickening.

◇　◇　◇

Lemon Mousse

Lemon mousse takes its flavor from both the zest and the juice of the lemon. The zest is the oil-rich outer rind of the lemon; it is best removed from the fruit with a vegetable peeler.

Serves 6

> 3–4 large lemons (approximately ½ cup juice)
> 1 cup milk, plus 2 tablespoons
> ½ package gelatin
> 4 eggs, separated
> ½ cup sugar
> 1 cup heavy cream
> 1 tablespoon Cointreau
> pinch of salt, pinch of cream of tartar for beating the whites
> candied violets for garnish
>
> 6 wine or martini glasses for serving

1. Remove the zest of the lemon in strips with a vegetable peeler. Infuse these in the milk for 20 minutes over a very low heat. Squeeze the juice from the lemons into a heatproof measuring cup (you should have about ½ cup), and sprinkle the gelatin on top. When the gelatin is soft and spongy, place the measuring cup in a pan of simmering water to melt it.

2. Prepare a *crème anglaise* as described above, using the milk, yolks, and all but 2 tablespoons sugar. Stir in the melted gelatin. Set the mixture over a pan of ice and stir it from time to time with a rubber spatula until it is on the verge of setting.

3. Whip the cream to stiff peaks and fold most of it into the lemon mixture, reserving a little for the garnish. Fold in the Cointreau. Beat 2 of the egg whites to stiff peaks, adding salt and cream of tartar after 10 seconds, sprinkling in the remaining sugar at the end. Fold the whites into the mousse mixture. Spoon the mousse mixture into the martini glasses and chill for at least two hours. (Lemon mousse can be prepared up to 24 hours ahead.) Just before serving, decorate each mousse with a rosette made from the rest of the whipped cream, and top with a candied violet.

CAFÉ AU LAIT MOUSSE

This unusual dessert recalls my student days in Paris. I was living on the narrow Rue Mouffetard, and every morning I would take my breakfast at a working-class bar. As I sipped my *café au lait,* I would watch my neighbors pour a shot of calvados (French apple brandy) into their empty, still-warm coffee cups—the combination was delicious. For an Italian accent, you could sprinkle the top with cocoa and cinnamon.

Serves 8

> 1 cup milk
> ½ cup sugar
> 6 egg yolks
> 1 cup freshly brewed espresso coffee
> 1 envelope gelatin
> 2 tablespoons calvados
> 1 cup heavy cream, beaten to stiff peaks with a little
>   confectioner's sugar
> 8 coffee beans (for decoration)
>
> 8 martini glasses

1. Prepare the *crème anglaise* as described on page 287, adding the coffee to the scalded milk. Meanwhile, soften the gelatin over the calvados and 2 tablespoons water in a heatproof measuring cup. Melt the gelatin in simmering water, and whisk it into the coffee mixture.

2. Set the coffee mixture over a pan of ice, and stir from time to time with a rubber spatula until it is on the verge of setting. Fold in most of the whipped cream, reserving a little for the garnish. Spoon the mixture into the martini glasses and chill for at least 2 hours. Decorate each mousse with rosettes of whipped cream, each crowned with a coffee bean.

PRALINE MOUSSE

Praline is a flavoring made from almonds and burnt sugar. The preparation is named for Plessis-Praslin, a seventeenth-century marshal of France, whose cook invented it as candy. When pulverizing praline in the food processor, run the machine in spurts and avoid overgrinding or you will turn the powder into a gummy paste. Frangelico is a hazelnut-flavored liqueur made in Italy. In its absence, use all rum.

Serves 8

FOR THE PRALINE:

1 cup sugar
1 cup unblanched almonds, plus 8 whole almonds for
    decoration
oil for the baking sheet

crème anglaise (see above) made with 2 cups milk, 6 egg
    yolks, and ¼ cup sugar
1 package gelatin
2 tablespoons Frangelico
2 tablespoons dark rum
1 cup heavy cream beaten to stiff peaks

8 martini or wine glasses

1. Make the praline. Lightly oil the *back* of a baking sheet. (Using the back will make it easier to pry off the praline.) Place the sugar and almonds in a non-tin-lined saucepan over high heat. Cook, stirring with a wooden spoon until the sugar melts and turns golden brown and the almonds start to snap, crackle, and pop (as the sugar heats the oil inside them). Immediately pour the almond mixture onto an oiled baking sheet.

Warning: Molten sugar is excruciatingly hot. Be careful not to let it touch your skin.

2. When the praline is cool (it will resemble peanut brittle), break it into small pieces, and pulverize these in a food processor. Run the processor in short spurts and don't overgrind: you want to wind up with powder, not paste. NOTE: The praline powder can be prepared ahead of time. Let it cool *completely,* then store in an airtight jar. It will keep for up to 2 weeks.

3. Prepare the *crème anglaise* as described on page 287. Meanwhile, soften the gelatin over the Frangelico and rum in a heatproof measuring cup. Melt the softened gelatin in a pan of simmering water and whisk it into the *crème anglaise.* Set the mixture over a pan of ice and stir it from time to time with a rubber spatula until it is on the verge of setting.

4. When the *crème anglaise* is on the verge of setting, fold in ¾ of the cream and half the praline powder. Spoon half the mixture into wine goblets, sprinkle with ½ the remaining praline powder, and add the remaining mousse mixture. Sprinkle the remaining praline powder on top, followed by rosettes made of the reserved whipped cream (see page 277). Crown each rosette with an unblanched almond. Praline mousse can be prepared up to 24 hours ahead of time.

VARIATION: To make a cold praline soufflé or chiffon pie filling, fold 4 stiffly beaten egg whites into the *crème anglaise* when you add the cream. Praline can also be made with hazelnuts.

FRENCH VANILLA ICE CREAM

Vanilla is an orchid native to Central America whose giant vine can grow to a length of 350 feet. Its fruit is a long, slender pod filled with tiny black seeds—the emblem of exceptional vanilla ice cream. When buying fresh vanilla, look for pods covered with a light white powder called "frost." This ice cream owes its richness to the high proportion of egg yolks. Ice cream machines vary according to the manufacturer: add the ice and salt as directed by the instruction manual of your particular machine.

Makes 1 quart (serves 4–6).

> 2 cups milk
> 1 vanilla bean, split
> 6 egg yolks
> 1 cup sugar
> 1 cup cream, beaten to soft peaks

1. Place the milk and vanilla bean in a large saucepan over the lowest possible heat and let the mixture infuse for 15 minutes.
2. Prepare a *crème anglaise:* Increase heat to high to bring the milk to a boil. Meanwhile, whisk the egg yolks with the sugar in a large bowl. Whisk the milk into the yolk mixture in a thin stream. Return this mixture to the saucepan. Have a strainer ready over the mixing bowl. Cook the yolk mixture for three to four minutes over medium heat, stirring constantly with a wooden spoon, until the foam subsides and the mixture thickens to the consistency of heavy cream. The classic test for doneness is to draw your finger across the back of the wooden spoon; if a clean line remains, the custard is cooked. Do not let the sauce boil, or it will curdle.
3. Remove the pan from the heat immediately and pour the thickened

custard through the strainer into the mixing bowl. Let stand till cool. Stir in the lightly beaten cream. Pour the mixture into your ice cream machine and churn, according to the instructions for your machine, until it is firm and frozen. If you have the patience, "ripen" the ice cream in the machine or in your freezer for two to three hours before serving. The cat's tongue cookies on page 322 would be an excellent accompaniment.

Dessert Soufflés

————————◇————————

Techniques:

BEATING EGG WHITES

MAKING PASTRY CREAM

FOLDING

MAKING STARCH-BASED SOUFFLÉS

MAKING FRUIT-BASED SOUFFLÉS

Master Recipe:

HOT APPLE SOUFFLÉ

Variations:

HOT PEAR SOUFFLÉ

HOT PEACH SOUFFLÉ

GRAND MARNIER SOUFFLÉ

◇　◇　◇

Soufflés are showstoppers any time during a meal but especially at dessert. Dessert soufflés fall into two basic classes: those that use pastry cream (the filling inside eclairs) as the base mixture, and those that use pureed fruit. Pastry cream soufflés are usually flavored with liqueurs. Fruit-based soufflés are popular with practitioners of *nouvelle cuisine* because they contain no flour.

Below you'll find detailed instructions on making the two base mixtures and on properly beating the egg whites. Pay particular attention to the latter, as egg whites are what make a soufflé rise. (For an explanation of *why* soufflés rise, see page 74.) Dessert soufflés rise higher than savory ones for two reasons: the base mixture is lighter and the whites contain sugar. (Sugar acts as a stabilizer on the whites.) Dessert soufflés can be baked in the traditional white porcelain dish, or in a charlotte mold (a metal mold with outwardly sloping sides). The latter is infinitely more chic. Remember to double-butter your mold (brush it once with melted butter, freeze the dish, and brush it again with melted butter) and completely line it with sugar.

BEATING EGG WHITES

When I was in cooking school, egg whites seemed invented expressly to torture the apprentices. There were endless quantities to be beaten by hand. The copper bowl had to be scrubbed with rock salt and vinegar, a mixture that blasted our nostrils and stung the small cuts on our hands. Beating egg whites by hand in a copper bowl remains the superior method (the copper imparts an electrostatic charge), but *only if* you have the stamina to beat them for the requisite five minutes.

The next best method is to use a machine with a planetary beater (that is, one whose beater both spins on its own axis and rotates around the bowl). Two excellent machines are made by KitchenAid and Kenwood. A hand-held mixer is adequate but not great.

Egg whites must be completely free of yolk. When separating more than one egg, separate each white into a small ramekin, before adding to the other whites. This way, you will catch any impurities, wasting at most one egg, without contaminating the whole batch. If you do see a tiny spot of yolk, you can try fishing it out with half an eggshell.

Machine Method

1. Make sure the bowl and beaters are immaculately clean. Beat the whites at low speed for 15 seconds. Add ¼ teaspoon each cream of tartar and salt. The salt helps break down the albumen (the gooey part) of the whites, so they will be smooth and even. The cream of tartar is slightly acidic (like the vinegar used for cleaning the copper bowl): it helps stabilize the whites. In the absence of cream of tartar, use a few drops of lemon juice or vinegar.

2. Increase speed to medium and beat the whites for 1½ minutes, or until they are light and billowy. Increase the speed to high, and beat for 20 seconds. If you are making a dessert soufflé, sprinkle in the sugar. Watch the whites with a hawk's eye, particularly at the edge of the bowl. Beat the whites until they are very smooth, stiff, and white; the whole process will take roughly 2 minutes. Stop the machine the moment the whites begin to look "grainy" (with uneven-sized bubbles) or watery. The disadvantage of machines is that they tend to overbeat the whites, causing the solids and liquids to separate. If the whites are not too far gone, they can be rescued by beating in sugar. If they look really watery, discard them and start over. Whites beaten by machine will never be as stiff and even-textured as those beaten by hand in a copper bowl. Nonetheless, you should be able to lift the whites on the beater of the machine.

Copper Bowl Method

1. Place 2 tablespoons each kosher salt and vinegar in a bowl. Using a paper towel, wipe the bowl with this mixture: the metal inside should be shiny. Rinse the bowl with cold water, and wipe it dry. Use a balloon whisk (a springy whisk with lots of tines), and be sure that it, too, is immaculately clean.

2. Place the whites in the bowl, and break them up by twirling the whisk between the palms of your hands. Lean the bowl over, and begin to beat the whites with the side of the whisk. Try to keep the whites in a confined

area. Start beating slowly, gradually picking up speed. After 3 or 4 minutes, the whites should be stiff. If you are making a dessert soufflé, this is the time to add sugar. Sprinkle it in gradually, and rotate the whisk in a circular motion around the inside of the bowl, working as fast as you can for 30 seconds. This is called "meringuing" the whites. The sugar acts as a stabilizer.

Note: When egg whites are properly stiff, you should be able to:
—invert the bowl;
—cut the whites with a knife;
—stand a whole egg on top of the whites without their sagging.

It is almost impossible to overbeat egg whites when working by hand. If you don't have a copper bowl, use stainless steel; plastic, glass, and aluminum produce poor results.

BEATING EGG WHITES

Egg whites will keep several months in the refrigerator and they can be frozen. Store egg whites in a *loosely* covered jar. In a tightly sealed jar they will acquire an unpleasant odor. Old egg whites beat better than new ones. (This is because some of the water has evaporated from the old ones, concentrating the white.)

Don't try to beat too many whites at once. It's hard to beat more than 6–8 egg whites by hand at one time; hand-held mixers can handle up to 6 whites, planetary-type machines, 8.

Start beating the whites slowly, picking up speed as you go along. Rapid beating at the beginning makes large bubbles, which are more apt to collapse later than small ones.

◇　◇　◇

Hot Apple Soufflé

This hot apple soufflé is simplicity itself, consisting of freshly made apple sauce leavened with stiffly beaten egg whites. Calvados is French apple brandy; it's available at any fine spirit shop. The cornstarch is added to prevent the fruit juices in the soufflé from separating. NOTE: if this is your first soufflé, or you want a fuller explanation of the techniques, see page 74.

Serves 4

1 pound firm, tart apples (like Granny Smiths or Northern
    Spys)
juice of ½ lemon
½ cup sugar
2 teaspoons cornstarch
1 tablespoon calvados
6 egg whites
    pinch of salt, pinch of cream of tartar

1 5-cup soufflé dish, double-buttered and sprinkled with sugar

1. Peel and core the apples, and finely chop or puree in a food processor, adding lemon juice to prevent the fruit from discoloring. Place the apples with ¼ cup sugar in a saucepan and cook over high heat, stirring from time to time, until most of the water has evaporated and approximately 1 cup puree remains. Dissolve the cornstarch in the calvados and stir it in, bringing the fruit pulp to a rapid boil. The recipe can be prepared up to 24 hours ahead to this stage.

2. Beat the egg whites to stiff peaks, adding salt and cream of tartar, and sprinkling in the remaining sugar at the end. Meanwhile, reheat the fruit puree if necessary: it should be very hot.

3. Stir ¼ of the whites into the hot fruit puree and gently fold this mixture into the remaining whites with a rubber spatula. Gently spoon this mixture into the soufflé dish. Smooth the top of the soufflé with a moistened spatula, and, if desired, make a design. Run your thumbs around the inside edge of the soufflé dish to keep the sides from sticking as the soufflé rises. Provided the whites are properly beaten and gently folded, the soufflé can be prepared up to 4 hours ahead and refrigerated.

4. Preheat the oven to 400°F. and bake the soufflé for 15 minutes or until cooked to taste. To tell if it is cooked, poke the side of the dish; the filling should be puffed but still wiggle ever so slightly.

Serving: For heightened drama, flambé the soufflé before serving: warm a few tablespoons of calvados in a saucepan and ignite with a match. Make a hole in the soufflé with two spoons and pour in the flaming calvados. See glossary for safety measures to be taken when flambéing.

◇   ◇   ◇

HOT PEAR SOUFFLÉ: Substitute 1 pound *ripe* pears for the apples, and Poire Williams (pear brandy) for the calvados.

HOT PEACH SOUFFLÉ: Substitute 1 pound *ripe* peaches for the apples, and Grand Marnier for the calvados.

GRAND MARNIER SOUFFLÉ

This is probably the world's most famous soufflé, and it differs from the previous recipes in that its base mixture is pastry cream, not pureed fruit. Pastry cream is best known as the filling inside eclairs. It is thickened with flour, which enables it to be boiled, unlike the *crème anglaise* (page 287).

Unfortunately, pastry cream scorches easily. For the best results use a heavy, nonaluminum saucepan, and whirl your whisk like a madman. If you should get a small burnt spot on the base of the pan, you may be able to rescue the pastry cream by transferring it, without scraping the bottom, to another pan. But sample it first, to make sure it doesn't taste scorched.

This soufflé will be even better if you have some leftover ladyfingers or sponge cake. Soak chunks of cake in Grand Marnier and layer them with the soufflé mixture. Grand Marnier differs from other orange-flavored liqueurs in that it is made with cognac, not grain neutral spirits. Grand Marnier soufflé takes minutes to make and is ideal for serving unexpected company.

Serves 4

> a few strips orange zest (removed with a vegetable peeler)
> 1 cup milk
> 4 eggs, separated, plus 2 whites
> ½ cup sugar
> 3 tablespoons flour
> pinches of salt and cream of tartar
> 3 tablespoons Grand Marnier or to taste
> 3–4 ladyfingers or a slice of sponge cake, broken into 1-inch
> pieces (about 1 cup)—optional
> butter and sugar for preparing the dishes
>
> 1 5-cup soufflé dish or charlotte mold, or 4 individual soufflé
> dishes

1. Warm the orange peel in the milk over a low heat for 10 minutes. Meanwhile, thoroughly whisk the yolks with 4 tablespoons of sugar in a large bowl. Gradually whisk in the flour. Double-butter the soufflé dish. Be especially thorough around the top inside edges. Line the inside of the dish with sugar. If you are using ladyfingers or cake pieces, sprinkle them with Grand Marnier.

2. Bring the milk to a boil, and strain it into the yolk mixture in a *thin* stream, whisking vigorously. Return this mixture to the pan, and cook it over high heat, whisking vigorously, for 3 minutes; it should boil for at least 2 minutes. Do not let it burn. The base mixture can be made ahead of time, but if you do, dot the top with butter to prevent a skin from forming. (To

do this, run the end of a stick of butter over it.) Reheat before folding in the egg whites.

3. Beat the egg whites as described on page 298, adding the cream of tartar at the beginning, sprinkling in the remaining ¼ cup sugar at the end. Stir ¼ of the whites into the *hot* base mixture to lighten it. Fold the base mixture as gently as possible into the remaining whites. Fold just to mix: underfolding is better than overfolding.

4. Spoon the soufflé mixture into the prepared dish(es) in three batches, sprinkling each layer with Grand Marnier or the liqueur-soaked cake pieces. To sprinkle liqueur, hold your thumb over the neck of the bottle to control the flow. Smooth the top of the soufflé with a wet spatula. Run your thumbs around the inside edge of the dish to prevent the sides from sticking as the soufflé rises. If the whites are properly beaten and folded with suitable finesse, the soufflés can be prepared up to 4 hours ahead to this stage, and baked at the last minute.

5. Bake Grand Marnier soufflé in a preheated 400° oven for 15 minutes or until cooked to taste. To tell when a soufflé is cooked, gently poke the dish: if the soufflé wiggles a lot, it is undercooked; if it wiggles just a little, it is slightly moist in the center—the way I like it. Open the oven door as little as possible: cold air makes a soufflé fall. Serve at once: guests may wait for soufflés, but soufflés wait for no one.

VARIATIONS: There is no limit to the flavorings that can be used with pastry cream soufflés. Drambuie, Frangelico, and Sambuca are but a few of the liqueurs that can be used in place of Grand Marnier.

LESSON 50

Fruit Tarts

◇

Techniques:
MAKING FRANGIPANE
MAKING TART TATIN
MAKING PASTRY CREAM

Master Recipe:
NORMANDY PEAR PIE

Variations:
ALMOND-PLUM TART
FRESH STRAWBERRY OR RASPBERRY TART
TART TATIN

◇   ◇   ◇

"**A**s American as apple pie?" A European might beg to differ. The French are particularly skilled in the art of making fruit tarts, as is seen in the recipes below.

The first two tarts are made with *frangipane*, a creamy filling made of almonds, sugar, and butter. (The term comes from Latin *frangibile* and *panis*, literally "frangible [breakable] bread"). Frangipane lends a fruit tart a rich, nutty flavor, and it also keeps the crust crisp and dry by absorbing any fruit juices. For this reason, tarts made with frangipane do not need to be blind-baked.

The tart Tatin is unusual in that the filling is cooked on top of the stove. Tart Tatin features apples caramelized with butter and sugar in a frying pan. The crust is baked on top of the apples and the tart is inverted for serving.

The fresh strawberry or raspberry tart uses a preparation we encountered in the soufflé lesson—pastry cream. The crust can be prepared ahead; so can the egg-rich filling. The fruit is arranged on top before serving and brushed with red currant glaze.

Complete instructions on making pie dough are found in Lesson 13.

◇   ◇   ◇

Normandy Pear Pie

This attractive tart can be made with any species of pear—bosc, Bartlett, or comice—provided it is ripe. Since ripe pears have become as elusive as truffles, we suggest poaching the pears till tender (see instuctions on page 284). Poire Williams is a pear *eau-de-vie* (fruit brandy); substitute any other fruit brandy or even Cointreau.

Serves 6–8

1 12-inch pie shell (blind-baking optional)

FOR THE FRANGIPANE:

⅔ cup almonds
½ cup sugar
5 tablespoons unsalted butter, at room temperature
1 egg, at room temperature
1 tablespoon flour
1 tablespoon Poire Williams

FOR THE PEARS:

3 ripe pears
½ lemon
½ cup sugar
2 cups water
2 strips lemon zest
½ vanilla bean (optional)

FOR THE APRICOT-BRANDY GLAZE:

3 tablespoons apricot jam
2 tablespoons Poire Williams, Cointreau, or water

1. Prepare the pie shell.

2. Prepare the frangipane. Grind the nuts with the sugar in a food processor. (When grinding nuts, run the machine in spurts. Do not overgrind, or you will reduce the nuts to an oily mess.) Add the butter, and blend until light and smooth. Blend in the egg, followed by the flour and brandy. (If you do not own a food processor, grind the nuts in a cheese grater or meat grinder. Cream the butter and sugar, and gradually whisk in the the nuts and other ingredients.) The frangipane can be made up to 48 hours ahead of time, but be sure to remove it from the refrigerator several hours ahead of time to ensure that it will be soft and spreadable.

3. Peel the pears and rub with cut lemon to prevent discoloring. Core the pears with a melon baller. If the pears are anything less than squishy ripe, poach them in syrup until soft. Bring the water, sugar, and flavorings to a boil, and poach the pears in this mixture for 5 minutes, or until the pears can easily be pierced with a skewer. Drain and cool on a cake rack.

4. Assemble the Normandy pear pie. Spread the frangipane evenly over the bottom of the pie shell. Arrange the pear halves on top, small ends toward the center. Try to have the pears as evenly spaced as possible—as in grade school, neatness counts!

5. Bake the Normandy pear pie in a preheated 400° oven for 30–40 minutes or until the frangipane is golden-brown and set. Remove from oven and cool on a cake rack, as described above. (Return the tart on the cake rack to the oven for 5 minutes if necessary to crisp the bottom crust.)

6. Meanwhile, prepare the glaze. Melt the apricot jam in a small saucepan and thin it with enough *poire* or other brandy to the consistency of light cream. Gently brush the glaze over the cooled Normandy pear pie. (Apricot glaze seals in freshness, as well as giving pastries an attractive luster.) Serve at room temperature.

Note: Normandy pear pie can be made up to 6 hours ahead.

ALMOND-PLUM TART

This almond-plum tart is similar to the Normandy pear pie but quicker and easier, as the plums need not be poached and sliced. Use any *ripe* plum: I like the large, purple Santa Rosa. Purists will wish to substitute a plum brandy, like French *mirabelle* or Yugoslavian *slivovitz,* for the *poire.*

Serves 8

5–6 large, ripe plums (more if you use a smaller species of plum; the important factor here is ripeness)
1 12-inch pie shell (blind-baking optional; recipe on p. 101)
1 batch frangipane (see above)
apricot-brandy glaze (see above)

1. Cut the plums in half lengthwise and remove the pits. (To split a plum, cut it around its midpoint to the pit. Grasp one half in each hand, and twist in opposite directions. This will be easy if the plum is ripe.)

2. Spread the tart shell with frangipane. Arrange the plums on top, evenly spaced, with one in the center. Bake and cool the tart as described in the master recipe. Gently brush it with glaze, and serve at room temperature.

FRESH STRAWBERRY OR RASPBERRY TART

There is nothing more refreshing on a summer day than this fresh strawberry tart. Complete instructions on making pastry cream are found on page 300. *Framboise* is an *eau-de-vie* (fruit brandy) made from raspberries.

Serves 8

1 12-inch pie shell (see recipe on page 101)
1½ pints fresh strawberries (or raspberries)

FOR THE PASTRY CREAM:

    3 egg yolks
    4 tablespoons sugar
    2 tablespoons flour
    1 cup milk
    1 tablespoon butter

    1 cup heavy cream
    2 tablespoons *framboise* or Cointreau

FOR THE RED CURRANT GLAZE:

    3 tablespoons red currant jam
    2 tablespoons *framboise* or Cointreau

1. Prepare and thoroughly blind-bake the pie shell. Wash and hull the strawberries. If using raspberries, do not wash but simply pick through them.

2. Prepare the pastry cream as described on page 300. Beat the heavy cream to soft peaks. When the pastry cream is cool, combine it with the whipped cream. Whisk in the flavoring.

3. To assemble the tart, spread the pastry cream inside the crust. Cut the strawberries in half (if using raspberries, leave them whole) and arrange them, rounded side up, on top. Melt the red currant jam with the *framboise* over low heat and brush this glaze on top of the berries. The tart should be assembled not more than 2 hours ahead.

TART TATIN

Tart Tatin, so the story goes, was invented and widely sold by two impoverished sisters from Soulogne (near the Loire). The secret lies in thoroughly caramelizing the apples over a *high* heat in a cast-iron skillet.

Serves 8

  6–8 small, firm, tart apples (Granny Smiths)
   ½ lemon
      basic pie dough made with 1 cup flour (see page 101)
    1 stick (8 tablespoons) unsalted butter
   ⅔ cup granulated sugar

1. Peel and halve the apples, and remove the cores with a melon baller. Rub them with cut lemon to prevent them from discoloring. Prepare the pie dough and chill for 20 minutes.

2. Thickly smear the bottom and sides of a 10-inch cast-iron skillet with ⅔ of the butter. Sprinkle with ⅔ of the sugar. Arrange the apple halves in

the pan in concentric circles, small ends down, the halves overlapping. Place one apple half, rounded side down, in the center.

3. Place the apples over *high* heat. Cook for 8–12 minutes, or until the sugar and butter form a golden-brown caramel, and the bottoms of the apples are browned. (Gently lift one of the halves at the end of a paring knife to check the bottom.) You must use a firm apple and cook it over high heat, or the apples will not caramelize but disintegrate into applesauce. If you have electric heat, turn the pan from time to time to prevent one spot from scorching. Preheat the oven to 400°F.

4. Dot the apples with the remaining butter and sugar. Place the frying pan in the oven and bake the apples for 15 minutes. Roll the pie dough into an 11-inch circle. Roll it up on a rolling pin, and unroll onto the skillet over the apples. Continue baking the crust for 30 minutes or until the crust is cooked.

5. Remove the pan from the oven and let it sit for 3 minutes. To unmold the tart, place a heatproof platter over the pan. Say the prayer of your choice and invert the pan, taking care not to burn yourself on the handle. The tart should slide out of the pan onto the platter. Many people like to serve tart Tatin with fresh whipped cream (see page 277.)

LESSON 51

Choux Pastry

◇

Techniques:
MAKING CHOUX PASTRY
PIPING CHOUX PASTRY

Master Recipe:
BASIC CHOUX PASTRY

Variations:
CREAM PUFFS
PROFITEROLES
WHIPPED CREAM DUCKS AND SWANS

◇ ◇ ◇

As a rule, we change our menus with each new session of the Taste of the Mountains. But there is one dish that has become as much a tradition of the school as our fondue welcome party and Bernerhof silk pie (see page 317). Every Saturday night at the end of dinner, a large round mirror is borne proudly into the dining room. A hush fills the room, then a round of applause— it's the moment of the whipped cream swans.

Whipped cream swans are a guaranteed showstopper, but despite their impressive appearance, they are as simple to make as cream puffs. Swans, cream puffs, eclairs, profiteroles, even French doughnuts share one thing in common: they are all made from *choux* pastry.

Pâte à choux means "cabbage dough," literally. (The French call their whipped-cream-filled shells little "cabbages" instead of cream puffs.) Choux paste is the easiest of all doughs to make, requiring neither rolling pin nor pastry marble but simply a saucepan and spoon. Unlike other pastries, the dough is cooked twice: once on the stove and once in the oven. When you have mastered choux pastry, and the related art of wielding a piping bag (see page 278), there are dozens of appetizers and desserts you can make. Following are instructions for making choux pastry, cream puffs (and profiteroles), and whipped cream ducks and swans.

◇ ◇ ◇

Basic Choux Pastry

The basic proportions for choux pastry are the same whether you are making appetizers or desserts. The number of eggs varies with the brand of flour —and with the weather (on humid days, flour is less absorbent). Let the consistency of the dough, rather than precise measurements, be your guide.

> 1 cup water
> 6 tablespoons butter, cut into small pieces
> scant ½ teaspoon salt
> scant ½ teaspoon sugar
> 1 cup flour
> 4–6 eggs, plus 1 egg beaten with a pinch of salt for glaze

1. Place the water, butter, salt, and sugar in a heavy-bottomed 2-quart saucepan. Bring the mixture to a *rolling* boil over a high heat. Remove the pan from the heat as soon as the butter melts and the water boils, or you will change the basic proportions of dry and wet ingredients.

2. Sift the flour through a strainer into the pan in one fell swoop. Using a wooden spoon, stir the ingredients together: you should wind up with a mixture that looks like mashed potatoes. Return the pan to a high heat and, stirring constantly, cook the mixture for 1 or 2 minutes, or until the excess moisture has evaporated and the dough comes away from the sides of the pan in smooth balls.

3. You are now ready to start adding the eggs. Beat them in one by one, until the dough is smooth, shiny, and the consistency of soft ice cream. Each time you add an egg, the mixture will disaggregate into slippery globules; do not add the next egg until you have beaten these into a smooth paste. To test the consistency of the dough, lift some with the wooden spoon. The dough should look soft and shiny and fall from the spoon with a *plop* after 5–10 seconds.

4. Eggs make choux pastry rise, so the more you add, the larger your puffs will be. More eggs make the puffs more fragile, however, and more likely to collapse when removed from the oven. As the dough approaches the proper consistency, you may wish to add the eggs half by half. To add a half egg, crack it into a cup, beat it with a fork, then pour half into the dough.

5. You are now ready to pipe the dough into the varous shapes. Preheat the oven to 400°F. Load the piping bag (see instructions on page 278). For the various shapes, see pages 309–10. Piping choux pastry is tricky; it helps to practice with instant mashed potatoes!

6. Despite its high butter content, choux pastry sometimes sticks— particularly on unseasoned baking sheets. Sprinkle a few drops of melted

butter on the baking sheet, and wipe most of it off with a paper towel. Anything more than the lightest buttering may cause the warm choux shapes to slide off the sheet. Pipe the shapes onto the back of the baking sheet: if any stick, it will be easier to slide them off with a knife.

7. Dip a fork in a cup of cold water, and with the flat side pat the tops of the choux shapes to smooth out any irregularities and lightly score the surface. (The water prevents the dough from sticking to the fork; the scoring helps the shapes rise more evenly.) Next, brush the tops of the shapes with egg glaze, taking care not to drip. (Glaze on a baking sheet prevents the shapes from rising.) Finally, sprinkle the baking sheet with cold water: the steam generated will help the pastries rise.

8. Bake the choux pastry in the top third of the oven for 20 minutes at 400°F. Try not to open the oven during the first 20 minutes of baking, and if you do, open it quickly—just a crack—and close it as gently as possible after you've satisfied your curiosity. The pastries are extremely fragile during the first 20 minutes of baking and a blast of cold air will deflate them.

9. Reduce the heat to 375° and continue baking for 25–35 minutes, or until the shapes are puffed and nicely browned all over. Invariably, choux pastry is underbaked, and, as is the case with most pastry, it tastes better cooked a little too long than not quite long enough. When choux pastry is completely cooked, the cracks on the surface will be the same brown color as the high points. Holes in the bottom of the choux pastry indicate the oven was too hot. If the pastries start to burn on the bottoms, place a cold baking sheet under the hot one. Do not bake choux pastry on more than one rack in the oven.

10. Once the choux shapes are thoroughly browned and crusty, remove them from the oven. All choux pastry shapes must be opened to release the steam, which would otherwise make them soggy. Make a 1-inch incision with a serrated knife in small shapes, like *profiteroles* and cream puffs. Cut the tops completely off larger shapes like swan bodies and duck bodies. Should the pastries feel soggy even after the steam has been released, return them to the oven for a few minutes at 375° to dry them out. All shapes should be transferred to a cake rack to cool.

◇   ◇   ◇

PIPING CHOUX PASTRY

As a rule, we pipe choux pastry with a bag fitted with a ½-inch round tip. The basic shapes are the ball (used for cream puffs), the stick (used for eclairs), the oval (used for duck bodies), and the teardrop (used for swan bodies). Ideally, the cooked choux pastry will puff 3–4 times the size of the original shape.

BALL: This is the easiest shape. To make a ball, hold the bag vertically, ⅓ inch above the baking sheet. Squeeze gently, stop, curl the tip around in a tight circle, and lift: you should wind up with a small, round dome of dough. Lower the bag closer to the baking sheet for smaller circles; raise it for larger.

STICK: Sticks are piped the same way as circles except that you move the bag in a straight line as you pipe, holding the bag at a slight angle. When you reach the desired length, stop squeezing, gently rotate the bag 30 degrees, or pull the tip back toward you, then lift.

OVAL: Ovals are piped the same way as sticks except that you move the bag only a little way in a straight line, and you squeeze harder to make a wider shape.

TEARDROP: To make a teardrop, squeeze the bag hard as though you were going to make a large cream puff, then move the bag in a straight line, gradually reducing the pressure. This will cause the shape to become progressively narrower. The result should look like a teardrop.

Note: When piping choux pastry, try to make all the shapes the same size so that they will cook evenly. Try to pipe in neat rows, leaving 2 fingers between each shape. French pastry chef Albert Jorant used to say that a properly piped baking sheet should be as neatly arranged as a cemetery!

CREAM PUFFS

Cream puffs (pastry balls filled with whipped cream) are the easiest choux pastry dessert to make. Profiteroles are cream puffs filled with ice cream and topped with hot chocolate sauce. Swans and ducks are nothing more than fancifully shaped cream puffs. Review the notes on using a piping bag and making whipped cream on pages 277–280 before you start.

Serves 8

1 batch choux pastry (see master recipe)
  egg glaze
2 cups heavy cream
½ cup confectioner's sugar (or to taste) for the cream, plus ½
  cup for sprinkling

½ teaspoon vanilla

1 tablespoon Grand Marnier (or spirit of your choice)

2 piping bags, ½-inch round tip for piping the choux pastry,
    ½-inch star tip for piping the cream

1. Prepare the choux pastry and, using a bag fitted with a round ½-inch tip, pipe out 24 1-inch balls. Brush these with egg glaze, bake, split, and cool as described in the master recipe.

2. Meanwhile, beat the cream to stiff peaks, adding the sugar and flavorings as it thickens.

3. Not more than 1 hour before serving, gently separate the top and bottom of each puff, and, using a piping bag fitted with a ½-inch star tip, fill each with whipped cream. Just before serving, sift confectioner's sugar on top.

PROFITEROLES

Profiteroles can be filled with either whipped cream or ice cream. For the sake of convenience, you can fill the shells ahead of time and store them in your freezer. A purist would insist on warming and filling the shells at the last minute. The delight comes from the contrast of temperatures: the icy filling, the hot chocolate sauce.

Serves 8

24 cream puff shells (see recipe above)
 1 pint vanilla ice cream (see recipe on page 294, or use store-bought)
 1 batch chocolate sauce (see page 316) made with bittersweet or semisweet chocolate (see pages 314–15), or your favorite chocolate sauce
 4 tablespoons chopped almonds

1. Prepare the cream puff shells as described above. Prepare the ice cream and the chocolate sauce. Toast almonds in a shallow pan in a preheated 400° oven for 2–3 minutes or until lightly browned.

2. Just before serving, warm the shells in a hot oven. Fill each with a spoonful of ice cream. Place profiteroles on glass serving plates (3–4 per person) and top with hot chocolate sauce and toasted almonds.

WHIPPED CREAM DUCKS AND SWANS

These fanciful creatures are guaranteed to bring down the house. Ducks are easier to make than swans: making the necks for the latter requires a little practice. The heads and bodies can be prepared ahead, but the birds should be assembled not more than ½ hour before serving.

Makes 8–10 swans, 16 ducks, or 6 and 10, respectively, of each

1 batch choux pastry (see master recipe)
   egg glaze
   small handful of slivered almonds
2 cups heavy cream
½ cup confectioner's sugar (or to taste), plus sugar for
   sprinkling
½ teaspoon vanilla
1 tablespoon Grand Marnier (or spirit of your choice)

2 piping bags, ½-inch round tip, ⅛-inch round tip for the
   necks, ½-inch star tip for the cream

1. Prepare the choux pastry as described in the master recipe. To make duck bodies, using a bag fitted with a ½-inch tip, pipe the dough into ovals 2 inches long and ¾ inch wide. Reserve ¼ of the dough for the heads.

2. To make swan bodies, using a bag fitted with a ½-inch tip, pipe the dough into 3-inch teardrop shapes. The easiest way to make a teardrop is to squeeze the bag hard at first, as though you were going to make a large cream puff, then pull it toward you, gradually decreasing pressure, to taper the end. Reserve ¼ of the dough for the necks. Duck bodies and swan bodies can be piped on the same baking sheet.

3. To make duck heads, place the ⅛-inch round tip over the large one, and pipe a series of tiny cream puffs, each ½ inch across. Insert a slivered almond in each, parallel to the baking sheet, to form the "bill." Pipe more heads than you have bodies, in case some of them burn or break.

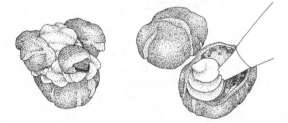

4. To make swan necks, place the ⅛-inch round tip over the large one, and pipe a series of 3-inch S-shapes. Pipe onto the back of a baking sheet (*lightly* greased). As you finish each S-shape, squeeze the bag a little harder to make a slight bulge. This will be the head. Cut the slivered almonds into

⅛-inch strips, and insert these in the heads for "beaks." It is easier to pipe the S-shapes when the bag is half full, making the remaining bodies afterward. Pipe 3 times as many necks as you have bodies, as they tend to break. Pipe the duck heads and swan necks on a separate baking sheet, as they cook much more quickly than the bodies.

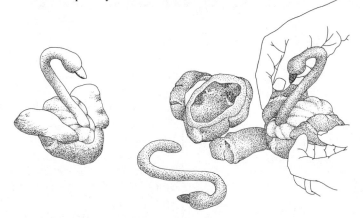

5. Brush the bodies with glaze, and bake as described in the master recipe. Glaze the duck heads, but not the swan necks (they are too thin). Bake them for 8–10 minutes, until the bodies are puffed and golden. WARNING: Swan necks burn like kindling—watch them carefully.

6. When the bodies are cooked, cut off the top third, and cut it in half lengthwise. These halves will be the wings. Remove any uncooked dough from the bodies with a fork. Return the bodies to the oven for 2–3 minutes, to crisp. Cool on a cake rack. Cool the heads and necks as well. The recipe can be prepared to this stage up to 6 hours ahead.

7. Not more than 1 hour before serving, beat the cream to stiff peaks, adding sugar and flavorings as it thickens. Not more than ½ hour ahead, assemble the birds. To assemble the ducks, using a bag fitted with a ½-inch star tip, pipe swirls of whipped cream into the bodies. Stick the two top halves in the cream to form the wings. Set the heads in the center.

8. To assemble the swans, fill the bodies with cream. Set the S-shape in the cream to form the neck. (It should be pointing *away* from the narrow end of the body!) Stick the two top halves in the cream to form the wings. Sprinkle the swans with confectioner's sugar to make them white; leave the ducks brown.

Serving: Arrange the birds on a silver platter, or better yet, a mirror. Play Tchaikovsky's *Swan Lake* as you serve!

Working with Chocolate

◇

Techniques:

MELTING CHOCOLATE

DISTINGUISHING CHOCOLATE TYPES

COOKING WITH CHOCOLATE

Master Recipe:

CHOCOLATE FONDUE BERNERHOF

Variations:

SILK PIE

BILL BERGMAN'S CHOCOLATE MOUSSE

CHOCOLATE TRUFFLES

GRAMMIE ETHEL'S FUDGE

ITSY-BITSY BETSY BROWNIE

◇   ◇   ◇

Chocolate. Imagine life without it. Yet chocolate is a relative newcomer to the Western food scene. Indeed its discoverers, the Aztecs, mixed it with chili and spices and didn't even use it for dessert.

Chocolate comes from the seeds of a tropical tree whose Latin name is *theobroma*, "food of the gods." The seeds must be harvested, fermented, dried, roasted, shelled, and crushed to turn them into chocolate. The Spanish added sugar and water to this New World ingredient, thereby inventing hot chocolate. In 1828 a Dutch chemist contrived a way to press the cocoa liquor out of the beans to make cocoa powder. This led the way for the first "eating chocolate" (candy bars) in 1847, made by mixing cocoa liquor and sugar with a paste of ground beans. In 1875 the Swiss invented milk chocolate, the result of adding condensed milk to cocoa butter and cocoa. The Swiss still lead the world in chocolate consumption: an impressive 22 pounds per person a year.

There are seven basic types of chocolate used for cooking:

Cocoa: An unsweetened powder made from cocoa beans from which all the cocoa butter has been extracted.

Unsweetened Chocolate: A blend of cocoa butter, cocoa liquor, and cocoa.

Bittersweet chocolate: An eating chocolate made with less sugar than semisweet.

Semisweet Chocolate: Contains at least 35 percent cocoa butter, cocoa, and sugar. This is the chocolate most often used for cooking.

Semisweet Chocolate Bits: Like the above, but with less cocoa butter, so the chips don't melt when baked.

Milk Chocolate: Contains cocoa butter, cocoa, sugar, and a minimum of 12 percent milk solids. Seldom used for cooking.

White Chocolate: Contains sugar, milk, cocoa butter. Legally this is not chocolate at all, because it contains no cocoa.

"Covering" Chocolate: A high-grade semisweet chocolate used for candy making. Its high proportion of cocoa butter makes it soft and malleable for coating candies.

COOKING WITH CHOCOLATE

Chocolate is a temperamental ingredient, reacting adversely to subtle changes in temperature and moisture. Heating chocolate too much will make it hard and crystalline. A few drops of water can turn smooth melted chocolate into a hard, clumpy mess.

The best way to melt chocolate is in a large bowl over a pan of hot (120°) water. (Hot tap water will suffice.) Chop the chocolate finely and don't stir until at least a quarter of the pieces have melted. Above all, don't let even a drop of water touch the chocolate, or it will "block" (turn hard and grainy). For this reason, I melt chocolate in a high-sided bowl over water in a low-sided pan. Do not cover the bowl lest condensation from the water fall in the bowl. (Curiously, chocolate will melt fine with lots of liquid.) Chocolate can also be melted in a microwave oven.

If chocolate does block, it can be rescued by whisking in a spoonful of clarified butter or vegetable oil.

When using chocolate to cover candies, such as the chocolate truffles in the recipe on page 319, it is common to "temper" the chocolate; that is, melt it, let it cool, and melt it again. This helps produce a smoother, shinier coating. A few drops of oil will give a similar effect. NOTE: Tempering chocolate is very tricky. Consult a book written by a specialist, like Maida Heatter (see Bibliography).

Below are six recipes for chocolate desserts. The Aztecs didn't know what they were missing.

◇   ◇   ◇

Chocolate Fondue Bernerhof

The secret to this delectable fondue is the chocolate, Toblerone from Switzerland. According to Bernerhof owner Ted Wroblewski, chocolate fondue should be enjoyed with your favorite companion in the intimacy of a sauna!

Serves 6

FOR THE FONDUE:

    ½ cup heavy cream
    8 ounces Toblerone or semisweet or milk chocolate, finely
        chopped
    2 tablespoons Grand Marnier

FOR THE GARNISH:

    1 pint strawberries
    2 bananas
    2 ripe pears
    2 oranges or tangerines, peeled and broken into segments
      lemon juice
      ladyfingers, tiny meringue stars, etc.

1. Bring the cream to a boil. Stir in the chocolate off the heat (if necessary return the pan to a low heat—the chocolate should be completely melted). Stir in the Grand Marnier. The fondue is now ready but can be kept warm in a double boiler.

2. Wash and hull the strawberries and peel and slice the other fruits, rubbing lemon juice on the pears and bananas to prevent discoloring. Arrange the fruits and cookies in a pretty pattern on a platter. To eat the chocolate fondue, each diner skewers a piece of fruit or cake and dips it in the chocolate. When serving chocolate fondue, it is not necessary to put a flame under the fondue; on the contrary, it will burn the chocolate.

VARIATIONS: Substitute bittersweet chocolate for the milk chocolate and calvados (French apple brandy) for the Grand Marnier. Serve with Granny Smith apples.

CHOCOLATE SAUCE

Made the same way as the chocolate fondue above, this concoction goes well whenever a rich chocolate sauce is needed.

Serves 6–8

    ½ cup heavy cream

8 ounces semisweet chocolate, finely chopped

2 tablespoons Grand Marnier, or alcohol of your choice

Bring the cream to a boil. Stir in the chocolate off the heat (if necessary return the pan to a low heat—the chocolate should be completely melted). Stir in the Grand Marnier. The sauce is now ready but can be kept warm in a double boiler.

SILK PIE

This chocolate silk pie is another great dessert from the Bernerhof Inn. There is nothing "gourmet" about the Oreo cookie crust, but that does not make it any less delicious. All the ingredients must be at room temperature or the filling may separate.

Serves 8–10

FOR THE CRUST:

8 ounces Oreo cookies (½ package)

3 tablespoons melted butter

FOR THE FILLING:

2 ounces semisweet chocolate

2 ounces unsweetened chocolate

6 ounces (1½ sticks) unsalted butter, at room temperature

1 cup superfine sugar

3 eggs, at room temperature

FOR THE DECORATION:

1 cup heavy cream, whipped to stiff peaks with 4 tablespoons confectioner's sugar and 2 tablespoons rum

1 ounce semisweet chocolate for shaving

1 8-inch pie pan

1. Prepare the crust. Pulverize the cookies by hand or in a food processor. Combine the crumbs with the melted butter and press the mixture into the bottom and sides of the pan. Chill for 10 minutes.

2. Meanwhile, prepare the filling. Melt the chocolates over warm water and let cool. Cream the butter with the sugar in an electric mixer, a food processor, or by hand. (Run the mixer at high speed.) Beat in the melted chocolate. Finally, beat in the eggs one by one, waiting until each is thoroughly blended before adding the next. Beat the mixture for 2–3 minutes, or until it forms stiff peaks.

3. Spoon the filling into the pie shell and freeze it for at least 3 hours, preferably overnight. Decorate the silk pie with stars of whipped cream and chocolate shaved with a vegetable peeler. Use a sharp knife dipped in hot water for slicing.

BILL BERGMAN'S CHOCOLATE MOUSSE

This recipe came to us from Bill Bergman, a fine septuagenarian cook and longtime friend of Taste of the Mountains, who passed away in September 1984. Bill possessed virtues much appreciated in the kitchen: patience, humility, a sense of humor, and an endless capacity for hard work. He delighted in sharing his vast experience with cooking but was the first to admit the gaps in his knowledge. It's an honor to print his recipe.

Serves 4–6

8 ounces semisweet chocolate, finely chopped
1 cup heavy cream (plus ½ cup for decoration)
4 egg whites
  pinch of salt
  pinch of cream of tartar
2 tablespoons sugar for "meringuing" the whites
1 tablespoon (or to taste) whiskey, Grand Marnier, Kahlua, or
  the spirit of your choice

1. Melt the chocolate over hot water, stirring until smooth. Let cool. Beat the cream to stiff peaks and keep refrigerated.
2. Add the salt and cream of tartar to the egg whites and beat until you have almost stiff peaks. Meringue the whites: sprinkle in the sugar and continue beating, for about another 30 seconds, until shiny.
3. Fold the melted chocolate into the whites, followed by the cream and spirit. Spoon the mousse into ramekins or wine glasses and chill for 2 hours.

Serving: Decorate the mousse with whipped cream and perhaps pieces of chocolate or coffee beans. You could use the leftover yolks to make a *crème anglaise* (see page 287) to be served as a sauce for the mousse.

VARIATIONS: This simple chocolate mousse is protean in its uses. It can be served as is, spooned into a pie shell (see page 101), or used for icing a cake. It can be spiked with brandy-soaked sultanas (yellow raisins) or layered with praline powder (page 293).

CHOCOLATE TRUFFLES

True truffles are expensive black fungi that grow underground. Chocolate truffles are made to look like them by rolling the candies in cocoa. These rich treats are a chocoholic's paradise: a sweet filling, semisweet chocolate shell, and bitter cocoa coating. Refrigerated, truffles will keep for up to two weeks. The flavor improves with age. This recipe is dedicated to Barbara Klein.

Makes 36 truffles

FOR THE FILLING:

> 6 ounces semisweet chocolate
> 4 tablespoons butter, at room temperature
> 2–3 tablespoons whiskey, Grand Marnier, raspberry *eau-de-vie,*
>   or spirit of your choice
> ¾ cup confectioner's sugar, sifted
> 2 tablespoons heavy cream

TO FINISH THE TRUFFLES:

> 6 ounces semisweet chocolate
> 1 teaspoon vegetable oil
> ¾ cup unsweetened cocoa

1. Prepare the filling. Melt the chocolate over warm water and let cool. Beat in half the butter, followed by the alcohol and half the sugar. Beat in the remaining butter, followed by the remaining sugar, and last, the cream. Chill the filling for 10–15 minutes or until firm enough to shape.

2. Using spoons or your fingers, shape the filling into ¾-inch balls. Set these on an oiled baking sheet and chill for 1 hour.

3. Finish the truffles. Melt the remaining chocolate over warm water. Whisk in the vegetable oil and let cool. Put the cocoa into a shallow bowl or cake pan. Use a fork for dipping the truffles, and take the phone off the hook, as the dipping procedure is *very* messy. Dip each ball of filling in melted chocolate until completely coated, then transfer to the cocoa powder, and shake the bowl or pan to completely coat the truffle with cocoa.

Serving: Shake the excess cocoa powder off the truffles before serving. Chocolate truffles make a nice present for the holidays; serve them with plenty of strong coffee.

GRAMMIE ETHEL'S FUDGE

The best chocolate dessert in the world is neither an exquisite *gâteau* from France, nor a torte from Austria, nor even a hand-dipped Swiss candy.

Rather, it is the fudge made by my grandmother, Ethel Raichlen. After decades of pleading, I finally cajoled the recipe from her.

  1¼ cups sugar
  ¾ cup milk
  4 ounces unsweetened chocolate
  5 tablespoons butter
  ½ tablespoon vanilla extract

  a lightly oiled baking dish

1. Combine the sugar and milk in a heavy saucepan and bring to a rolling boil. Add the chocolate off the heat, and stir with a wooden spoon until melted. Boil the mixture, stirring, for 1 minute. Stir in the butter and vanilla. Reduce heat to medium, and simmer the fudge, beating it vigorously, for 10–15 minutes, or until it becomes as thick as sour cream or caramel and the butter *begins* to separate out in shiny beads.

2. Remove the fudge from the heat and beat it with a wooden spoon for 2 minutes, or until slightly thickened. The mixture should remain soft and creamy; if you overbeat, it will become crumbly. Spoon the mixture into the oiled baking dish and cut it into squares or diamonds while still hot.

The appropriate beverage? A glass of milk, of course!

ITSY BITSY BETSY BROWNIE

This is the fudgiest brownie I have ever tasted. It was first made for me by a little girl who stood vigil while the brownies baked. She said that the brownies improve with age, if by some miracle you have any left the next day.

Serves 4

  1 stick (½ cup) unsalted butter, plus butter for greasing the
     pan
  3 ounces unsweetened chocolate
  1¼ cups sugar
  ¼ cup flour
    pinch of salt
  ½ teaspoon vanilla
  3 eggs, beaten
  ½ cup coarsely chopped pecans (optional)

  1 8-inch-square cake pan

1. Double-butter the cake pan. Preheat the oven to 350°F. Melt the butter and chocolate in a large bowl over a pan of gently simmering water. Remove the bowl from the heat and whisk in the sugar. Fold in the flour, salt, and vanilla. Finally, fold in the eggs and nuts.

2. Spoon the batter into the cake pan and bake the brownie for 18–20 minutes in the center rack of the oven. Do not overcook: the center should remain very moist. Let cool and cut into squares.

L E S S O N 5 3

Cookies and Petits Fours

———————◇———————

Techniques:

PIPING EGG WHITE COOKIES

Master Recipes:

CAT'S TONGUE COOKIES

LADYFINGERS

MADELEINES

◇　◇　◇

Cookies are as American as apple pie and ice cream. Or are they? Our word cookie comes from the Dutch *koekje,* "little cake." (Another favorite dish of the Dutch settlers of Manhattan was *koolsla,* "cabbage salad," whence our ubiquitous coleslaw.) And speaking of little cakes, no serious French meal would be complete without a tray of *petits fours,* tiny cookies and cakes named for the *petit four,* the low oven (or miniature oven, depending on whom you read) in which they were traditionally baked.

In this lesson we take up two kinds of cookies: crisp, flat cookies, like cats' tongues, which derive their crispness from egg whites; and cakelike cookies, like ladyfingers and madeleines, which owe their chewy moistness to the presence of whole eggs.

◇　◇　◇

Cat's Tongue Cookies

Cats' tongues (*langues de chats*) are tiny, flat sugar cookies that are ideal for serving with mousses and frozen soufflés. Watch them closely as they are very prone to burning. This recipe comes from Bernerhof chef Rick Spencer.

Makes 60 2-inch cookies

½ cup unsalted butter, at room temperature
½ cup sugar

the grated zest (oil-rich outer rind) of 1 lemon
½ teaspoon vanilla
3 egg whites
1 cup flour

3 baking sheets
3 sheets parchment paper
piping bag fitted with a ¼-inch round tip

1. Preheat the oven to 425°F. Cream the butter with the sugar and flavorings and beat until very light and fluffy. Add the egg whites one by one and beat the mixture for 30 seconds. Add the flour and beat just to mix.

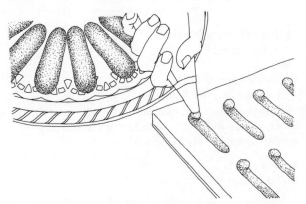

2. Line the baking sheets with parchment paper. (A dab of butter in each corner will help hold the paper to the baking sheet.) Pipe the batter into 1½-inch strips, leaving two fingers' width between each. Bang each baking sheet once to flatten the batter, and bake the cats' tongues for 5 minutes, or until golden brown. Transfer the cookies to a cake rack to cool as quickly as possible.

Note: When the cookies are in the oven watch them like a hawk. The difference between undercooked and burnt-to-a-crisp is often a matter of seconds.

VARIATION: Pipe the batter into hazelnut-sized mounds to make round cookies. Place a currant or sultana in the center of each. The French call these tiny cookies *palets de dames,* a palet being an iron disk used in the game of quoits.

◊　◊　◊

Ladyfingers

Cats' tongues, ladyfingers . . . my, aren't we morbid? These chewy, finger-sized cookies—actually a cross between a cake and cookie—are a culinary tour de force. Like sponge cake, they owe their lightness to thousands of tiny air bubbles in the batter. For this reason, the egg whites must be perfectly beaten (see page 296 for instructions). I learned this recipe at La Varenne cooking school in Paris, where pastry chef Albert Jorant would horrify students by banging the filled baking sheet upside down to knock off excess sugar.

Makes 36 ladyfingers

butter for the baking sheet
4 eggs, separated
½ cup sugar
½ teaspoon vanilla
grated zest of a small lemon
¾ cup all-purpose flour, plus flour for the baking sheets
pinch of salt and cream of tartar for the whites
confectioner's sugar for sprinkling

2 baking sheets
piping bag fitted with a ½-inch tip

1. Double-butter the baking sheet. Preheat the oven to 350°F. Whisk the egg yolks with half the sugar and flavorings for 3 minutes or until the mixture falls in a thick, silky ribbon when the whisk is raised. (We beat the yolks first, because they are less likely to fall than the whites.) By now the butter on the baking sheet should be cool. Sprinkle with flour and tip the sheet to knock off the excess.

2. Beat the egg whites to stiff peaks, adding salt and cream of tartar after 20 seconds. When the whites are almost stiff, gradually whisk in the remaining sugar.

3. Stir ¼ of the whites into the yolk mixture to lighten it, then gently fold it back into the remaining whites, gradually sifting in the flour. (To sift in flour, shake it through a strainer.) Fold the mixture as little as possible, for each pass of the spatula knocks out air bubbles.

4. Spoon the batter into the piping bag and pipe it into 4-inch "cigars," leaving two fingers' width between each. (For instructions on piping, see page 278.) Thickly sprinkle the ladyfingers with confectioner's sugar. Hold your breath, quickly invert the baking sheets, and gently tap to shake off excess sugar. (NOTE: I have never lost a batch, but you must tap gently.) Bake the ladyfingers for 12–15 minutes or until golden brown. Remove from

oven, let cool for 60 seconds, then gently pry the ladyfingers off the baking sheet and cool on cake racks.

Serving: One of my favorite ways to end a meal is with ladyfingers and champagne.

VARIATION: Ladyfinger batter can be piped in circles or squares and baked like the layers of a cake. Garnish with whipped cream, fruit mousse, etc.

Ladyfingers are also the key ingredient in *charlottes* (molded Bavarian creams). To make a charlotte, trim the edges of a batch of ladyfingers with a serrated knife and wedge them vertically around the inside of a charlotte mold (a cylindrical mold with outwardly sloping sides), filling any gaps with slivers cut from the extras. Fill the mold with any of the Bavarian creams in Lesson 48. Chill until firm. To unmold, dip the bottom of the pan into hot water for a few seconds, then unmold the charlotte onto a platter. Decorate the top with whipped cream.

◇　◇　◇

Madeleines

Madeleines are small, shell-shaped, chewy cookies. The taste of one was enough to set Proust reminiscing about his childhood for seven novels! Orange flower water is a perfumy orange extract popular in Middle East baking. (It entered French cooking via Italy during the Renaissance. Look for it in Middle East grocery stores. If you can't find it, substitute an orange-flavored liqueur like Triple Sec.) You will also need madeleine molds, available at most gourmet shops.

Makes 24–30 madeleines

  2 eggs
  ¾ cup sugar
  1 teaspoon orange flower water, or 1 tablespoon orange
      liqueur
    grated zest of one lemon and one small orange
  4 tablespoons heavy cream
  1 cup flour plus 2 tablespoons
  ½ teaspoon baking powder
  6 tablespoons melted butter, plus butter for the molds
  ½ cup confectioner's sugar for sprinkling (optional)

    madeleine molds

1. Whisk the eggs with the sugar and flavorings till very light and fluffy. Stir in the heavy cream. Sift one cup flour with the baking powder, and gently fold it into the egg mixture. Gently fold in the butter. Preheat the oven to 350°F. Let the batter sit for 5 minutes.

2. Brush the madeleine molds with melted or softened butter and dust with flour. Pipe the batter into the molds, filling each ¾ full. Bake the madeleines for 15 minutes, or until puffed, firm, and just beginning to brown. Transfer the madeleines to a cake rack to cool, and store in a plastic bag until you are ready to serve them. If you like, you can sprinkle the madeleines with confectioner's sugar.

GLOSSARY

◇

al dente: literally, "to the tooth"; pasta cooked briefly enough to remain slightly chewy. See crispy-tender.

beard: to remove the lacy "fringe" (black membrane) encircling the mussel inside the shell; bearding is optional but makes the mussel more appetizing (Lesson 21).

blanch: cook in rapidly boiling water for 15 seconds.

blender: ideal machine for pureeing sauces and soups. Poor for pureeing or grinding thicker substances.

blind-bake: to prebake a pie crust lined with foil filled with beans or rice. The beans or rice hold the crust in shape during baking (Lesson 13).

bouquet garni: an herb bundle comprised of bay leaf, thyme, parsley, black peppercorns, cloves, and allspice berries. For convenience these ingredients are wrapped in foil; the foil is perforated with a fork to release the flavor (Lesson 1).

braise: to cook pieces of fish, poultry, or meat in a covered pan with relatively little liquid. Braising is usually done in the oven, but it can also be done over a low heat on the stove.

broth: stock made with a whole chicken or beef shin instead of bones (Lesson 1).

candied violets: candied flowers used for decorating desserts. They are available at gourmet shops.

capers: the small, pickled buds of a trailing shrub with a tart, tangy flavor. The smaller the buds, the better.

cheese: in this book we use many different kinds of cheese. When a recipe calls for grated cheese, try to grate it freshly. (To grate Parmesan or Romano in a food processor, have the blade running, and add the cheese in small cubes.) Among the cheeses most frequently called for are:

> *chèvre:* French goat cheese. Mild types include montrachet and lingot; stronger varieties include bûcheron and crottin de Chavignol.
> Gorgonzola: a pungent Italian blue cheese made from cow's milk.

Gruyère: a Swiss-type cheese with tiny holes and a strong pungent flavor.

Parmesan: an Italian grating cheese made from cow's milk. (The best is Parmigiano-Reggiano; look for these words on the rind.)

Romano: an Italian grating cheese made from sheep's milk.

Roquefort: French blue cheese made from sheep's milk and ripened in limestone caves. There is no substitute.

chef's knife: see French knife.

China cap: a fine-meshed conical strainer (so called because it resembles a pointed coolie's hat.

chopping: cut into small pieces with a knife. Detailed instructions for chopping are found in Lesson 2. Specific cuts include:

coarsely chopped: cut into ¾-inch pieces.

chopped: cut into ½-inch pieces.

finely chopped: cut into ¼-inch pieces.

very finely chopped: cut into ⅛-inch pieces.

diced: cut into ¼-inch cubes.

minced: chopped as finely as possible. To mince garlic we smash it with the side of a knife.

"circumcise": to remove the small, opaque, thumbnail-shaped muscle on the side of a scallop.

clam broth: a good substitute for fish stock, but you must cut back on the salt in a recipe because bottled clam broth is already quite salty.

clarified butter: butter from which the water and milk solids have been removed. Clarified butter is ideal for pan-frying because it has a higher burning temperature than regular butter (Lesson 30).

coating consistency: a sauce that is thick enough—and just thick enough —to coat a spoon. Your finger should leave a clean path when drawn across the back of the spoon.

coriander leaf: also known as cilantro or Chinese parsley, this herb has a flat, scalloped leaf and a unique pungent flavor. There is no substitute.

cream (as in "to cream butter"): to beat butter (and often sugar) with a whisk until it is light and airy. It helps to start with butter that is at room temperature.

cream of tartar: a natural fruit acid derived from grapes. It helps stabilize egg whites during beating. Baking powder is made by adding cream of tartar to baking soda.

crème anglaise: custard sauce made of egg yolks, cream, and sugar (Lesson 47).

crispy-tender: the vegetable equivalent of al dente; vegetables cooked in rapidly boiling salted water until they are completely cooked yet ever so slightly crisp or resilient when bitten. Do not rely on a timer: test the texture with your teeth as the vegetables cook.

croûtes: bread slices brushed lightly with butter and baked crisp in a hot oven (see Lesson 33). Croutons are made by cutting *croûtes* into ½-inch squares.

curry powder: a blend of as many as 30 spices, including cumin, coriander, cardamom, cayenne, cloves, cinnamon, fenugreek, and pepper.

deglaze: to dissolve juice congealed on the bottom of a pan with an acidic liquid, like wine or vinegar. The pan must be hot when the liquid is added; working over high heat, scrape the bottom of the pan with a spoon or spatula to dislodge the juices.

double boiler: used for warming or cooking heat-sensitive mixtures. There is no need to buy a special double boiler—any bowl or pot placed in or over a large pot of simmering water will do.

double-butter: to brush a mold or baking dish twice with melted butter, freezing the dish between coats. Double-buttering is used for any preparation that tends to stick to a pan.

duxelles: mushroom forcemeat (Lesson 41).

eau-de-vie: "water of life," literally: a true fruit brandy (not to be confused with "fruit-flavored brandy," which is actually a sugary fruit liqueur. *Eau-de-vie* contains no sugar. Among those commonly used in this book are:

> *calvados:* an apple brandy that is aged in wood.
> *fraise:* a clear strawberry brandy.
> *framboise:* a clear raspberry brandy.
> *kirsch:* a clear cherry brandy.
> *Poire Williams:* a clear pear brandy.

egg glaze: egg beaten with a pinch of salt. Egg glaze is used both as glue (to attach pieces of dough) and as "shellac" (to give baked pastries an attractive sheen).

emulsion: a stable mixture of two liquids that would normally remain separate. Mayonnaise is an emulsion; so is hollandaise sauce (Lessons 6 and 29).

escallope: a thin (¼-inch) diagonal slice of fish or veal.

extra-virgin olive oil: a highly fragrant oil made from hand-culled, cold-pressed olives (Lesson 5).

filleting knife: distinguished by a long (6–10 inch), very flexible blade, which follows the contours of bones when filleting fish or poultry; also useful for chopping onions.

flake (as with fish): the classic test for doneness for fish. When pressed with a finger, fully cooked fish will break apart into opaque flakes.

flambé or flame: literally, to ignite a wine or spirit. Flambéing has two purposes: to burn off alcohol (which has a harsh taste) and to impress your guests. The first can be accomplished simply by bringing the booze to a boil. For the second, you must bring the spirit in contact with an open flame. Alcohol must be warm (at body temperature) before it will ignite. Don't heat it too much, however, or the flammable alcohol will evaporate. To flambé over gas heat, add the liquid to the pan, warm for a few seconds, then tilt the edge of the pan toward the flames. To flambé with electric heat, add the liquid, warm for a few seconds, then hold a lit match over the pan. Be careful: alcohol sometimes ignites with an explosive woosh. (Use baking soda to extinguish any accidents.)

fluting knife: a knife with a short blade with a U-shaped loop at the end. This loop is used for removing long thin strips of peel from an orange or lemon.

fold: to incorporate one mixture into another by gently mixing with a rubber spatula.

food processor: ideal for grinding nuts and bread crumbs, pureeing fish and poultry, and chopping and grating cheese and vegetables. Does not work well for pureeing soups. The best models are those made by Cuisinart and Robotcoup.

forcemeat: a stuffing (usually made of ground meat).

French knife: distinguished by a long (over 8 inches), wide, rigid blade; used for chopping long, thin vegetables and herbs.

gratin: topped with bread crumbs or melted cheese. The term comes from the French *gratter,* literally to "scratch" or "scrape."

green peppercorns: the pickled fruit of the pepper tree. When dried, they become black pepper; when peeled and dried, they become white peppercorns.

hot chili oil: a Chinese flavoring made by cooking hot chilis in sesame oil or vegetable oil. It is sold at Oriental markets. If unavailable, use a pinch of cayenne pepper.

julienne: to cut into matchstick-sized slivers (Lesson 19).

juniper berries: small, blue-black berries with a flavor we associate with gin. (Juniper berries are, in fact, the primary flavoring of gin.) Juniper berries are sold in jars at specialty shops—if unavailable, use gin.

lemon wedges: proper lemon wedges have been cut so that the ends are blunted to give your fingers a place to squeeze (Lesson 17).

meringue (as in "to meringue the egg whites"): to sprinkle granulated sugar into stiffly beaten egg whites. Meringuing helps stabilize stiffly beaten whites, making them firm and glossy.

mirin: sweet rice wine from Japan; substitute white wine with a little sugar.

mixer: invaluable for creaming butter, kneading yeast doughs, and stiffly beating cream and egg whites. Get a model with a dough hook (and a motor powerful enough to drive it). Avoid machines with plastic bowls.

nouvelle cuisine: a "new" style of cooking that revolutionized French cuisine in the 1970s, characterized by unusual flavor combinations, exotic ingredients, starchless sauces, small portions, and painterly plate presentations. Nouvelle cuisine profoundly influenced contemporary French and American cooking, however much the term and some of the more outlandish flavor combinations may be out of vogue today.

pancetta: Italian-style, dry-cured, rolled belly bacon. Its flavor resembles that of prosciutto.

parboil: to partially cook by boiling. Parboiling is similar to blanching, but the food is cooked slightly longer.

parchment paper: a heatproof, silicon-based paper used for lining molds and baking sheets. Unlike waxed paper, it will not melt when baked.

paring knife: distinguished by a short (up to 4 inches), rigid blade; used for trimming vegetables and boning.

pastry brush: the cook's equivalent of a paintbrush, used for brushing away excess flour and applying coats of melted butter and egg glaze. No kitchen should have fewer than three. Buy brushes with natural bristles.

pastry wheel: a hand-held device used for cutting pastry dough. It consists of a thin metal disk with a straight or fluted edge rotating at the end of a handle. It is quicker to use than a knife.

pâté: a considerable amount of confusion exists between the terms pâté and terrine. Historically, a pâté was a forcemeat baked in pastry (the French word for which is *pâte*), while a terrine was baked in an earthenware mold. (*Terre* is the French word for "earth.") Today, the terms are used interchangeably. Pâtés come in two basic forms: sliceable loaves and spreadable pastes.

pipe: to force a semi-liquid mixture, like cookie batter or whipped cream, through a metal nozzle via a cone-shaped bag, called a piping bag. The nozzle is called a piping tip, which comes with two basic ends: smooth (a "round" tip) and fluted (a "star" tip). For a complete discussion of piping, see Lesson 45.

poach: to cook in gently simmering liquid.

purge: to remove sand from clams and mussels by soaking them in salt water with cornmeal. (The shellfish ingest the cornmeal and spit out the sand; see Lesson 21.)

reduce: to diminish the volume of a liquid and intensify its flavor by boiling it down. This technique is often used to make sauces.

refresh: to rinse boiled vegetables or pasta under running cold water to stop the cooking, and, in the case of green vegetables, to fix the bright-green color.

render: to cook bacon, pancetta, or other fatty meat over medium heat to melt out the fat.

roux: a thickener consisting of equal parts butter and flour.

sauté: to cook in a relatively small amount of fat over a brisk heat. The term comes from the French word *sauter,* literally "to jump." Some people claim that the "jumping" refers to the individual pieces of food in the hot fat; others to the action of giving the pan a quick flick of the wrist to brown the food evenly on all sides.

scald: to bring milk or other liquid to a gentle boil.

season: to add salt and freshly ground black pepper (and often cayenne pepper and freshly grated nutmeg). It is my belief that a cook should fully season a dish before it leaves the kitchen. Correct seasoning can only be done by tasting.

set: a term used to describe doneness in a custard. Poke the side of the crust or dish. When the filling no longer ripples or wiggles, it is set (i.e., cooked). You can also test doneness by inserting a skewer or slender knife tip. When it comes out clean, the mixture is cooked.

simmer: to cook at just below boiling. Bubbles should barely but steadily break the surface.

skim: remove fat or foam from simmering stock. Use a ladle for skimming and hold it just beneath the liquid's surface (see Lesson 1).

smash (as in garlic): reduce to a fine paste with the side of a knife or cleaver.

soy sauce: a salty brown sauce made from fermented soy beans, wheat, and salt. Soy sauce is used throughout the Orient: there are numerous types. Because it contains more wheat, Japanese soy sauce tends to be sweeter and less salty than Chinese. There are two basic kinds of Japanese soy sauce: light and dark. The former is thinner, lighter in color, and saltier than the latter. I prefer dark Japanese soy sauce; a good brand is Kikkoman, which is manufactured under Japanese supervision in the United States. I also like *tamari*—a very dark, intensely flavored sauce made from cultured, fermented soy beans.

special flour: a home version of commercial pastry flour made by cutting 2 parts all-purpose flour with 1 part cake flour. This helps reduce the gluten in the flour—an enemy of rolled doughs because it causes them to shrink.

steam: to cook over boiling water in a sealed pot.

stiff peaks: as egg whites are beaten, they gradually become firm, white, and much increased in volume. After 2–3 minutes, the whites will form "soft" or droopy peaks, when lifted with a whisk or spatula. When fully beaten, the whites will form stiff peaks: they will support the weight of a whole egg and can be cleanly cut with a knife. If you continue beating, the solids will separate from the liquids, a state known as "grainy." It is better to underbeat rather than overbeat egg whites, for once graining occurs, the whites are useless (see Lesson 49).

stir-fry: to cook small pieces of meat, seafood, or vegetables in a small amount of hot fat over high heat, stirring constantly. Stir-frying originated in China, and it is usually done in a wok.

stock: stock is a liquid infusion of herbs, aromatic vegetables, and animal bones, added to soups, sauces, and stews. Stock is easy to make and very ecological (it's a good way to use up leftovers). For full instructions see Lesson 1. In this book we use three types of stock:

light stock: made from uncooked bones (usually chicken or veal).

dark stock (or brown stock): made from roasted bones (usually veal—sometimes chicken or beef).

fish stock: made from the bones of firm white fish. (Fish stock is simmered for only 20 minutes, unlike veal or chicken stock, which is cooked for 2–3 hours.)

sun-dried tomatoes: a specialty of the Italian Riviera, sun-dried tomatoes are made by salting and drying vine-ripened tomatoes. The result has an intense flavor not unlike that of prosciutto. Oil-packed sun-dried tomatoes are the best but also the most expensive. Straight dried tomatoes are cheaper and can be marinated at home (see Lesson 19).

sweat: to cook vegetables in a tightly sealed pan over a low heat, so that they stew in their own juices.

tart pan (French-style): a pan with low, fluted sides and a removable bottom. The latter makes it easy to unmold the tart.

terrine/terrine mold: traditionally, a forcemeat made of pork, baked in an earthenware mold, and served cold. Although earthenware terrine molds are widely available, you are better off with metal ones, which won't break when tapped. You can also use a loaf pan.

toasted (as in nuts or bread crumbs): toasting brings out the flavor of nuts and bread crumbs. Almonds, walnuts, pecans, and bread crumbs should be toasted on a baking sheet in a preheated 400° oven. Sesame seeds can be toasted on a baking sheet or in an ungreased frying pan over medium heat. Pay attention when toasting nuts or crumbs: they have a nasty habit of burning.

turn (as in vegetables): to carve chunks of root vegetables into attractive, 7-sided shapes.

wash in several waters (as for lettuce or mushrooms): agitate an ingredient in a deep bowl of cold water. The dirt falls to the bottom. Lift the ingredient out of the water into a strainer; don't pour it in, or you will wash the dirt back onto it. Change the water two or three times, or as necessary.

water bath: a roasting pan filled with 1 inch of boiling water, in which a custard, mousseline, or other delicate mixture is baked. The water keeps the heat moist, even, and relatively low.

well (as in "a well in flour"): a 4–6-inch depression in a round mound of flour, made with the bottom of a measuring cup. The liquid ingredients are placed in the center.

yeast: a one-celled organism used as a leavening agent. Yeast transforms the sugars in dough into carbon dioxide and alcohol. When the dough bakes, the bubbles or carbon dioxide expand, causing the dough to rise.

Yeast is sold in a state of suspended animation. To "activate" it, we mix it with warm water and a little sugar. To "raise" the dough, we leave it in a warm, draft-free spot covered with plastic wrap and a dishcloth, usually until it has doubled in volume. The dough is then "punched down" to knock out the excess carbon dioxide, which would make the dough taste gassy. For a full discussion of yeast doughs, see Lesson 15.

zest: the oil-rich outer peel of a citrus fruit. It is best removed with a "zester," a hand-held instrument with a small flat blade, the end of which is perforated with small holes. As the zester is pulled over the rind, it removes hair-thin strips of zest. (A grater serves the same purpose, but it is harder to clean.) A vegetable peeler works well for removing wide strips of zest. Whatever you use, avoid the bitter, white pith just below the zest.

BIBLIOGRAPHY

◇

When lauded for his discovery of the laws governing heavenly bodies, Sir Isaac Newton observed, "I stand on the shoulders of giants." Although writing a cookbook is considerably less lofty a pursuit than explaining astrophysics, I am no less indebted to numerous writers and chefs who came before me. Below are some of the references I found useful in writing this cookbook.

THE BIBLES (GENERAL BOOKS ABOUT COOKING)

Child, Julia. *Mastering the Art of French Cooking* (vols. 1 & 2). New York: Alfred A. Knopf, 1961.

Fisher, M.F.K. *The Art of Eating.* New York: Vintage Books, 1976.

Haller, James. *The Blue Strawbery Cookbook.* Harvard: Harvard Common Press, 1976.

Hillman, Howard. *Kitchen Science.* Boston: Houghton Mifflin Co., 1981.

Kamman, Madeleine. *The Making of a Cook.* New York: Atheneum, 1971.

Rombauer, Irma, and Marion Rombauer Becker. *The Joy of Cooking.* Indianapolis: Bobbs-Merrill, Inc., 1964.

Townsend, Doris McFerran. *The Cook's Companion.* New York: Crown Publishers, 1978.

Willan, Anne. *The La Varenne Cooking Course.* New York: William Morrow & Co., 1982.

ETYMOLOGY AND FOOD HISTORY

Beck, Leonard. *Two Loaf Givers.* Washington, D.C.: Library of Congress, 1984.

Castelot, André. *L'Histoire à Table.* Paris: Prisma, 1962.

Root, Waverley. *Food.* New York: Simon & Schuster, 1980.

Soyer, Alexis. *The Pantropheon.* New York: Paddington Press, 1977.

Trager, James. *Foodbook.* New York: Grossman, 1970.

Wheaton, Barbara Ketchum. *Savoring the Past.* Philadelphia: University of Pennsylvania Press, 1983.

Willan, Anne. *Great Cooks and Their Recipes.* New York: McGraw-Hill Book Co., 1977.

ETHNIC CUISINES

General Books on Ethnic Cooking:

Rozin, Elisabeth. *Ethnic Cuisine: The Flavor Principle Cookbook.* Brattleboro: Stephen Greene Press, 1983.

The Time-Life *Foods of the World* cookbook series. New York: Time-Life Cookbooks.

Asian:

Solomon, Charmaine. *The Complete Asian Cookbook.* New York: McGraw-Hill Book Co., 1976.

Chinese:

Simonds, Nina. *Classic Chinese Cuisine.* Boston: Houghton Mifflin Co., 1982.

French:

Kamman, Madeleine. *When French Women Cook.* New York: Atheneum, 1976.

Willan, Anne. *French Regional Cooking.* New York: William Morrow & Co., 1981.

―――. *La Varenne's Basic French Cookery.* Tucson: H.P. Books. 1980.

Israeli:

Nathan, Joan, and Judy Stacey Goldman. *The Flavor of Jerusalem.* Boston: Little, Brown & Co., 1975.

Italian:

Hazan, Marcella. *The Classic Italian Cookbook.* New York: Alfred A. Knopf, 1976.

BOOKS ABOUT INDIVIDUAL FOODS

Cheese:

Marquis, Vivienne, and Patricia Haskell. *The Cheese Book.* New York: Simon & Schuster, 1964.

Chocolate:

Heatter, Maida. *Book of Great Chocolate Desserts.* New York: Alfred A. Knopf, 1978.

Filo Dough:

Sousanis, Martin. *The Art of Filo Cookbook.* Berkeley: Aris Books, 1983.

Fish:

Davidson, Alan. *North Atlantic Seafood.* London: Macmillan London, Ltd., 1979.

Hooker, Richard J. *The Book of Chowder.* Harvard: Harvard Common Press, 1979.

Levy, Faye and Fernand Chambrette. *La Cuisine du Poisson.* France: Flammarion, 1984.

McClane, A. J. and deZanger, Arie. *The Encyclopedia of Fish.* New York: Holt, Rinehart & Winston, 1977.

Mitcham, Howard. *Provincetown Seafood Cookbook.* Reading, Mass.: Addison-Wesley, 1975.

Pasta:

Del Conte, Anna. *Portrait of Pasta.* New York: Paddington Press Ltd., 1976.

Vegetables:

Bianchini, Francesco, et al. *The Complete Book of Fruits and Vegetables.* New York: Crown Publishers, 1976.

Harris, Lloyd J. *The Book of Garlic.* New York: Holt, Rinehart & Winston, 1974.

Hazelton, Nika. *The Unabridged Vegetable Cookbook.* New York: Bantam Books, 1980.

Morash, Marian. *The Victory Garden Cookbook.* New York: Alfred A. Knopf, 1982.

WINES AND SPIRITS

Doxat, John. *The Book of Drinking.* London: Triune Books, 1973.

Henriques, E. Frank. *The Signet Encyclopedia of Whiskey, Brandy and All Other Spirits.* New York: Signet, 1979.

Johnson, Hugh. *The World Atlas of Wine.* New York: Simon & Schuster, 1971.

INDEX